Under Egypt's Spell

UNDER EGYPT'S SPELL

*The Influence of Egypt
on Writers in English
from the 18th Century*

Mursi Saad el Din
& John Cromer

BELLEW PUBLISHING
London

First published in Great Britain in 1991 by
Bellew Publishing Company Limited
7 Southampton Place, London WC1A 2DR

Copyright © Mursi Saad el Din and John Cromer 1991

ISBN 0 947792 54 6

Phototypeset by Input Typesetting Ltd, London
Printed and bound in Great Britain by
Billings & Sons

Contents

Acknowledgements   vii
Prologue   1

1   The Early Years   5
2   The British in Egypt and the First World War   19
3   The Inter-war Years   46
4   The Second World War – The Cairo Scene   63
5   The Second World War – The Publications   97
6   The Second World War – Music, Drama and Other Entertainment   132
7   The Aftermath   164
8   The Continuing Interest   175
9   Alexandria   192
10   Under Their Own Spell – Egyptian Writers   203

Epilogue   223
Appendix – Art and Architecture   227
Bibliography   237
Index   243

Illustrations

illustrations appearing between pages 148–149

The Victory Club, Cairo
Erik de Mauny and G.S. Fraser
The Founders of the Salamander Society
John Gawsworth, Cairo
Saleh Mursi
Youssef Idris
Youssef el Sebai and Mursi Saad el Din
Neguib Mahfouz
Mahmoud Teymour
Abbas el Aqqad
Tewfik el Hakim

Acknowledgements

The authors wish to express their thanks to all those who have helped them with advice, information and material, in particular Leslie S. Barnard, Erik de Mauny, the directors of the Mathaf Gallery, London and the following members of the Savage Club: the late Noel Barber, Ronnie Burgess, John Hillaby, Alan Jenkins, Peter Kingsbury, Bob Leach, the late Reg Lever (and his widow, Elsie Winsor), Barrie Pitt and Alan Wykes.

Thanks are also due to Leicester University Press for permission to reproduce 'An Elegy for Keith Bullen' from *Poems of G. S. Fraser*; to Paddy Fraser for permission to reproduce extracts from *A Stranger and Afraid* by G. S. Fraser (1983); to Andre Deutsch Ltd and Laurie Devine for permission to reproduce extracts from *Nile* (1983); and to Macmillan Publishers Ltd and James Aldridge for permission to reproduce extracts from *Cairo: Biography of a City* (1970).

The bibliography has been arranged in continuous numerical order, sources being marked by superior figures on their first reference in the text.

Prologue

This book began as a review of the cultural life in Egypt during the Second World War as seen through the eyes of an Egyptian writer and a British writer, both of whom were there at the time. Our aim was to reveal some of the facts behind the fictionalised versions of the period, for these latter have tended to obscure the real significance of this epoch, when a unique cultural life was created and flourished locally during a time of world upheaval. As we progressed, however, it became apparent that to take merely those few years in isolation from the longer period of cultural interchange between the Egyptians and the British would be to give a false perspective and an almost incomprehensible view of a much longer-standing relationship.

Since time immemorial, Egypt has attracted foreign visitors: poets, writers, philosophers, scientists, politicians and artists. So much has been written about Egypt that it would be a daunting task to compile a definitive bibliography. There are books on its ancient history, its Islamic culture, its political role, about the Nile and its flora and fauna and, of course, about modern Egypt.

The English Egyptologist H. S. Smith wrote in his introduction to *Ancient Centres of Egyptian Civilisation*:[1]

> How is it that, in an age of atomic fission, space shuttle and other wonders, each year many more thousands of people from all over the world visit Egypt to see its ancient temples, tombs and cities? Why have vast crowds waited patiently so many hours at the British Museum, the Louvre and elsewhere to see the treasures of Tutankhamun? What is it that makes the demand for University degrees, for external courses, for exhibitions, for films and books concerned with the civilisation of Ancient Egypt so intense, above all to English-speaking countries?

Writers in English have been particularly fascinated by Egypt since the early nineteenth century, producing both fact and fiction, and it is primarily upon this work that we wish to concentrate, spreading a little into the other arts as well.

Once we have painted the backdrop of more distant years in the early chapters, we shall try to recapture something of the great cultural activity that was going on in Egypt while armies were fighting round it. We shall view this from two sides, one the intruder in uniform, striving to preserve his culture in an alien land, the other a national of the host country, responding to the foreign influences around him.

Much has been written about the Second World War by historians, war correspondents, military strategists, novelists, biographers, diarists – indeed it would seem that little remains to be said. Despite this, there is still more to tell, records to be corrected and an account to be rendered of some scenes in the great drama which were enacted in a particular theatre of war. The Middle East covered a large spread of territory and several countries but the hub of much of the war effort of the Allied Armies was Cairo – the throbbing heart of Egypt. Alexandria too had its own share of the effort. It is of Egypt that we wish to tell, not as a military headquarters or the target of spies and counter-spies but as a land and host of culture.

We have another reason for writing this book. As time has gone by, the participants in this period of upheaval have gradually left the scene. There are few of us left who remember those days sufficiently clearly to recapture something of the flavour of the time. Writers and commentators there have been in plenty who have touched on this forgotten aspect of events and some have not always been accurate. Younger writers have emerged, many of whom were not even born at the time, who have researched and fed upon second-hand information and have not always got it right. Theses mushroom in the fields of Academe. Before we, too, pass on, we would like to give our own version of the facts behind the fiction, of what made up the cultural life of Egypt during the Second World War.

Too little is known in the Western world of modern Arabic, and more particularly, of Egyptian literature. We have therefore devoted one chapter to this, focusing on the way in which Egyptian writers have been fascinated and influenced by European literature. We see this cross-fertilisation of cultures as a hopeful harbinger of closer relationships between the peoples of the two continents and a bridge across the ravines of mis-understanding and even distrust.

We have also added an appendix on the Egyptian influence on British art and architecture as we felt that these fields pro-vided further examples of the extraordinary power which Egypt has exerted.

1

The Early Years

In July 1956 Mursi Saad el Din was returning by sea to Egypt after a 12-year appointment as Secretary of the Egyptian Institute in London. The night before the ship reached Port Said it was announced over the radio that President Gamal Abdel Nasser had nationalised the Suez Canal Company. The subsequent intervention by British, French and Israeli forces has no place in this narrative, but the immediate effect was the sequestration of British and French properties, including schools and cultural centres. These latter were not closed down; they were simply placed under Egyptian direction.

British and French officials were asked to leave, including teachers and lecturers. The British Council was one of those institutions affected by the decision. Mursi was chosen to be one of the sequestrators. The other was the late Abdel Rehim Rashwan, who was the chief inspector of English in the Ministry of Education and a great enthusiast for the English language and culture. The British Institute had been burned down in 1952 and was then housed in a modern block of flats in Adly Street.

Mursi and Rashwan, being great believers in cultural exchanges and admirers of the English language and literature, and realising the importance of learning foreign languages, embarked on a policy for the British Council which followed to the letter its previous activities under British control. English classes continued and so did the lectures and other activities, such as poetry-reading groups, drama, theatre and film shows, without any interference, directions or instructions on the part of the Government. The two sequestrators were astonished to see the rush for what was on offer.

Mursi was responsible for the extra-curricular activities such as lectures, poetry, drama and films. He rummaged through the stores and found a treasure of recordings, poetry recitals, new

films and batches of newly-arrived books. The printed programmes were facsimiles of the past ones. At that time the
standard of Egyptian teachers of English was still high. Most
of them, if not all, had graduated from Exeter University or
Trinity College, Dublin and their command of English was
superb. Many of them were recruited and lecturers were found
who could fulfil the programme.

Mursi found a new recording of *Richard III* with Laurence
Olivier and other leading British artists. When this was
announced, the hall was packed and it had to be given daily
for a whole week. He also discovered Benjamin Britten's *Let's
Make an Opera* and a record of William Butler Yeats reading
'The Lake Isle of Innisfree'. The British Council and Institute
became, once again, a centre for cultural and artistic activities.
One achievement was the production of Shakespeare's *A Mid-
summer Night's Dream*, with an all-Egyptian cast. Mursi
directed the play, having previously been responsible for drama
production in the English Department at Cairo University. It
was a somewhat amateurish production but drew large audiences and it had to be given on three successive nights. The
leading star eventually received a British Council scholarship
and is now teaching at Cairo University.

The library of the Council was another active area. Hundreds
of students from the English departments of the universities
were regular borrowers from the library since its shelves contained much that was not available in their libraries.

Sequestration was lifted in 1958 and this remarkable period
came to an end, as did the British Council until its resumption
later. The library went to Ain Shams University, lock, stock and
barrel.

This virtually unrecorded aspect of Anglo-Egyptian relations
and the fascination of the English language for Egyptian students lies at the heart of this book, as does the equally strong
fascination of Egypt for writers in English. To trace how this
came about, we must look back a long way.

Egypt has had the good fortune to have been well documented
and described since its earliest days, through the hieroglyphics
and papyri which have given so graphic a picture of the past,
and wall paintings which have been equally rich in showing life
as it was in colour which remains good to this day. It is not
our purpose to encroach into these fields and what follows is
intended to serve only as a backdrop to the cultural period we

shall depict later. Almost from the beginning, the facts behind the fictional glamour of those early and subsequent days have shown two levels of life: the real and the imagined.

One of the first to write about Egypt was Herodotus, who was also one of its earliest visitors. He is the author of the well-known saying that Egypt is the gift of the Nile. Although a great deal of what he wrote is now being questioned, he still holds a leading position among travellers to Egypt.

A supercilious questioner was Lord Curzon who, as well as being a statesman and a Viceroy of India was also a winner of the Gold Medal of the Royal Geographical Society for exploration and research. His observations on Egypt reveal the keenness of his eye and the jaundice of his mind. In his *Travels with a Superior Person*,[2] he revealed both:

> The Egyptian atmosphere had never been very favourable to the truth. In the book of Exodus there are traces of exaggeration, if not worse. Herodotus, the Father of History, had made some startling discoveries in Egypt and been told a good many lies by the Egyptians; he had himself told a few more, and perhaps this had set the ball rolling so that Egypt had acquired a reputation in these respects which it was necessary to maintain, and which, I am bound to say, its inhabitants up to the latest hour have never done anything to impair.

Curzon's questioning only increased as he went further into Egypt.

> From that time forward I never felt or expressed astonishment at any discovery of the kind I was fortunate enough to make, but merely recorded it with delight in my notebook. For instance, when I came to Assouan I found with no surprise that the first Cataract of the Nile, even as it then existed, was not a cataract at all, but only a rapid a few yards wide, with a fall in 150 yards of not more than six or seven feet. But then Herodotus also made a discovery about this same cataract; for hereabouts were his two famous hills of Crophi and Mophi, between which lay the unfathomable fountains of the Nile.

One should read Curzon for his comment about place rather than for his judgements on people.

Successive invasions have brought different masters and different cultures to Egypt and the genius of the country, albeit unwitting, has been to absorb the domination of foreigners and turn upon them the mystique which has led to an aura of romanticism, thus disguising the true nature of the country and its people. Although the Western world has tended to judge Egypt by what has been written about it by Western historians and writers, the indigenous literary world has a long tradition.

As an example of story-telling on the grand scale, what could be more exotic than the *Tales of the Arabian Nights* (known in Arabic as *The Thousand and One Nights*)? Douglas Sladen, to whom we shall return later, having already published *Queer Things about Egypt* and *Egypt and the English*, in 1911 brought out his book *Oriental Cairo*,[3] which he sub-titled 'the City of the "Arabian Nights" '. He justified this by referring to Edward Lane, whose translation of the *Arabian Nights*[4] he considered to be the greatest 'foreign classic' after the Bible. The collection of tales, the first manuscript of which was bought in Aleppo by a French diplomat in the palmy days of the Ottoman Empire, was first translated into French in the early eighteenth century, then into English and other European languages. In a reasoned Appendix, Sladen quotes from Lane to show that it was sixteenth-century Cairo which supplied the local colour of that classic, and proclaims that no one who means to study Oriental Cairo seriously should go there without the three precious volumes. 'It clothes with life a multitude of grand old mosques and palaces, neglected, decayed or in ruins, by showing the tragedies and comedies and everyday existence which went on in them 350 years ago.'

Sladen goes on to quote from Stanley Lane-Poole, who waxes lyrical on the same theme in his *Cairo*,[5] later to be expanded into *The Story of Cairo*.[6]

For Cairo is still to a great degree the city of the *Arabian Nights*. And as we thread the winding alleys, where this streak of sky marks the narrow space between the lattice-windows of the overhanging stories, and dive under a camel here, or retreat into a narrow recess there, to escape destruction under the feet of the apparently impassable crowd of beasts of burden, we may fancy ourselves in the gateway of the Aly of Cairo, and in that stall round the corner we may perhaps find the immortal Barber Brothers; within the grated lattice over the way, the three Royal Mendicants may at this moment be entertaining the Portress and her fair sisters with the history of their calamities; and if we wait till night we may see the good Harun El-Rashid (newly arrived from Baghdad) stealthily pursuing his midnight rambles, with Ja'far at his heels, and black Mesrur clearing the way.

The tales are a history of the everyday life of the people of Cairo and not of the lives of the great, as the Arab historians claim, and the tales relate to the merchants of Cairo, its shopkeepers and sailors who had to match their wits against the evil djinns who could almost be identified with the unpredictable Mameluke overlords. The descendants of these shopkeepers are to be found in the Khan el Khalili today.

As we progress into our theme, we must look back at some of the names who have brought the spirit of Egypt into the mainstream of European scholarship and culture. Sir John Gardner Wilkinson, who has written one of the best books on ancient Egypt, *Manners and Customs of Ancient Egyptians*,[7] was the great pioneer of Egyptology. He first became interested in ancient Egypt when he was at Harrow School. This led him to visit the country in 1821 at the age of 24. He settled for 12 years, building himself a house of mud-brick near Thebes. Without any government support during that time, he managed to learn a great deal about the past and came to be recognised as a leading authority on the culture of Egyptian antiquity. He was an artist as well as a scholar, an ability which made his work in the field especially valuable.

The outcome of his researches and the goal to which he was moving was an extraordinary book, containing original analysis and all-embracing synthesis. Its title, quoted above, gives a fair idea of its content, including, as it does, the private lives of Egyptians, their government, arts, manufactures, religion and early history, all derived from a comparison of the paintings, sculptures and monuments still existing, with the accounts of ancient authors.

The historical development seen through Egyptian eyes was explored by Ahmed Ibn Ali el Makrizi in his many works, in which he featured, in various aspects, life under the Mamelukes and the place of the Copts. As a chronicler of *la condition humaine*, none was better than Abdel Rahman Ibn Mohammed (Ibn Khaldun) whose *Prolegomena*, translated into French by Baron MacGuckin de Slane (1862–8),[8] applies as much to the life of the people today as it did when it was written. Life under the Turkish occupation and a blow-by-blow account of the invasion by Napoleon has been provided by Abd el Rahman Ibn el Jabarti, whose nine-volume work, translated by several hands, was published in Cairo between 1888 and 1896.[9]

It is already clear that at this time there was no cross-fertilisation of cultures. Strangers to the country wrote about what they saw through their own eyes. They were recorders of what they saw and heard, not creators. For their part, the Egyptian writers followed a similar path. They told about their own people, they recorded the impact made by their conquerors. The stream of creative invention and decoration had hardly begun its early trickling.

The Rev. Thomas Shaw was one of the first of the travelling scholars to record his descriptions of Egypt when he visited the country in 1721. The second edition of his book, *Travels or Observations Relating to Several Parts of Barbary and the Levant*,[10] which was published in 1757, includes an engraving of the famous Roman mosaic from the temple of Fortuna Primigenia at Palestrina, representing the inundation of Egypt by the Nile, together with buildings and strange animals. He was closely followed in the late 1730s by another cleric, the Rev. Richard Pococke, who was the first of three travellers to progress any further south than Saqqara, all three reaching Aswan. His book, *A Description of the East*,[11] Frederick L. Norden's *Travels in Egypt and Nubia*[12] and Dr Charles Perry's *A View of the Levant*[13] all had engravings of the monuments of Middle and Upper Egypt, thus setting the pattern for the many who followed.

The mid-eighteenth century saw further publications, the traders and scholars being followed by the *jeunesse dorée* who took in Egypt as part of the Grand Tour. Among them were John Perceval, 1st Earl of Egmont, James Caulfeild, 1st Earl of Charlemont, John Montagu, 4th Earl of Sandwich and his cousin Edward Wortley Montagu. In November 1741, an Egyptian Society was founded in London, the leading members being Lord Sandwich, who was President, and the three travellers, Pococke, Perry and Norden. The Society lasted two years before folding.

Twenty years later, the German, Carsten Niebuhr, in his book, *Voyage en Egypte*,[14] first brought to European notice the Egyptian dancing girls 'with their yellow hands, spotted faces, absurd ornaments and hair larded with stinking pomatum . . . their movements graceful though indecent'. A French traveller, Count Constantin François de Volney, writing twenty years later still (1783–5),[15] had a very different impression of Cairo and the Egyptians. Hard on his heels came W. G. Browne, whose *Travels in Africa, Egypt and Syria from the Year 1792*

to 1798,[16] described pre-Napoleonic Cairo and foresaw the
French general's defeat of the Mamelukes. Browne saw Cairo
as a city on the verge of social disintegration.

Then came Napoleon and with him writers, artists, scientists
and a new wave of culture. Egypt was never the same wholly
Oriental country again. The French influence had, perhaps, an
even greater impact than the British, who came 100 years later.
Both Cairo and Alexandria, as the most important cities, Port
Said and other towns looked, and continue to look, more French
than British in those sectors where European architecture pre-
vails over Egyptian.

The great contribution which Napoleon made lay in the way
in which he approached the country – apart from his naval and
military dispositions, which were unsuccessful. He brought with
him 100 *savants*, who were responsible for that compendium
of observation and research which still stands as probably the
greatest European work on Egypt, *Description de l'Egypte: un
receuil des observations et des recherches qui ont été faites en
Egypte pendant l'expedition de l'armée française*, a collection
of 20 volumes, published in Paris between 1809 and 1828 and
24 volumes published between 1821 and 1829.[17]

Napoleon took up residence in Cairo in July 1798 in a newly-
built palace which Mohammed Bey el Elfi had spent a lot of
money on building but had not yet occupied. It stood in its own
gardens which later became the site of the Shepheard's Hotel,
known to so many travellers and servicemen in both world wars
and which was burned down in 1952. Napoleon had hardly
settled into his headquarters when he set up his famed Institut
d'Egypte, putting to work the 100 *savants* he had brought
with him to study and analyse Egypt both historically and
contemporaneously. Two houses in the Nasriya quarter of Cairo
were set apart for them and the Institute itself was divided into
four sections: industry, health, science and mathematics, art and
literature. Accounts written at the time were *Bonaparte au Caire*
by R. Luis de Boisey, published in Paris in 1799[18] and *Napoleon
I and Louis Berthier*, an account of the French Expedition in
Egypt (with Sir William Sidney Smith's letters), published in
Leeds in 1800.[19]

When the French were expelled from Egypt, an account of
the campaign which led to their defeat was written by Sir Robert
T. Wilson in his *History of the British Expedition to Egypt*,[20]

published in London in 1802. This was the official account in which he said that 'the French had expected much of Cairo but the British expected nothing and even that was pitching their hopes high'. A less official account of the campaign was written by 'a private on board the *Dictator*',[21] doubtless a marine, whose book *A Faithful Journal of the Late Expedition to Egypt* was published in London in 1805.

For the British, the military exploits were of less interest than the performance of their hero Admiral Nelson, whose spectacular victory in the Battle of the Nile was a masterpiece of naval strategy and daring. The battle inspired Mrs Dorothy Hemans to immortalise not a British sailor but a Frenchman, in her poem 'Casabianca', based on the midshipman of that name who died with his father on the burning deck of the French flagship, *L'Orient*, when it blew up. If Lady Hamilton had had her way, she would have heaped upon Nelson titles which would have associated him for ever with Egypt. She said that if she had been King of England, she would make him Duke Nelson, Marquis Nile, Earl Alexandria, Viscount Pyramid, Baron Crocodile and Prince Victory.

The romantic movement in poetry of the early nineteenth century could not fail to find inspiration in the exotic images of Egypt, even though the poets did not go there. John Keats was sufficiently inspired in 1818 to write seven poems during the year with references to Egypt, no doubt as a result of visiting the British Museum, as his letters record, to see the antiquities which had recently been installed there. It will be remembered that in the same year, he, Shelley and Leigh Hunt competed with each other in writing a sonnet entitled 'To the Nile'. It cannot be said that any of them were the best that these poets have written. Keats did better with some of the passages in 'Hyperion' which were clearly inspired by his visits to the Museum; and Shelley's sonnet, 'Ozymandias' must have sprung from reading about the arrival of the head known as 'Young Memnon', described in the *Quarterly Review* of January 1818 as 'without doubt the finest specimen of an ancient Egyptian sculpture which has yet been discovered'. The Egyptian flame also burned in the heart of the young Alfred Tennyson who, in 1824, at the age of 15, was describing a 'bloodred Pyramid' and 'obelisks bloodred' in his poem 'The Coach of Death'. His prize poem 'Timbuctoo', written at Cambridge and published five years later, contains a reference to the lighthouse of Alexandria.

Although D. A. Cameron's book *Egypt in the Nineteenth Century*[22] was published much later chronologically, in London in 1898, he dealt thoroughly with Egypt under Mohammed Ali, a period which followed Napoleon's. This was a time when European influence and culture was encouraged but the real goal was trading and investment. As Cameron said, 'The Pasha and the foreigners were drawn together by a mutual necessity: they both wanted money.' It was then that Europeans took their place as the privileged class, particularly in Cairo and increasingly in Alexandria. As the profit motive drove the trading interests along, the peasant classes suffered.

From the 1830s onwards, the writers came into their own, amateurs for the most part with some professionals among them. Travellers' tales abounded through to the 1850s and beyond. Mohammed Ali's Cairo ceased to be a city of Eastern Mystery and blossomed as a stopping-off place for every traveller bound for the glories of Egypt. The English were predominant among these literary visitors and among the amateurs was the professional A. W. Kinglake. He wrote in his preface to *Eothen*:[23]

> My excuse for the book is its truth . . . my narrative is not merely righteously exact in matters of fact (where fact is in question) but it is true in this larger sense – it conveys, not only those impressions which ought to have been produced upon any 'well constituted mind' but those which were really and truly received at the time of his rambles by a headstrong and not very amiable traveller, whose prejudices in favour of other people's notions were then exceedingly slight. As I have felt, so I have written; and the result is, that there will often be found in my narrative a jarring discord between the associations properly belonging to interesting sites, and the true tones in which I speak of them.

Kinglake, writing of his tour in 1834 (the book was published ten years later, having been rejected by several publishers before becoming a bestseller, its title *Eothen* being taken from the Greek 'from the early dawn' or 'from the East') makes other relevant remarks about travel writers, whose approach has always been different from that of novelists and poets. For example:

> A traveller is a creature not always looking at sights; he remembers

(how often!) the happy land of his birth; he has, too, his moments of humble enthusiasm about fire and food, about shade and drink . . . but it seems to me that this egotism of the traveller, however incessant, however shameless and obtrusive, must still convey some true ideas of the country through which he has passed.

These are the ideas of a man whose picture of Cairo was very much of his time. Egypt takes up only a small portion of the book. 'Cairo and the Plague' is the longest chapter and has much descriptive matter. He arrived in Cairo across the eastern desert and was immediately struck by the city's beauty:

There appeared the dark line upon the edge of the forward horizon and soon the line deepened into a delicate fringe that sparkled here and there as though it were sown with diamonds. There then before me were the gardens and minarets of Egypt, and the mighty works of the Nile and I had lived to see, and I saw them.

Of all that Kinglake saw in Egypt, it was the Sphinx that impressed him most. He writes:

And near the Pyramids, more wonderous and more awful than all else in the land of Egypt, there sits the lonely Sphynx. Comely the creature is, but the comeliness is not of this world. Laugh and mock if you will at the worship of stone idols; but mark ye this, ye breakers of images, that in one regard the stone idol bears awful resemblance of Deity – unchangefulness in the midst of change – the same seeming will and intent for ever and ever inexorable.

'Cairo to Suez' describes the journey by dromedary and the chapter is more about people than place. This typifies the writing of most Europeans – they were travellers, the early tourists, looking at the country with a more discerning and educated eye than the package tourist of today, but their records are still largely descriptive and anecdotal.

W. M. Thackeray put his visit to Egypt to good account, not in a novel, but in his travel piece *Notes of a Journey from Cornhill to Grand Cairo*[24] published in 1846. He was particularly intrigued by the part played by Thomas Waghorn, the forerunner to Thomas Cook in making travel arrangements for voyagers. Waghorn's Overland Route, as it was known, had been started in 1837 when he was Deputy Agent of the East India Company in Egypt for the superintendence of mails. He also arranged for the transport of British coal overland by barge and camel. He had competitors for passengers and baggage between Cairo and Suez in the form of Mr Hill and Mr Raven, who had formed the Bombay Steam Company, operating a hotel at each end of the run, with rest-houses in the intervening desert. Waghorn decided not to try to beat the competition but to join it and the partnership became known as J. R. Hill & Co. As a result, the route became reliable and safe, so that Waghorn could honestly claim that 'even ladies, alone with infants, could pass to and fro with ease and security, in that desert between England and India, as in Europe'.

We find Thackeray in the hotel in Cairo, watching with amused eye the scene around him, a babble of Anglo-Indians and their retinue en route to and from the homeland, complete with nurses and 'little white-faced babies that have seen the light of day at Dumdum or Futtyghar'. He continues:

> The bells are ringing prodigiously and Lieutenant Waghorn is bouncing in and out of the courtyard full of business. He only left Bombay yesterday morning, was seen in the Red Sea on Tuesday, is engaged to dinner this afternoon in the Regent's Park, and (as it is about two minutes since I saw him in the courtyard) I make no doubt he is by this time at Alexandria or Malta – say, perhaps, at both. *Il en est capable.* If any man can be at two places at once (which I don't believe or deny), Waghorn is he.

Thackeray goes on to ask:

> What are Napoleon's wonders, compared to those of Waghorn? Nap massacred the Mamelukes at the Pyramids; Wag has conquered the Pyramids themselves – dragged the unwieldy structures a month nearer England than they were, and brought the country along with them . . . All the heads that Napoleon caused to be struck off . . . which would not elevate him a monument as big. Be ours the trophies of peace! O my country! O Waghorn! *Hae tibi erunt artes.* When I go to the Pyramids I will sacrifice in your name, and pour out libations of bitter ale and Harvey sauce in your honour.

It was good of De Lesseps later to ask the Empress Eugénie to unveil a monument at Suez to Thomas Waghorn.

It is difficult to keep track of the many privately printed and subscription list books of travellers' tales which were published throughout the nineteenth century. One such, bearing a subscription list for over 200 copies, is *Letters from the Nile* by J. W. Clayton, 13th Light Dragoons – no rank volunteered – which appeared in 1854.[25] The style is typical of the time. Starting with the departure from England, the overland journey to Marseilles and the sea trip to Alexandria, the over-lush prose continues in the form of a letter from Memphis:

> At last we are fairly upon the bosom of the sacred river, which every infant lisps – the river that bore the cradle of Moses and the gilded barge of Cleopatra, which washed the land of bondage of the children of Israel, and was crimsoned by the victory of Nelson, and now glittered in the sun, flowing as fast and bright as when its waves swept past Memphis.

The reception in Luxor describes what must have been a routine affair:

> On approaching Luxor, the general harbour for the Nile boat, we were saluted rather feebly by a seedy double-barrel from an English boat at anchor, which we returned by twenty rounds from all our guns and pistols, and hoisting our private flag, were soon at anchor opposite the old Temple of Luxor.

The Sphinx is all things to all people. This author felt let down:

> I myself was disappointed at the comparative smallness of the Sphinx to what I read of and expected; it stands an eighth of a mile from the Pyramids; the countenance, from a severe blow on its nose and other contusions, renders it not unlike a prize-fighter's after his thirtieth round, and still serenely smiles amidst the surrounding desolation.

American literary travellers were now beginning to appear on the scene and to add their contributions to the bookshops. In an article written by Munroe Berger about American travellers in the nineteenth century, he says that there were at least 200 books written by Americans during that period about Egypt and particularly about Cairo. That spate of books reflected the growing interest in the country and the desire of Americans to know the origins of Western civilisation. This interest helped to initiate later greater cultural and political exchanges between the two countries.

Beginning in the 1830s, American visitors tended to make Egypt, and Cairo in particular, their final port of call after exploration of the Holy Land, and they were typically American in their down-to-earth approach. John Lloyd Stephens in his book, *Incidents of Travel in Egypt, Arabia, Petra and the Holy Land*, published in Edinburgh in 1839,[26] led the way in this respect. Then came James Ewing Cooley, another pathfinder for his countrymen. He railed against high hotel prices and rip-offs. His book *The American in Egypt*[27] contained the sentences later quoted by James Aldridge:

> The natural consequences of those long ages of despotism and slavery are that the people themselves, accustomed to be plundered by the government and its officers, and unused to its care and protection, have lost all moral courage, and are strangers to every principle of honesty.

In the face of this growing interest and the increasing number of American travellers, one of them wrote: 'The Nile has become nearly as much travelled by Americans as the Rhine.' A decade later, a diplomatic despatch from Egypt to Washington reported that from the 1850s, the number of Americans in Egypt rose from twenty or thirty to four or five hundred at the end of the century.

The list of American travellers compiled by Berger includes Herman Melville and Mark Twain. Melville, seeing the Pyramids for only a few moments on his last day there in 1856, wrote in his notebook: 'After seeing the Pyramids, all other architecture seems but pastry. Its simplicity confounds you. It refuses to be studied or adequately comprehended.'

Perhaps the most famous American traveller to Egypt was Mark Twain. Late in 1867 he and about 65 other Americans spent a few days there. Twain's book *Innocents Abroad*[28] was a great success. It may be described as a humorous travel book, aiming not only at serious discussion but also to stress the light and ironical side of groups of American tourists making their first contact with other people. His description of Shepheard's was 'the worst hotel on earth except the one I stopped at once in a small town in the United States'. The Pyramids impressed Mark Twain and yet he showed irreverence and sarcasm. This is what he wrote:

> At a distance of a few miles, the Pyramids rising above the palms looked very clean-cut, very grand and imposing, and very soft and filmy as well. They swam in the rich haze that took from them all suggestion of unfeeling stone and made them seem only the airy nothings of a dream structure which might blossom into tiers of vague arches or ornate colonnades may be and change again into all graceful forms of architecture, while we looked, and then melt deliciously away and blend with the tumultuous atmosphere.

How poetic Twain can be in describing the great wonder of the world. And yet almost with the same breath, he returns to his sarcastic humour. When he came close to the Pyramids, they were no longer a fairy vision but 'a corrugated, unsightly mountain of stones'. Then he describes how the tourist was besieged with beggars and donkeys to which he gave his utmost attention. Twain thought that the donkeys were the best he had ever seen. He did not fail to leave his mark there. Napoleon, Gladstone, and later, Churchill were all names given by the donkey boys to their animals. But the name most commonly used became Mark Twain.

2

The British in Egypt and the First World War

The Englishman Edward William Lane came to Egypt for the first time in 1825, rented a house in the native quarter, donned Egyptian dress and called himself Mansour Effendi. His much-acclaimed record of Egyptian culture and folklore, *Manners and Customs of Modern Egyptians*, was published in London in 1836[29] and who better to expand on this seminal work than Mursi Saad el Din, who wrote an introduction to the Everyman edition of 1954, from which we now quote:

> There are very few books on nineteenth-century Egypt that can be regarded as classics. This is certainly one of them. Modern Egypt has suffered greatly from two types of books; the one which is written by the hasty traveller who does not bother to record more than what he sees in the Mousky Bazaar, the other by the well-meaning European once in the service of the Egyptian Administration who assumes a patronising attitude. It would be difficult to say which of the two has done Egypt more harm; certainly neither of them has done her justice. Egypt needs explaining, not defending.
>
> Lane's book is an essay in objective social research. The author was, in modern sociological jargon, a 'participant observer'. In many ways his approach would have satisfied the most up-to-date ideas of social research. He chose a role which was acceptable to the Egyptian community, without arousing their suspicion. Lane's excellent knowledge of Arabic and his adoption of Egyptian attire helped him greatly in achieving his task. In this was he able to share in the life of the community and gain their confidence. This book covers a period of the greatest importance in the life of modern Egypt; a period which was, from almost every viewpoint, the dawn of a new civilisation. If the influences of Europe were already beginning to be felt, it is also true that Egyptian life was straining to emerge from behind the hitherto impenetrable edifice of traditions, and to cultivate, albeit apprehensively, the new culture from the West. This period was, in fact, a watershed in the history of Egypt;

so much was changing, so much was new, and the atmosphere was being slowly charged with a new vitality.

To the reader who has not been to Egypt in modern times – the soldier, the tourist, and the official – there may seem to have been great changes since the days when Lane wrote his book, and great changes there have been, indeed. A closer examination reveals, however, that these changes are often superficial and result almost entirely from the impact of the West.

The historical significance of Lane's book derives from its accuracy and from the fact that Lane was the last and the greatest writer to describe at first hand a society that is now gone. It provides us with a most valuable record of Egypt's culture, its songs and legends, its folklore and superstitions, in short, of all that is part and parcel of the Egyptian heritage.

One of the most distinguished European writers who visited Egypt in the mid-nineteenth century was Gustave Flaubert, extracts from whose correspondence is contained in Francis Steegmuller's book, *Flaubert in Egypt*.[30] Travelling with Maxime Du Camp, he landed in Alexandria in November 1849, describing the scene later in a letter to his mother as follows:

> Landing took place amid the most deafening uproar imaginable: negroes, negresses, camels, turbans, cudgelings to right and left, and ear-splitting guttural cries. I gulped down a whole bellyful of colours, like a donkey filling himself with hay. Cudgelings play a great role here; everyone who appears in clean clothes beats everyone who wears dirty ones, or rather none at all, and when I say clothes I mean a pair of short breeches.

By December he was in Cairo and wrote to Louis Bouilhet: 'One of the finest things is the camel – I never tire of watching this strange beast that lurches like a turkey and sways its neck like a swan.' His travel notes reveal sharp observations: 'Everything in Egypt seems made for architecture – the planes of the fields, the vegetation, the human anatomy, the horizon lines.' The noise in Cairo hardly changed. Flaubert's experience in 1850 is set out in a letter to Dr Jules Cloquet:

> So here we are in Egypt. What can I say about it all? As yet I am scarcely over the initial bedazzlement. It is like being hurled while still asleep into the midst of a Beethoven symphony, with the brasses at their most ear-splitting, the basses rumbling and the flutes sighing away; each detail reaches out to grip you; it pinches you; and the more you concentrate on it the less you grasp the whole.

Du Camp was not to be outdone in descriptive matter. In

their journey up the Nile, they were struck by the Khamsin, which he describes thus:

> Here they call this wind the 'Khamsin' (fifty) because it usually blows for fifty days. It is the ocean of dust borne by a hurricane; the sky turns a leaden grey, and the sun, behind a dark veil and shorn of its rays, looks like a great shield of dull silver. The sand, whirled about by the wind, covers everything and penetrates every- thing. At Philae, after a Khamsin whirlwind, I found a powdering of sand even in the springs of my watch, which was inside a double case in a buttoned-down pocket.

Flaubert was no less affected, as his travel notes reveal:

> Khamsin. We shut ourselves in; sand grits between our teeth and makes our faces unrecognisable, it gets into our tin boxes and spoils our supplies – cooking is impossible . . . Great whirlwinds of sand rise up and beat against the sides of our cange [a light Nile boat]; everyone takes to his bed.

Finally, here is Flaubert describing the Nile in a letter to Louis Bouilhet, written in March 1850 from somewhere beyond Assuan:

> It is a crazy, magnificent river, more like the ocean than anything else. Sandy beaches extend as far as the eye can see on both its banks, blown about by the wind like sea beaches; it is so enormous that one doesn't know where the current is, and sometimes you feel enclosed in a great lake.

Maxime du Camp was a skilled and tenacious photographer and his pictures, particularly those of the temples between Cairo and Thebes, have achieved fame as the first photographic record of many of the monuments before they were cleared of sand later in the century. For his great work he was awarded the Cross of the Legion d'Honneur.

A few years later, in 1858, an equally distinguished English writer, Anthony Trollope, was interrupted while writing *Dr Thorne*, by being, as he says in his *Autobiography*,[31] 'asked by the great men at the General Post Office to go to Egypt to make a treaty with the Pasha for the conveyance of our mails through that country by railway. There was a treaty in existence, but that had reference to the carriage of bags and boxes by camels from Alexandria to Suez. Since its date, the railway had grown, and a new treaty was wanted.' His opposite number in the negotiations was Nubar Bey, 'a most courteous gentleman, an

Armenian. I never went to his office, nor do I know that he had an office. Every other day he would come to my hotel, and bring with him his servants, and pipes, and coffee. I enjoyed his coming greatly; but there was one point on which we could not agree.' This was the length of time in which the mails should be carried through Egypt. Trollope insisted on 24 hours, Nubar stuck to 48, threatening to resign his post, forecasting that loss of life and bloodshed would follow. The threats were met not by 'oriental quiescence but British firmness'. Finally Trollope won. He had been told privily that the 48-hour ploy was at the behest of the P & O Steamship Company, great paymasters of the railway, for their own reasons. It was not Egyptian guile that had confronted Trollope at that time. As he reminisced later, 'I often wondered who originated the frightful picture of blood and desolation. That it was an English heart and an English hand I was always sure.' In later years, Nubar Pasha, as he became, related how bullying Trollope had been, saying that he, the Pasha, 'had been treated as a peccant publisher might be treated by an expensive author'.[32]

The meetings had taken place at Shepheard's Hotel and it was there, as well as on the journey there and back, that Trollope steadfastly continued his daily stint on *Dr Thorne*. As one biographer, James Pope-Hennessy, has written, 'he had the amazing ability to abstract himself from his surroundings and be lifted by the imagination back into Barsetshire'.[32] That imagination kept him in a cathedral town in England while he visited Saqqara, the tombs of the Caliphs, the Pyramids of Giza, the mosque of Sultan Hassan and Heliopolis, which last he said was 'a humbug'. He went off to the Holy Land, leaving a message at Shepheard's for his colleague Yates, announcing that he was taking a flying trip to Jerusalem and advising Yates to see the Pyramids.[33] On the way home to England he visited Malta and Gibraltar to inspect their post offices. Some of his adventures during his trip to Egypt appear in his short stories such as 'Tales of All Countries'.

Meanwhile women writers from both sides of the Atlantic were beginning to succumb to the lure of Egypt, the manners and customs of the people holding as great an attraction as the antiquities. The Hon. Mary G. E. Dawson Damer followed the tracks of John L. Stephens and her contribution, published in 1841 in two volumes two years after her visit, was entitled *Diary of a Tour in Greece, Turkey, Egypt and the Holy Land*.[34]

This was a factual, virtually non-contentious approach, which could hardly be said for that of her American counterpart, Sarah Haight, whose *Letters from the Old World*[35] were published in New York in 1840. She was very much for bringing the natives to heel by means of the bastinado or sterner military measures. Sophia Poole, Stanley Lane-Poole's grandmother, with *The Englishwoman in Egypt* (1844–6)[36] and Harriet Martineau with *Eastern Life*,[37] a three-volume work published in London in 1848, represented the distaff view of Egyptian life.

One of the most outstanding women of her time, and a revered name today, was Florence Nightingale, who was 29 when she visited Egypt in the winter of 1849–50 with her friends, Charles and Selina Bracebridge, arriving in Alexandria at almost the same time as Flaubert and du Camp. Her letters home were edited and privately printed by her sister, Parthenope, in 1854. The original collection has been edited and introduced by Anthony Sattin in a beautifully illustrated modern edition under the title *Letters from Egypt: A Journey on the Nile*.[38]

By the time Amelia Edwards went up the Nile, 25 years later, travel had changed considerably and Thomas Cook & Son were already running package tours from London to steamers on the Nile. Florence went by *dahabieh* [a large Nile sailing boat]. She would never go on a steamer. Her subsequent work in the Crimea seems to have been anticipated by her Egyptian experience:

> The state of things here is horrible. Every man is a conscript for the army and mothers put out their children's right eye, cut off their forefingers, or lamed them, to save them from conscription, till Mehemet Ali, who was too clever for them, had a one-eyed regiment, who carry the musket on the left shoulder. The number of one-eyed men you see is frightful.

She had a good eye:

> Cairo . . . is . . . the rose of cities, the garden of the desert, the pearl of Moorish architecture, the fairest, really the fairest, place of earth below . . . From the terrace of the Mehemet Ali mosque is what I should imagine is the finest view in the whole world. Cairo, which is immense, lies at its feet, a forest of minarets and domes and towers.

But can one recognise the later Florence from this self-description? 'They call me "the wild ass of the wilderness, snuffing up the winds", because I am so fond of getting away.'

She ponders: 'I really think a traveller should consider the question, whether it is not less painful to him to travel in America, where there is no Past, an ugly and prosperous Present, but such a Future! or in the East, where there is such a Past, no Present, and, for a Future, one can only hope for extinction!' – and philosophises: 'The Egyptian mind, with its satire and subtlety, reminds me of Pascal, and shows, as he did, how truly earnestness may be allied with these.'

She was by no means starry-eyed, quite the opposite: 'Dendera is a vulgar, upstart temple, covered with acres of bas-reliefs which one has no desire to examine; built without faith or purpose.' We have quoted Mark Twain's views on the Pyramids. Florence Nightingale, there before him, was even blunter:

> Hardly anything can be imagined more vulgar, more uninteresting than a Pyramid in itself, set upon a tray, like a clipt yew in a public-house garden; it represents no idea; it appeals to no feeling; it tries to call forth no part of you, but the vulgarest part – astonishment at its size – at the expense. Surely size is a very vulgar element of the sublime . . . There is nothing to compare the Great Pyramid with; you remain from first to last insensible of its great size, which, as it is its only quality, is unfortunate.

Flaubert and his companion apostrophised the Khamsin. So did Florence: 'Let an European wait till he has seen the Nile in a Khamsin before he speaks uncivilly of a London Fog.' Yet, at the end of her visit, she reveals her great sympathy and respect for the country:

> So, farewell, dear, beautiful, noble dead Egypt, the country which brought forth a race of giants – giants in war, art, science and philosophy. Farewell, without regret, without pain (except a merely personal sorrow), for there is nothing mournful in the remains of a country which, like its own Nile, has overflowed and fertilised the world, and to which you can plainly hear its Maker saying 'Well done'.

It is paradoxical (but then Egypt is a land of paradox), that some of the most revealing and descriptive scenes of the country were depicted by women, whose place was very much in the background in the mid-nineteenth century. European ladies, as they were, went to Egypt as travellers, consorts to their consular husbands, for their health, and inevitably, at some time or other, to do 'good works'. Lady Lucie Duff Gordon was one such who went there primarily for health reasons. Suffering from tuberculosis, her doctors advised her to live in a warm climate. Noble and kind as she was, she did not want to live among her family, husband and children, for fear of infecting them with the disease.

She was 40 when she arrived in Egypt, where she lived until her death seven years later. She was a typical Victorian aristocrat and yet when she arrived in the country, she decided to live with the peasants, the fellaheen as she called them. She loved the simple people and they loved her. She mixed with them and shared their life. She got to know them at first hand, their joys and their sufferings, their feasts and their funerals, their moulids (birthday festivals) and folklore. She lived most of the time on a boat, moving from one town in Upper Egypt to another, following the sun, as it were. She lived with those simple people, the backbone of the country, eating their food and sympathising with their troubles. No wonder her book is a genuine record of an Egypt which no longer exists.

Lady Duff Gordon's *Letters from Egypt* were first published in 1865. The introduction, written by George Meredith, gives a sympathetic pen-picture of her and her character, concluding with the words: 'Lucie Duff Gordon was of the order of women of whom a man of many years may say that their like is to be met once or twice in a lifetime.' This edition was edited and prefaced by her mother, Mrs Austin, who omitted those passages which might have given offence both to Egyptians and others, about whom Lucie wrote so freely. The letters were next published in 1875 with 'Last Letters from Egypt' being added as well as 'Letters from the Cape', together with memoirs by Lady Duff Gordon and by her daughter Janet Ross. In 1969 a centenary edition, entitled *Letters from Egypt 1862–1869*[39] was brought out, edited by Lady Duff Gordon's great-grandson, Gordon Waterfield, to which he added a new introduction. The latest version to appear was in 1983, in the Virago Travellers series, edited this time by Sarah Searight, who has written yet another introduction of her own but also restored George Meredith's original and Janet Ross's memoir.

It is interesting to compare the two versions. They have about the same number of pages but Waterfield includes about 200 letters whereas Searight has only 165. The latter names all addressees, the former does not, explaining that the letters are to Lucie's mother, husband and children, the names of recipients being included where necessary. Searight omits family matters which she considers to be of no interest to the public. Waterfield has rearranged some of the letters to follow the sequence of the writer's travels and not always in date order. He has also brought together several letters on the same subject when they were written within a few days or weeks of each other. He retains some of Lucie's Arabic spelling of names and places; Searight spells the villages according to the atlas published by the Egypt Exploration Fund. Waterfield is generous with explanatory but not excessive footnotes; Searight gives none.

After her first winter, in 1863, Lady Duff Gordon wrote to her husband, Sir Alexander, 'I long to bore you with traveller's tales', but as Sarah Searight has written: 'If that was really her intention, she failed dismally to achieve it. There are library shelves laden with books about nineteenth-century Egypt – discoveries and re-discoveries, archaeology, anthropology, the political assessment, leading to the patronisingly imperial tract.'

Lady Lucie was a shrewd observer and one of the first writers, perhaps, to reveal some of the facts behind the romantic fiction which sometimes passed as a fact, resulting from the seven years she spent in Upper Egypt, a longer time than any other European up to that date. She wrote of a book by her distant cousin, Harriet Martineau:

> It is true as far as it goes, but there is the usual defect – the people are not real people, only part of the scenery to her, as to most Europeans. The descriptions are excellent, but she evidently knew and cared nothing about the people, and had the feeling of most English people here, that the difference of manners is a sort of impassable gulf, the truth being that their feelings and passions are just like our own.

She felt a kinship with her Egyptian hosts which can only be developed by living among them for a period.

She was not put off by the lower side of life:

> The more I see of the back slums of Cairo, the more in love I am with them. The dirtiest lane of Cairo is far sweeter than the best street in Paris. Here there is the dirt of negligence and the dust of a land without rain, but nothing disgusting; decent Arabs are as clean in their personal habits as English gentlemen.

But there were other aspects of life to distress her. 'The system of wholesale extortion and spoliation has reached a point beyond

which it would be difficult to go,' she wrote in one of her letters
dated January 1865. 'I still grieve more over the daily anguish
of the poor fellahins who are forced to take the bread from the
mouths of their starving families and to eat it while toiling for
the private profit of one man.' Then she begins to criticise the
English attitude:

> These are no sentimental grievances; hunger and pain, and labour
> without reward, and the constant bitterness of impotent
> resentment ... To you this must sound remote and almost
> fabulous ... I know the cruel platitudes about governing the orien-
> tals by fear which the English pick up like mocking birds from the
> Turks.

Lady Lucie tried hard to bridge the religious gap with a deep
sincerity. In one letter home she explains the similarities in the
moral codes of both Islam and Christianity.

> In fact I am very much puzzled not to discover the slightest differ-
> ence between Christian and Muslim morality or belief. No one
> attempts to apply different standards of morals or of piety to a
> Muslim and a Copt ... East and West is the difference, not Muslim
> and Christian. There is no hope of a good understanding with
> Orientals until Western Christians can bring themselves to recognise
> the common faith contained in the two religions; the real difference
> consists in all the class of notions and feelings that we derive not
> from the Gospel at all – but from Greece and Rome and which, of
> course, are altogether wanting here.

In his book *Foreign Travellers to Egypt*, one of Egypt's leading writers and historians, Dr Sarwat Okasha, describes Lady
Lucie as 'The Angel of Compassion'.

The religious schism theme was echoed by D. A. Cameron,
quoted earlier, when writing in 1898 of the years between 1849
and 1882:

> We who call ourselves Christians cannot but feel ashamed when
> we learn how during the thirty years Christian adventurers victim-
> ised the Muslims of Egypt, not shooting them down, but neverthe-
> less cruelly wronging them by the abuse of privileges and capitu-
> lations, by the mysterious processes of European law to which the
> Orientals were quite unaccustomed.

The year 1877 saw the first publication of *A Thousand Miles
up the Nile* by Amelia B. Edwards, described by Quentin Crewe
in a much later (1982) edition[40] as 'one of the most engaging
chronicles of the Nile ... one of those intrepid Victorian

spinsters who is a delight to read about but who, one fears, might have been a considerable trial to know'. The greater part of the book is devoted to the ruins and monuments of ancient Egypt and it is this aspect of the country that has given rise to most literature about it. Volumes, papers, studies, theses and collaborations on every aspect of ancient life have abounded and continue to appear as excavations of an almost inexhaustible number of buried cities continue. Amelia Edwards herself became an authority on Egyptology. She founded the Egypt Exploration Fund, left her library to University College, London and money enough to found the first Chair in Egyptology in England.

Tribute should also be paid to Sir Ernest A. T. Wallis Budge, an Egyptologist who did much to popularise ancient Egypt. Among his books was *The Nile: Notes for Travellers in Egypt*[41] first published in 1890, with many later editions running through several years. It is of interest because it was commissioned by Thomas Cook and Co. A copy was given to every one of their customers who travelled up the Nile – as is still done today. It set out to inform them so that they would 'no longer be able to be misled (unintentionally) by Dragomans'.

Rider Haggard was a frequent visitor to Egypt, his fascination with the country stretching over many years. *She*, which virtually created a new literary genre of lost races, with the descendants of the ancient Egyptians living in the hidden heart of Africa ruled over by an immortal queen, Ayesha, was published in 1887 and *The Tale of Philo*, another Ayesha story, appeared in *Hutchinson's Magazine* as late as 1922. His portrayal of this extraordinary woman – 'She who must be obeyed' – was so beautiful that Haggard was forced to say: 'Language fails me when I try to give some idea of her loveliness.' *She* and its followers could not have been written had Haggard not travelled extensively in Egypt and researched among the tombs and relics which were being discovered there.

Rider Haggard dedicated *Cleopatra*, published in 1889, to his mother, writing: 'I trust you will receive from my romance "Cleopatra" some such pleasure as has lightened the labour of its building up; and that it may convey to your mind a picture, however imperfect, of the old and mysterious Egypt in whose lost glories you are so deeply interested.' He was particularly concerned with the old religious rites and was much more than a mere storyteller. He realised very well that not all his public

would share his enthusiasm for symbolism and old beliefs, as
is clear from the author's note preceding the novel:

> Unfortunately it is scarcely possible to write a book of this nature
> and period without introducing a certain amount of illustrative
> matter, for by no other means can the long-dead past be made to
> live again before the reader's eyes, with all its accessories of faded
> pomp and forgotten mystery. To such students as seek a story only,
> and are not interested in the faith, ceremonies or customs of the
> Mother of Religion and Civilisation, ancient Egypt, it is, however,
> respectfully suggested that they should exercise the art of skipping,
> and open this tale at its Second Book.

It was during one of his trips to Egypt, in 1904, that Rider
Haggard was angered by what he called 'the wholesale robbery
of the ancient Egyptian tombs and the consequent desecration
of the dead who lie therein'. So angry was he that he wrote an
article on the subject for the *Daily Mail* in the hope of stirring
up public attention. This appeared on 4 June 1904 under the
title, 'The Trade in the Dead':

> Of those million tombs, scarce any remain unviolated, and we
> Christians hunt over what the Persians, the Romans, the Mohamme-
> dans and desecrating thieves of all ages have left us. See the spot
> today! Everywhere groups of blue-robed fellahin, many of them
> children, are at work upon the mouths of or in the shafts of ancient
> sepulchres. Standing in a cloud of choking dust, the men loosen the
> rubble with their picks, while the children carry it away in
> baskets . . . Is it right that kings and queens, and high priests and
> priestesses, prophets and prophetesses of God as they understand
> Him, should be thus dragged from the sepulchres they fashioned
> with so much thought and care, and for so high a purpose; stripped,
> too, even of their shrouds and made a show of in the very land
> they ruled?

He referred to the subject again in his autobiography, *The
Days of My Life*, when he wrote: 'It did seem wrong that people
with whom it was the first article of religion that their mortal
remains should lie undisturbed until the Day of Resurrection,
should be hauled forth, stripped and broken up, or sold to
museums and tourists.'[42]

Let us backtrack a little to that great event of 1869, the opening
of the Suez Canal. The wheeling and dealing leading up to this
day has been well documented and we are not concerned here
with the political, strategic and commercial considerations of

the de Lesseps dream-become-deed or Disraeli's deal. In seeking connections with literature and the arts we are obliged to Lord Kinross for his colourful painting of the scene in his book *Between Two Seas*[43] published in 1968. After describing the efforts made by the Khedive, Ismail I, to secure the most illustrious persons in Europe as his guests, Lord Kinross writes:

Of the more distinguished guests, the majority came from France, but all countries were represented, with Ibsen from Norway, and Switzerland, on Ismail's explicit instructions, not forgotten, for 'by her commerce and her industry she is called upon to have frequent relations with Egypt'. This privileged selection of guests, which would hardly have shamed Napoleon's Institut d'Egypte, reached Alexandria in two ships from Marseilles, on October 15, 1869. They were met by de Lesseps in person and proceeded to Cairo by train. Next to Zola and Dumas, the most notable writer among them was Théophile Gautier, who observed his fellow-travellers with amusement, and was especially intrigued by the variety of hats which they wore . . . He found himself installed in Shepheard's, a hotel with which Cook was associated. It had been partially destroyed by fire earlier in the year, but hurriedly rebuilt and enlarged, and now resembled, to French eyes, an English barracks rather than an Eastern caravanserai. To Charles Blanc, another French writer, it was 'a vast convent, whose staircase and corridors are hardly lit at all, and whose enclosed rooms resemble monastic cells'. One understands here that light and heat are the same and that coolness is synonymous with night! He took pleasure in walking through the silent sombre corridors, imagining himself in a monastery. From time to time a ray of light shone suddenly – through the door of a cell which a monk had opened. He ran into one of his own party, dragging himself along with his arm in a sling and a companion supporting him. It was Gautier, who explained in his slow asthmatic voice: 'You see what comes of embarking on a Friday . . . I opened the door of a room which I took to be that of a friend: I fell into a coal hole and have broken my collar bone. So I am condemned to remain here.' Gautier thus spent most of his visit watching the world go by, with a none the less observant gaze, from the terrace of Shepheard's.

Entertainment was lavish, with a gala reception which included a performance of a 'Caprice' by Alfred de Musset, balls, concerts, and what was to have been the cultural *pièce de resistance*, a new opera by Verdi in the timber-built Opera House, constructed for the occasion. The story of the opening of the Opera House and the replacement of the unwritten *Aida* by *Rigoletto* has been written by Lord Kinross and other hands.

On 17 November 1869, de Lesseps' 64th birthday, the Suez Canal was formally opened, a convoy of 46 ships, led by the *Aigle*, with the Empress Eugénie on board, sailing through it.

It is not the purpose of this book to analyse or become involved in the ever-complicated political scene in relation to either Egypt and its European partners or rulers *de facto* and *de jure*, or to the internal religious or constitutional factional vicissitudes. However, these considerations cannot be wholly ignored because of the pressures they brought to bear on personalities and life as a whole. British and French rivalry continued through the nineteenth century, the French supplying those intangibles with which we are primarily concerned – language, culture, architecture, social graces and diplomacy; and the British the practicalities of engineering works, including the railway system, money (most important) and politicking. The down-to-earth bedrock of the last mentioned laid the foundation for eventual success and domination.

There were many other Europeans who came to and through Egypt at this time, Greeks taking hold mainly in Alexandria, Italians and Swiss bringing their architecture, Germans their scholarship and so on. Of 300,000 inhabitants in Cairo alone in the 1870s, 5,000 were non-Egyptians, either living permanently in the city or as visitors.

The British occupation in the 74 years from 1882, during which Egypt was under varying degrees of British political control, provided writers of differing talents, professional and amateur, with material of many kinds. The landscape itself, the people, the ebb and flow of travel, the growing interest in archaeology were spurs to the pens of the *literati*. In addition to purely literary contributors during this period, the political commentators and apologists for and critics of the regime were also writing, making speeches and talking in the salons.

One of the few professional writers of note to tell the inside story of Egypt during the period of British ascendancy over France and the setting up of its suzerainty was Wilfred Scawen Blunt, whose fascinating study in two parts, *The Secret History of the English Occupation of Egypt*, was published in London in 1907.[44] Describing himself as a Tory anti-Imperialist, he was, perhaps, an early example of a latter-day 'Wet' but with much more flamboyance and aristocratic disdain than his modern counterparts.

The British (not Blunt's limited nationalist 'English') supremacy was consolidated by that great proconsul Sir Evelyn Baring, later to become Lord Cromer. The half of this writing partnership of that name has to record with regret that he is in no way related to his late lordship, although he strongly suspects that the reason for the high turn-out of Egyptian notables at a lecture given by him at the Anglo-Egyptian Union in 1943 was due to a misplaced belief in some sort of kinship.

It was frequently the theme of late-Victorian statesmen that Britain would shortly be able to leave Egypt but there always seemed to be valid reasons why it should stay. In a footnote in his book *The British in Egypt*,[45] Peter Mansfield writes that according to one estimate, such a statement was made 72 times between 1882 and 1907. He does not say who was counting.

Baring had the nominal title of British Agent when he was appointed in 1883, but he became the virtual ruler of the country. He was given other titles and nicknames. 'Over-Baring' was an obvious reflection on his character, which had less of the cold aloofness of Curzon but some of the traits of a bully. One of the victims of his high-handedness was the irrigation engineer, William Willcocks, after whom the sporting club in Cairo was named. They had several brushes, culminating in a row over a book Willcocks was writing, 'a kind of comic history of Egypt under the English', a theme later to be developed by C. S. Jarvis, of whom more anon. Lord Cromer, as he then was, regarded this as subversive and threatened to dismiss its author from Egypt unless he signed a pledge not to write anything more. Willcocks could not refuse but even he agreed that though Lord Cromer was 'a brute, he was a just brute'. In the event, Willcocks did publish a book, *Sixty Years in the East*,[46] in 1935.

Another aspect of Lord Cromer is revealed in his treatment of Harry Boyle, who had never been to school but became an outstanding linguist. He arrived in Cairo in mid-1885 at the age of 25. Cromer's first address to him was, 'I suppose you speak Arabic fluently.' 'No, sir, hardly at all.' 'What the devil does White [who was the British ambassador in Constantinople] mean by sending that boy here? He'll be worse than useless.' He gave Boyle six weeks to learn Arabic, which he did by vanishing into the back streets of Cairo and returning five weeks later with a wide knowledge of the vernacular. It was not long before he was invaluable to Lord Cromer, later becoming Oriental Secretary. He was nicknamed 'Enoch' because 'he walked with the Lord'. There is no record of any published work by Boyle but his story has been told by Clara Boyle.[47]

The history of the literature inspired by Egypt from Lord Cromer's days on becomes later closely intertwined with education, secondary and post-graduate, and the work of the British Council and its representatives. One cannot ignore, therefore, the development of education in the country. It was not one of the highest points of the Cromer regime, and his firm supporters, Lord Lloyd, in his book *Egypt after Cromer*[48] and Sir Valentine Chirol in *The Egyptian Problem*[49] tend to leave the problem alone. Even Milner[50] could not make much of it, so we find education as no more than a part of a chapter headed 'Odds and Ends of Reform'. As Peter Mansfield notes in his book mentioned earlier, 'In all Cromer's years in Egypt, the amount spent on education did not exceed one per cent of the gross revenues.'

Lord Cromer himself said, in his farewell speech at the Cairo Opera House in 1907, 'I hear it frequently said that although the material prosperity has increased marvellously of late years, nothing has been done towards the moral and intellectual advancement of the people. What! gentlemen, has there been no moral advancement? Is the country governed, as was formerly the case, exclusively by the use of the whip?' He went on to enumerate the abolition of forced slavery, the decline of corruption and the reform of the prisons and hospitals but said nothing more about 'intellectual advancement'.

Because the main languages of books about or influenced by Egypt (apart from archaeological and historical treatises and commentaries) have been French and English, a brief traverse of the ground covered already by Peter Mansfield is called for here. When the British occupation started, itself following upon the previous French indoctrination, Egypt had a dual education system: the Islamic, based on the Kuttabs (schools) and working through the government primary and secondary schools, and the higher institutes of learning and foreign mission schools (Greek, Italian, French and American).

Upon this structure were imposed English methods of teaching and discipline so far as the Egyptian government schools were concerned. To run the departments of public instruction (the P I as it came to be called), Douglas Dunlop, a Scotsman who came out to Alexandria to teach in a missionary school, was brought in as a Chief Inspector. Although not a public-school man himself, he recruited a number of aristocratic Oxbridge graduates, known as Dunlop's Young Men.

It was not long before English replaced French as a second language in the schools. The statistics of the time show that between 1889 and 1898 the number of pupils in the government schools who studied the English language increased from 1,603 to 3,559, while those who studied French dropped from 2,994 to 1,881. The totals in any case are not large. The great incentive to learn English was not so much academic prowess as the practical necessity of the language in the government service, which was the Promised Land of security to the greater number of aspiring students. Culture remained more securely anchored in the French language and the salons, particularly in Alexandria.

It was during this period of the English language surge that the weekly magazine *The Sphinx* was founded in 1893 by an American, David Garrick Longworth. Primarily a chronicle of the comings and goings of English society, it was, and remained until its demise in 1952, a vehicle for prose and poetry. Longworth also started the Sphinx Bar near Shepheard's Hotel, which turned out to be a good source for chit-chat in the magazine. The readers of *The Sphinx* would be both European residents and tourists, mainly British and American, who would inevitably go on shopping expeditions, with or without a dragoman. Douglas Sladen devotes a few chapters to this subject in his *Oriental Cairo*[3] and his description of a transaction in the early 1900s could well stand today. It happened in the Street of the Camels in Cairo, when he was offered a scarab for £2.

> I confess that I am unable to detect a well-forged scarab. Some of the most valuable scarabs in the Cairo Museum look like clumsy and garish forgeries. But I knew that if he offered it to me for only £2 it must be a forgery, so I offered him two piastres for it. He said, 'Don't pay me now. Take it to the Museum, and if they say it is a forgery I will give you £10.' This man had not got £10, and he had never had £10, and never would have £10, and he knew that if I took it to the Museum the director would sweep it away in instant contempt. But he thought that if he bluffed me like this, I might try to buy it from him for some smaller price, a pound, or ten shillings, or even two shillings. But I said, 'For an imitation one piastre is enough. But this is a very cleverly made imitation, so I

will give you two for it. Do not bother me any more until you wish to take two piastres.' Of course he picked me up farther down the street and let me have it for two piastres; he was making a hundred per cent on it, or more, and probably had a pocketful.

When the shopping was done, the evening entertainment followed in due course and amidst the noise and light of the cafés and the bands, Sladen reminds us of the constant British presence:

The scarlet uniforms of Tommy Atkins recall you to a sense of reality. Tommy is for the most part behaving very well, doing nothing worse than singing uproariously in chorus, though occasionally he grows so 'blind' that he has to be taken home in a cab by his fellows. And an odd sight it makes to see half a dozen Tommy Atkinses, some 'blind' and some leading the blind, crowded into a Cairo arabeah with a tarbushed Jehu on the box lashing a pair of white Arabs into a gallop.

When Lord Cromer left Egypt and wrote his book *Modern Egypt* in 1908,[51] he wrote in all sincerity, 'The Englishman came to Egypt with a mission to perform', yet Anglo-Egyptian relations were uneasy, as Lord Edward Cecil was to disclose, albeit unconsciously, in his minor classic *The Leisure of an Egyptian Official*.[52] Lord Edward Cecil served in the Egyptian army from 1901 until his transfer to government service in Egypt, first as Under-Secretary for War (1904), Under-Secretary for Finance (1905) and Financial Adviser from 1912 until his death in 1918. His book was published by his widow in 1921 and consists of a series of sketches, primarily of his life in Cairo, written originally for the amusement of his family. They provide a light-hearted glimpse of officialdom at work and at leisure. His widow said of the book that 'it was written by the wittiest Englishman I have ever known'.

The two major sections are 'My Daily Life', divided into 12 chapters, taking him through the day from getting up and breakfasting, through office chores and meetings, lunch, golf, dinner, evening party, and supper through to bed and a dream of a Pharaoh; and 'Going on Leave', from planning and packing through every stage to the Paris to Calais rail journey, phased through 11 chapters. In between these two major sections are four cameos, one on Lord Kitchener, one about a day on the Suez Canal, a funeral, entitled 'A Well-managed Ceremony', and a very amusing sequence of telegrams passing between the Foreign Office and Cairo in 1916.

The following extracts give some of the flavour of his style, at the same time revealing glimpses of the mores of the period, thus:

> The custom of giving tips or commission runs through every class and every transaction in this country, from the superior irrigation engineer, who expects his 'present' from the landholder for giving him the water he has a right to, to the office-keeper, who expects a farthing tip from the poor petitioner who wishes his complaint laid upon the great man's table.

Lord Edward's assessment of his subordinates is all too familiar:

> The native officials are far too fond of referring questions to superior authority, partly because they are timid, and partly because they have no sense of proportionate importance. This is due to the undeveloped state of their intelligence, and to the tradition of bad government which makes them live like all those whose tenure of position or livelihood is precarious, in the present. The immediate effect, not the ultimate result, is what they care about.

After describing the balls given at the various hotels, Cecil continues:

> Of course there are other entertainments, whether of a recurrent nature – as, for example, the opera (which is usually like nothing on earth except a concert of cats) – or special festivities which are given from time to time, such as garden parties, concerts, etc.; but the balls are the standing dish, of which you can always partake if you can get nothing better.

The Cecil view of the Copts is severe:

> The Copts are liars because for years it has been dangerous for them to speak the truth; crooked and cunning because by those qualities alone they could get a living; proud in their contempt of the Moslem, servile in view of his power to oppress them, careless of their personal appearance from ages of concealment of their riches by this means.

This is not a view which is shared by those who know this hard-working sect.

Lord Edward was Kitchener's ADC during the Nile Expedition of 1896, and when he came to Egypt again in 1912 saw him practically every day until the First World War broke out in 1914. His judgement and appreciation is therefore based on observation and knowledge:

> No man was greater in one respect – he never ceased learning. He had none of that almost universal vanity which makes us conceal or slur over what we do not know. When he came to something he did not know, he immediately looked round for some one who did, and if the matter was one with which he saw he would be concerned in the future, he learnt as much as he could about it . . . What struck one almost first was the vitality of his mind. He was always doing something, planning something – and something big. He never was for a moment satisfied. No one understood more thoroughly and practically that life is far too short for all you ought to do. His mind was always devising something fresh, some new improvement, some move forward in the path he followed . . . He was naturally and ever on the side of the weak and the oppressed. No one was perhaps in a sense more dictatorial, but no one was more truly just or had more reverence for the rights of his poorer fellows. The oppression of the fellahin, and the way in which the half-civilised upper classes of Egypt regard them as little better than animals, stirred Lord Kitchener to the depths of his character.

The Egyptian University, denied by Lord Cromer, was founded, with the agreement of his successor, Eldon Gorst, at the end of 1908, financed at first solely from private funds until the Government later provided a small subsidy, which did not increase substantially for some time. Government scholarships for an education abroad had practically ceased and students seeking a liberal university education were obliged to go to European seats of learning at their own or their parents' expense.

As Sir Eldon Gorst succeeded Lord Cromer, so Ronald Storrs succeeded Harry Boyle as Oriental Secretary, after an apprenticeship in lower posts in what was then rather grandly called His Britannic Majesty's Diplomatic Agency and Consulate General. This title was changed to the Residency during the Protectorate (see p. 41) until the Anglo-Egyptian Treaty of 1936, when it became the British Embassy. It is to Sir Ronald Storrs that we look for vignettes of that uneasy period between 1908 and the outbreak of war in 1914. His book *Orientations*,[53] first published in 1937 and running through several editions, to be republished in a definitive edition in 1943, throws a clear light on official and social life in Egypt at that time:

> For Cairo Society, the golden epoch must have been the late 'eighties

and the 'nineties . . . 1904 may be said to have marked the decline, 1914 the fall . . . With the decline of foreign political influence and so of foreign social prestige; with the increasing numbers of minor British officials and the extension of the club and sport system; with the multiplication of the hotels, and the mass production of the peach-fed standardised tourist 'doing' the whole country in ten days and demanding indiscriminate hotel dances, there came less mixing with and understanding of Egyptians and foreigners, and a general diminution of social caste, cachet, and character.

Storrs was a man of culture, and music was one of his delights. There were not many concerts in Cairo before 1914 and no permanent orchestras. Gramophones were still scratchy and there was no radio. One made one's own music and Storrs, having been given a small Bluthner grand piano, contrived concerts after tea on Wednesdays to an exclusive audience of 12, his artistes being drawn from the best amateur talent of Cairo society. He records that one could get a reasonably good back stall in the Opera House for the equivalent of four shillings (1937 value): 'Italian and French companies were subsidised some four or five thousand pounds in alternate years, the Italians giving infinitely better value for opera and the French for drama.'

When stationed in Alexandria in the Customs Inspectorate, prior to his appointment as Oriental Secretary, Storrs became the operatic critic to the *Egyptian Gazette*, one of the two English-language newspapers, and enjoying his free stall seat, spent many nights at the little Zizinia Theatre for performances of *La Bohème*, *Tosca*, *Thaïs* and *Lohengrin*, the Wagnerian predecessor of subsequent renditions of *La Valkeria* and *I Maestri Cantori di Norimberga*. Some of his Cairo experiences at the Abbas Theatre were less happy: *Africans*, 'a piece which made yawn our grandsires', *Cavalleria Rusticana*, when the prima donna was hissed and booed because she had not tipped her claque; *Herodiade*, spoiled by a gesticulating John the Baptist who had not been given a limelight, and *Anna Karenina*, 'the worse opera I ever saw'. Storrs' musical taste was further slighted at the Memorial Service for Edward VII held in Alexandria: 'The massed bands were moderate only, lacking in Bass, and they contrived to lower the quality even of Chopin's "March", which one would have thought just suited to their taste. "Saul" we expected to be massacred, nor were we disappointed.'

Let us conclude this musical interlude with two more operatic experiences. The *Salome* of Richard Strauss had been successfully performed in the capitals of Europe, being a *succès de scandale* at the same time. When it came to Cairo, Storrs, for whom this was his first Strauss opera, attended all the rehearsals. Twice the conductor, Signor Bracale, flung down the score and fled from the theatre and at one rehearsal, the Salome 'completely losing her temper, so far forgot herself as to throw the Charger at J the B, who was talking in the wings'. The second item was of a much higher order – the visit of Dame Ethyl Smyth to Egypt in 1913 to complete her latest opera, *The Bosun's Mate*. While her music was not to everyone's taste, Storrs enthused, stating that he could not have enough of it:

> She seemed to bring the atmosphere of the hunting field, Johannes Brahms, John Sargent and our friends in Paris with her every time she came into the house – and it was life ... with the face of a battered Sphinx, eyes like blue spinels, clothes of a District Visitor, she plays and makes others play like Seraphim.

By now, time for leisure was running out. Eldon Gorst had died and Lord Kitchener had been appointed in his place. Unlike Lord Cromer, he was neither a scholar nor a writer, nor even a serious reader. He had none of Gorst's taste for music and science, nor the love of sport and poetry of that later hero, Lord Allenby. In the estimation of Ronald Storrs, however, 'in his love and pursuit of fine arts, especially the decorative and the antique, Kitchener surpassed all who had gone before or have come after him'.

Ronald Storrs was informed during Kitchener's first week in Cairo that a number of British officials might be tendering their resignations; some because they disliked him, others to forestall compulsory retirement. Storrs goes on to relate:

> When (without mentioning individuals) I warned him of this tendency he significantly tapped a drawer in his desk and said: 'You'd better go down to the Club and let it be generally known that I've always kept printed acceptance forms for resignations, only requiring the name to be added to become effective.' I duly circulated this news and need hardly say that, for whatever reason, not one single resignation was submitted. Next day, curious to see how the forms ran, I opened the drawer and found it to contain a box of cigars.

Nevertheless the fear of dismissal was a real one. In his biography,[54] Russell Pasha relates the tale of Captain Hubbard of the Interior who, losing his temper over a matter of rolling stock, slapped the face of the stationmaster of Dab'a. Kitchener was reported to be very annoyed and intending to sack Hubbard. As Russell writes:

> A few days later the Khedive came out from Alexandria in his special train to inspect the Maryut estates, and on slowing up at the station noticed drawn up on the platform a curious guard of honour composed of a tall soldierly British officer, half a dozen odd Camel Corps police, and a bugler who sounded the Khedivial salute. The Khedive called the officer up and asked him who he was, to which Hubbard, who stammered badly, replied: 'Your H-H-Highness, I am C-C-Captain H-H-Hubbard who smacked your stationmaster's face. L-L-Lord K-K-Kitchener wants to sack me, and I appeal to Your H-H-Highness to protect me.' The Khedive was so amused at being appealed to against the all-powerful Kitchener that he intimated in the proper quarter that he wished no more done in the matter of Captain Hubbard and the stationmaster.

This pre-war period was drawing to a close. John Galsworthy came for a holiday and was reported to have been seen camping with H. W. Massingham near the Pyramids; Storrs was delighted to sit for two hours with Amir Abdallah, later to become King of Transjordan, while he intoned the Seven Suspended Odes of Pre-Islamic Poetry, the Glories and the Lament of Antar ibn Shaddad; Kitchener returned to England to become War Minister and the First World War began.

The First World War did not produce much in the way of a cultural life in Egypt. The main interest was in politics and the relationship of the country to its British 'protectors'. Immediately before the outbreak of war, the servicemen coming to Egypt, whether their work was military or diplomatic – the main objective of which was the defence of the crucial lifeline to India – were intent on stamping their superiority upon the land, as noted by James Aldridge.[55]

With Turkey's entry into the war on the side of Germany on 6 November 1914, the whole of the Middle East immediately became a chess board on which the pieces were moved constantly by the diplomatic and military hands which were shaping the destiny of the area. Martial law was proclaimed in Egypt, which was still, technically, a province of the Ottoman Empire and the debate about the status of the country rapidly developed. The decision had been taken in London for Annexation to be proclaimed and an Order in Council was actually drafted. The Egyptian Ministers viewed this step with horror and the British diplomatic team on the spot (still awaiting a replacement for Kitchener) were nonplussed and pressed for Protectorate status. As Storrs himself wrote:

> I am anti-Annexation and pro-Protectorate. It is too late, in the twentieth century, to denationalise and attempt to absorb races; and even if it were practicable elsewhere, the Nile Mud, which has absorbed Hebrews, Persians, Greeks, Romans and Turks so completely as to efface every trace of them, is not a suitable medium for any such experiment.

Happily, the British Government opted for a Protectorate and Prince Hussein Kamel was installed on the throne in place of the Khedive Abbas who was in Turkey, while the Residency was put into the hands of Sir Henry MacMahon, who took the title of High Commissioner. He it was who, in 1916, had the foresight to purchase the property adjoining the Residency, thus adding the present Chancery and almost doubling the size of the garden.

The military threat to the British at this time lay in the Turkish forces who were in Palestine and Syria. It was anticipated that they would advance across the Sinai Desert to the Suez Canal and immediate steps were taken to forestall such action by strengthening the Canal defences. These lay in the hands of the professional army. Behind the lines in Cairo, a volunteer reserve unit had been formed by members of Gezira Sporting Club, known as 'Pharaoh's Foot' by the heartless locals.

There was to be virtually no military action on the Egyptian side of the Canal but the activities to the north and north-east would become known the world over, particularly through the exploits of one man. In the winter of 1914, the now almost legendary T. E. Lawrence appeared on the Middle Eastern scene, becoming a member of the Intelligence Branch of the Egypt Defence Force. The books about him have been many and varied, providing information, speculation and many an apocryphal story about this strange, complex character. But this book is about Egypt and its influence, not the wider issues of Britain against Turkey, Arab against Arab and Arab against Jew, or the more scattered geographical range of the Hashemite

Crescent. Sir Ronald Storrs saw him at close quarters, when Lawrence would wander in and out of his flat reading or borrowing books for further reading:

> We had no literary differences except that he preferred Homer to Dante and disliked my placing Theocritus before Aristophanes. He loved music, harmony rather than counterpoint, and sat back against the cushions with his eyes half-closed, enduring even the meandering stream of musical consciousness which I dignified by the name of improvisation.

Lawrence was horrified at the thought of being cooped up in Cairo. In a letter to Lord Lloyd, he wrote: 'My statement, when they offered me the succession to Allenby, was that I'd shut up the Residency, except as offices, take a room at Shepheard's and ride about Cairo and the Delta on my motorbike; and yet "run" the Government from underneath.'

There were few others to grace the scene with cultural pretensions. Storrs found one such in Mark Sykes, who did not appear in Cairo until 1916 – that other half of the Sykes–Picot agreement which planned the tri-partite division of non-Turkish Turkey between France, Russia and England but was nullified by the fall of Russia. Sykes was a man of many parts; caricaturist, political cartoonist, actor (even music-hall comedian), he dictated into a dictaphone for Storrs a three-act Drury Lane melodrama. He was an entertaining writer but has made no lasting impression on the literary scene.

It was in the spring of 1916 that Storrs felt moved to take some steps to ensure recognition of the tercentenary of Shakespeare:

> I telephoned to the Bishop, Rennie MacInnes, suggesting that he should work the thing into his Easter Sermon. Similar injunctions through the Coptic Patriarchate obtained an honourable mention from every Coptic pulpit in the realm; I next binged up the Minister of Education to the tune of a memorial lecture in every school, and finally, telephoned to the English, French, Italian, Greek, Arabic and Armenian Press, provoking a flow of leading articles, prize poems, and enthusiastic correspondence.

Thus did one man stir up a proper appreciation of the Bard in the middle of the First World War.

The disastrous Dardanelles campaign ended in a stream of wounded and shattered men leaving Gallipoli in hospital ships, many bound for Alexandria. Here, schools and hotels were taken over as hospital and convalescent areas. Into this network of sickbeds came E. M. Forster, arriving in the autumn of 1915 as a Red Cross volunteer. In his introduction to the 1961 edition of his *Alexandria – a History and Guide* he wrote: 'What had begun as an outpost turned out something suspiciously like a funk-hole, and I stuck it for over three years, visiting hospitals, collecting information and writing reports.' This edition was published in New York. The book itself was first published in Alexandria in 1922, in circumstances described by Forster in his introduction. A second edition, also published in Alexandria in 1938, proved as difficult to obtain subsequently as the first, as Lawrence Durrell notes in his introduction to the first British edition, published in 1982.[56] Further reference to the book and its contents will be made later in the chapter devoted to Alexandria.

One of those wounded at Gallipoli by 'a mild dose of shrapnel' was Joseph McPherson, whose life in Egypt, based on letters home and collected by his family in 20 bound volumes, was published as *Bimbashi McPherson, a Life in Egypt* in 1983.[57] These letters were never intended for publication but they give a vivid picture, not only of life in Egypt before the war, but in this particular context, of the activities of the Camel Transport Corps, which had been formed following the decision to change military tactics from a defensive line along the Suez Canal to a harassing operation by which the Turks would be faced in the Sinai Desert and thrown out of the positions they occupied in strategic oases and along the coast. The CTC were to act as logistics support, supplying the fighting troops in the desert with water and stores and bringing the wounded back to base. The two chapters in the book under the headings 'The Battle for Sinai' and 'The Battle for Gaza' show McPherson at his decriptive best.

The Camel Transport Corps was only one of many military offshoots which made Egypt the centre of activities. The Army of Occupation, itself augmented by Imperial Service troops from India, Australia and New Zealand, needed depots, training centres and barracks. The Egyptian Army also was no mean size. In addition, there were the Egyptian Expeditionary Force, the Arab Bureau (controlling the Hejaz campaign) and various Intelligence Bureaux. Ronald Storrs described this period thus:

Sport, racing and dances for civilians continued . . . I clung to my

Wednesday Musics so long as I remained in Cairo, reinforced often by varied accessions of War talent, and had once, during an afternoon of Brahms songs, to prefer the room to the company of two visitors who objected to the use of the German language.

One of the soldiers who came to Egypt in the middle of the Dardanelles campaign and lived on there after the war to carry on engineering work, was Major C. S. Jarvis, CMG, OBE, who wrote a number of books in humorous vein, mostly sketches and vignettes of the country and its people, the first being *Oriental Spotlight*, published in 1937 with caricature-type illustrations by R. A. Young, the two collaborators taking the pseudonyms of 'Rameses' and 'Roly'.[58] From this and three other books by the same duo – *The Back Garden of Allah*,[59] *Heresies and Humours*[60] and *Happy Yesterdays*,[61] we have been able to cull a few more facts about the period.

Most of what Jarvis wrote was in a light-hearted vein but a serious underside would break through now and again. He spent what he called a long and boring period of the war, so far as the Palestine campaign was concerned, between the unsuccessful second battle of Gaza and the very successful third battle in September 1917. Spots of leave were taken in Cairo, as full of brigadiers then as it was in the Second World War. Jarvis sets the scene by observing that:

> On the whole Egypt had a very good war . . . the two big hotels in Cairo, Shepheard's and the Continental, were full winter and summer, a state of affairs that has never occurred before and never will again unless there is another war, whilst all the other hotels were rented at the most generous prices to be turned into hospitals and offices. There was a constant stream of officers coming down on leave from the front with pockets full of unspent pay and allowances and an enormous capacity for enjoyment; and Cairo experienced an unbroken season of four years instead of a short three months annually . . . Racing went on as usual and every place of amusement was packed to the roof nightly with enthusiastic troops.

Storrs confirms the prosperity brought to Egypt through the war. His account of 1917 reflects the scene:

> In Cairo and Alexandria civilian life glided tranquilly forward into the making and spending of fortunes . . . Stocks in the bazaars had fallen in quality as well as in quantity but not, it seems, quite so quickly or so low as the critical faculty of gallant purchasers.

There was little to add to cultural life, even the charity shows

being limited largely to light-hearted revues. There was nothing
of the wide-ranging choice of alternatives which were so much
a feature of the Second World War.

Jarvis draws down the curtain on the Middle East campaigns
and their effect on Egypt:

> By the autumn of 1919 every soldier desiring demobilisation had
> been shipped off home, but it was not until the year 1922 that the
> huge ordnance dumps and camps all over the country were finally
> broken up and Egypt emerged from the War with her manhood
> practically intact, her finances flourishing, and the price of cotton,
> her staple product, soaring to unprecedented heights – without a
> doubt Egypt had a very good war.[58]

3

The Inter-war Years

Two of the personalities to whom we have introduced you – Bimbashi McPherson and Major Jarvis, are archetypal examples of that particularly British phenomenon, the ex-pat, as the expatriates are familiarly known. They appear all over the world, a legacy of the Imperial days when the globe was coloured with the pink of British possessions or influence and the colonies became the refuge of the younger sons, the not so successful and the bad hats. But those sterling characters who remained in Egypt because they loved the country and had something useful to contribute to its well-being, were of a particular quality. It was this attraction which lies at the heart of our theme – the spell that the country casts over those who first visit, then stay there. The land and its people draw out of the visitor a desire to depict and enshrine the qualities that attract them. Many of them are amateurs in the true sense but often they become professional in their skill and the magic goes on working.

Jarvis reflects this love/hate relationship between the expatriate and the Egyptian government service in his record of his experience immediately after the First World War:

When I started my service in Egypt after the last war, it coincided with a new order of things – the adoption of mechanical transport on the frontiers and the gradual elimination of the camel and pony. In this respect I may say that the elimination has been very gradual indeed, as when I retired (in 1937) there were still more than 250 police and gendarmerie mounted on camels in the Sinai . . . The Egyptian government has always been remarkable for the strict economy it exercises over desert administration, the argument being that a man who is fool enough to put up with the desert will put up with anything. For this reason in 1919 we did not get new cars for our service, but second-hand ones from the bargain basement of the Army Disposal Board which had already seen three years of service. They had therefore been thoroughly run in.

The anecdotes which follow from this economy of service-ability are humorous indeed, but the thrust of the text is all too familiar when, at any time from then on until the present day, the ramshackle, run-down state of almost every public service from sewage to transport bears the mark of endemic poverty, parsimony and, perhaps, peculation at certain levels, which deny the services the full value of the monies allotted or donated. These reflections are not really digressions from our theme because the end product of experience is the literature which lies at the heart of this book.

McPherson was not, of course, a writer. He was, however, a classical scholar with an Oxford degree and a natural story-teller, so his letters (he wrote no books) have a quality of their own. Between 1918 and 1924 he was first put in charge of a political prison at Giza but after a few months was appointed Acting Mamur Zapt, or Head of the Political CID and Secret Police of Cairo, under the authority of Russell Pasha, who was Commandant of Police.

Mursi and his generation remember Bimbashi McPherson, who was often to be seen during the Second World War riding a white donkey with his sayes [groom] striding alongside. He took no notice of the traffic and wherever his donkey led him he was greeted by many Egyptians. Going through the book which reproduces his letters, one cannot fail to detect two separate and, at times contradictory, lines of thought. He could make and praise friends as individuals but at the same time he was contemptuous of the people. Perhaps it was his work in the police and intelligence which gave him an inside knowledge of the unsavoury characters and rogues he found around him. Certainly, during this period he saw at first hand the corruption that existed among the high-ranking officers, who were mostly foreigners.

The colonialist nature of McPherson is reflected clearly when he deals with the 1919 Revolution. McPherson explains that nobody took the Revolution seriously. The British accounts of the events in Egypt in 1919 refer to them as 'disturbances'. This is what McPherson wrote to his friend Dougal in that year:

For nearly twenty years now, I have been sending home scraps of information about the East; and I suppose I ought not to be silent

on the recent events in Egypt, though it is as depressing to write
about those days of shame as it will be for you to read the
unpleasant facts.

I do not know what damned political game may supply a key of
sorts to this interregnum of impotence. Politics is a form of immor-
ality, from which, thank God, I have kept clean. I assume, however,
that as Roosevelt put it: 'As long as we are in Egypt, we are here
to govern it; otherwise we should clear out.' At present we are
doing neither.

McPherson tries either to philosophise his colonialist attitude
or to find an excuse for it. When he is asked by an Egyptian
friend: 'How it is that you, our friend, almost an Egyptian in
many ways, would hesitate to give us complete independence?'
McPherson answered in his patronising manner: 'Because I love
you too well to give you what would harm you, on the same
principle that I would hesitate to lend you my sailing boat,
without someone on board to manage her, lest you should come
to grief.'

Yet in spite of this patronising, colonialist attitude, the Bimbashi expressed sympathetic, almost loving feeling towards the
people of Egypt, especially the peasants:

> Next to Father Nile, it is the fellah who matters. He is to all intents
> and purposes voiceless in the nation, and there are many in the
> noisy minority who would fain batten on him again as in the
> past. By such he has been misled, and at times even excited into
> compromising action, but there is something pyramidal in his solid-
> ity and simplicity of character, and happily he still remains what
> he has been through the ages. His ideals are perhaps not high, but
> they are natural and peace-loving; he loves to employ his wonderful
> physical strength in tilling the land, and is contented if he may keep
> a modest share of what he produces for his own simple needs: a
> share sufficient to enable him to marry, to keep up a mud hut for
> his family and domestic animals, and to supply himself and them
> with food; and he likes, after working from dawn till sundown, a
> little leisure for his evening prayers and his evening meal, and to
> linger in a café, and listen to some raconteur, or a few musicians.
> Almost above all he loves to talk . . .

If we forget the patronising, we cannot but agree with Mc-
Pherson. One can detect some kind of torn loyalties. He is,
without a doubt, sincere, in both his colonialist belief and his
love for Egypt and the Egyptians. The 'disturbances' were a
series of strikes and demonstrations sparked off by the arrest

and deportation of Saad Zaghlul Pasha who, following the lead given by President Wilson and his Fourteen Points, claimed Egypt's right of self-determination as one of them. All the cities and towns were taken over by Egyptians, and in Cairo trains and trams stopped and nobody went to work. On 18 March 1919 eight English soldiers were killed on their way to Cairo and the rioters dug trenches to prevent mounted police and troops from operating. Lorry loads of troops were attacked with sticks and stones, provoking them to open fire, killing 13 and wounding 30. On 9 April a further 30 people were executed for killing British officers. General Allenby was despatched as High Commissioner to replace the Resident and restore order.

His first act was to release Saad Zaghlul from exile in Malta. The delegation which he led to the Residency with his demand for independence was called the Wafd and that became the name of the political party founded to negotiate terms with the British. Allenby declared martial law and took little time to crush the strikes. Any hope that the Wafdists, directed by Zaghlul from Paris, might have had in relying on the Wilsonian doctrine to support their cause was swiftly dispelled by a declaration made by the United States on 20 April recognising the British Protectorate of Egypt.

Lord Milner was sent out to Cairo with the object of working out a constitution for Egypt, but his mission was boycotted, the women playing a conspicuous part in hijacking tramcars, shouting 'Down with Milner' and thrusting slogans into the faces of would-be passengers. In his book[49] Sir Valentine Chirol says that the schoolgirls of Cairo were much more violently anti-Milner than the boys. Education was, in any case, at a low ebb and as Chirol says, 'was unquestionably the worst of our failures'. The Milner mission failed also and went home. Zaghlul was allowed to present his case in London and to return to Cairo in 1921 to lead the Wafd. He was uncompromising in his demands for independence. 'Not a single British soldier must remain on Egyptian soil. If negotiation fails, Egypt will fight like Ireland.' The outbreaks of violence which followed in Cairo, Alexandria and elsewhere in Egypt, goaded Allenby to order the arrest and deportation of Zaghlul, this time to the Seychelles.

Allenby then took his own initiative, forcing the British Government to grant independence to Egypt, at the same time reserving some powers to itself for future negotiation. He had pushed the Government further than it had wanted to go and Lloyd George said of him to King George V, 'I know now why he is called the Bull; he has got into our Eastern china shop and is breaking everything up.' Nevertheless, the declaration terminating the British Protectorate and establishing the independence of Egypt was made on 28 February 1922. The powers reserved to Britain were: security of the communications of the British Empire in Egypt; the defence of Egypt against aggression; the protection of foreign interests and minorities in Egypt; and control over the Sudan. A government was formed which was prepared to work under these conditions and the Khedive, Fuad, assumed the title of King.

Violence continued, 17 British officials being assassinated and as many more attacked during the following 18 months. British civilians and Egyptian cabinet ministers were also attacked. In September 1923 Saad Zaghlul was allowed to return from exile, became Prime Minister after the elections and inveighed against the reserved clauses. On 19 November 1924 Sir Lee Stack, the Sirdar or Commander-in-Chief of the Egyptian Army, was shot as he was driving through Cairo by assassins who escaped in a taxi. On the day of his funeral, Allenby drove with an escort of cavalry to the Egyptian Parliament with a list of demands, including an apology for the murder. Six months later, he resigned, to be replaced by Lord Lloyd. Although Bimbashi McPherson had little good to say of Allenby, calling him 'a vacillating jackass and do-nothing King Log', General Wavell later said of him that 'he had recognised in Egypt the awakened spirit of a people'.

A serving officer who was also an academic and an intellectual was Lt-Col. P. G. Elgood, whose first book, *Egypt and the Army*, appeared in 1924. Four years later, *The Transit of Egypt* was published, followed by *Bonaparte's Adventure in Egypt* in 1931. In 1935 came *Egypt – a Brief History from Ancient until Modern Times*, reprinted in Cairo in 1943, with a new edition in 1949. His last book was *The Ptolemies in Egypt*, published in 1938, but it is the *History*, bringing the story of Egypt, through its last edition, up to 1942,[62] that has fascinated Mursi, who has appreciated Elgood's confidence in the country and its people, particularly the women. 'Tradition may still oblige the women of the village to wail and sob, but the tears here lost their poignancy, and the mourners are paying no more than a tribute to convention. Noticeable, also, is the restlessness of the younger upper-class women. If they do not claim equality with me, they are moving towards that goal.' Elgood also stresses the point which has been made by earlier writers, the unity of religion: 'Moslem and Copt live side by side in peace. The Moslem invokes the name of the Almighty in the mosque, the Copt in the Church, otherwise the two are hardly distinguishable one from another.'

We come now to Robert Graves. Martin Seymour-Smith remarks in his biography,[63] that when he left the army, Graves would never 'take orders', a vow which in 1920 gave him strength and which remained unbroken except for the short period when he worked in Egypt. To preface that, we must look back to when his interest in the country had been kindled by his half-brother Philip, who when home on leave from Cairo in June 1916 had spoken of Second Lieutenant T. E. Lawrence, with whom he then worked in Military Intelligence. In November 1919, Graves and his father had been given places of honour at the High Table of All Souls, and in the coffee room after dinner were introduced to Lawrence, then a full Colonel working at the college on *Seven Pillars of Wisdom*. There was something of mutual admiration in their relationship, Lawrence praising Graves for his poetry which he said he read in Egypt during one of his flying visits from Arabia, and confessing that he was deeply interested in writers and reading. He saw Robert as a useful link with the younger poets. For his part, Graves was delighted to meet the man who had become a legend in his own lifetime.

In the period following October 1920, Graves introduced Lawrence to such literary figures as Thomas Hardy, Edmund Blunden and Siegfried Sassoon. Graves made frequent visits to All Souls to discuss poetry and the two became firm friends but did not meet after 1922, by which time Lawrence had enlisted in the RAF and later in the Tank Corps as T. E. Shaw.

Further detail on this period has been provided by Richard Percival Graves in the first volume of his biography.[64] By October 1925, Graves was at a low ebb financially and worried because of the illness of his wife, Nancy Nicholson. He had been turned down for a post at Cornell University in June and had been passing the word round that he was looking for work. Nancy's doctor had advised that she should spend the winter in a dry, warm climate and within a week or so, Graves received post comprising one letter from Liverpool University asking him to stand as a candidate for the Professorship of English and three more inviting him to apply for the Professorship of English at Cairo University. Graves applied for both jobs but preferred Cairo because of the climate plus the relatively good salary and light teaching duties, which would give him time to carry on with his writing. In a letter to Siegfried Sassoon, Graves said that the letters about the post, a Foreign Office appointment, came from 'Sir Sidney Lee, Sir Izzy Gollancz and my brother Philip who has secured George Lloyd's backing (isn't he High Commissioner of Egypt or something?). And apparently the "little ray of sunshine" as I once heard T. E. L. queerly but accurately called, has been stirring in the matter.' He also had letters of commendation which had been written earlier, no doubt for the Cornell post, by Robert Bridges, the Earl of Asquith and Oxford and the Vice-Chancellor of Oxford. He was afraid that Arnold Bennett might have been against him, so wrote to him asking him 'not at any rate to curb my chances', but he need not have worried as Bennett, too, had recommended him.

He tried to get Siegfried Sassoon to join him, asking him, 'I suppose it would be hopeless to suggest you coming to Cairo with us? It would make it so much more attractive for both of us. I suppose you wouldn't consent as my assistant, and pool the salaries?' Sassoon would not. On receiving the formal letter of appointment at the end of November 1925, Graves thought the starting salary of £900 too low and the sum of £75 towards his passage insufficient. He therefore turned down the offer but changed his mind and accepted, when the offer was increased to £1,200 per annum payable monthly, with a month's salary in advance to help with the travelling expenses.

There was much activity preceding the Graves family's move to Egypt. Money was raised by loans, Graves senior, Alfred Percival, was busy pulling strings and in the middle of it a transatlantic bomb dropped – Laura Riding Gottschalk arrived from America. The two writers had been corresponding and the visit had been planned for some time. At a dinner party in January 1926, when Laura met the Graves family, another guest was E. M. Forster who, since his return from Egypt, had kept in touch with a number of Egyptians and had been one of those who had recommended Graves for the job to which he was going. Forster poured out advice on the country. Siegfried

Sassoon was at the docks to see Graves and his family off on their journey, accompanied by Laura.

It is that last name that must be the key to unlock the mystery of the failure of Egypt to bring Graves under its spell as it had always done with writers, actual and potential. Instead of a burst of literary activity, there was dissatisfaction and disillusion. Both he and Seymour-Smith gloss over the issue. The biographer says nothing because he does not know; the author/poet says nothing because he will not tell. Whatever else he may not have taken with him from Egypt, Graves clearly assimilated the inscrutability of the Sphinx. In *Goodbye to All That* the period becomes a 'story' which Graves will not tell. His autobiography is a matter of 'history' in which he does not consider that Laura plays a part, the only reference to her being in the epilogue, the omission of this period being because it is, in his own words, 'dramatic but unpublishable'.

Both biographers make the same point − that the Egyptian interlude came at a critical juncture in Graves's career and the combination of several factors turned the scale against the country. To take the words of the latest chronicler, Robert's nephew Richard Percival Graves:

> Since [his Copthorne days], certainty after certainty had been stripped away, until in recent years, he had begun to feel as though a process of personal disintegration had begun . . . As he leaned over the ship's rail, waving goodbye to Sassoon, Robert was fortunate not to know where that process of disintegration would end. He was still more fortunate that he was sailing to Egypt with the woman who would one day help him to become whole again . . . whether Robert would remain an interesting minor poet or whether he would achieve something more, must have seemed an open question in January 1926. He needed above all some strong and self-reliant person upon whose judgement he could rely, and in whose affection he would feel secure. Such a person was to hand in Laura Riding. It was she who showed him the way out of his emotional and intellectual impasse.

Had Egypt anything to do with it at all? Would it have been the same if Graves had gone to Liverpool instead? Egypt became in his eyes a symbol of the blackness of the world around him. He wrote in *Goodbye to All That*: 'By the summer of 1926 the disintegration was already well advanced.' He elaborates to 'disintegration of my post-war personality'. He saw only the dark side of Egypt. The sun failed to set light to his creativity.

His social realism could not take the surrealist life of the country. The conditions disgusted him – the strikes, students' essays, the political situation, the Belgian-made architecture of Heliopolis, his wife's failure to improve in health and, perhaps the last straw, the neglect of his son, Sam, in an isolation hospital with measles, from which he returned with a scarred eardrum and permanently affected hearing.

This preamble will, it is hoped, explain why Egypt had so little effect on the literary output of Robert Graves. He wrote the final draft of 'Lars Porsena or the Future of Swearing' in Cairo but it was not published until April 1927. It was there, too, that he arranged his first retrospective collection of poems, *Poems 1914–1926*, to be published in June 1927. The dedication is to N[ancy] and L[aura]. *Res ipsa loquitur.*

A writer of an entirely different kind, Agatha Christie, did draw upon her experience in Egypt. In 1910, when she was 20, her mother became seriously ill and no doctor seemed able to diagnose what was wrong. Her mother made her own decision, believing that she needed a change and finding a doctor who advised sunshine and a warm climate. Egypt was the chosen location, so mother and daughter sailed out there and stayed at the Gezira Palace Hotel for three months. Agatha enjoyed herself, spending many evenings dancing, under the watchful eye of her mother. This period has been recorded in Agatha's photograph album, showing Cairo races, spring manoeuvres, a Review, polo, croquet, tea parties, picnics in the desert and tours of Cairo. She was not at that time interested in the antiquities and turned down invitations to visit Karnak and Luxor.

After her return to England, she began writing poems and short stories but her first attempt at a novel was set in Cairo, based on three people she had seen in the hotel. After a false start, she abandoned the book but started again with a Cairo setting and a deaf heroine. Putting the two together and calling the result 'Snow upon the Desert', she sent it to several publishers, all of whom sent it back.

It was not until 1933 that Agatha Christie returned to Egypt, when she took a trip up the Nile with her second husband, Sir Max Mallowan, the archaeologist. The following year she published a collection of short stories entitled *Parker Pyne Investigates*, one of which was called 'Death on the Nile', a tale of poisoning aboard a steamer. She was clearly fascinated by the Nile journey and returned to it for a play, 'Moon of the Nile', which she gave up without finishing. The idea of using the river steamer as the locus for a murder story remained with her, however, and in 1936 she used the SS *Karnak* as the centre of her successful novel, *Death on the Nile*, the title she had used already. In this, the Belgian detective Hercule Poirot has his holiday interrupted by five violent deaths on board.

Agatha Christie was more interested in characters than in places. As with *Murder on the Orient Express*, *Murder on the Nile* is a study of people and motives for murder. The descriptive matter is minimal — a line here, two lines there, snatches of conversation, as when Poirot tries to enthuse one of the young girls on board: '. . . it enchants me. The black rocks of Elephantine, and the sun, the little boats on the river. Yes, it is good to be alive. Do you not find it so, Mademoiselle?' Rosalie Otterbourne did not. 'It's all right, I suppose. I think Assuan's a gloomy sort of place. The hotel's half empty and everyone's about a hundred.' The girl's mother is a novelist. She tells M. Poirot, 'I don't mind telling you, I am partly here for the local colour. "Snow on the Desert's Face" — that is the title of my new book.' Here is a flashback to Agatha's own ill-fated novel which was never published. Another character, Mrs Allerton, did not take wholly to the country:

> If there were only any peace in Egypt I should like it better. But one can never be alone anywhere — someone is always pestering you for money, or offering you donkeys, or beads, or expeditions to native villages, or duck shooting.

When the book was made into a film in 1978, with screenplay by Anthony Shaffer, the immense scope for evocative background was used to the full. The Pyramids and the Sphinx, broad sweeps of the Nile and the busy quayside are all actuality. The scene of the attempted murder by falling rock is changed from the Abu Simbel location of the book to the towering columns of Karnak, where the Hitchcockian build-up and dénouement have a powerful effect. One of the difficulties was to find a steamer of the right size and layout, as the allocation of passengers to cabins is one of the keys to the plot, so important that a sketch of the promenade deck and cabin distribution is included in the book. While the screenplay stuck to the main outline of the story, it shuffled round some of the characters, dropping a few of them altogether and re-allocating their roles among the remaining passengers. The casting of Peter Ustinov as M. Poirot was central and the presence of David Niven, Bette Davis, Mia Farrow, Angela Lansbury and Maggie Smith among others in the cast ensured that the characterisation gave life and depth to the Christie originals.

Returning to the 1930s, Agatha had then become most interested in Egypt and its history. As her biographer, Janet Morgan, writes:[65]

> In the ancient Egyptian religion she found something sinister – a strange mixture of human and animal in the deities, an emphasis on death and the ritual surrounding it – but also reassuring, the 'comfortable structure', as she called it, of 'the old gods'. She had also been thinking about parallels between the past and present, the similarity of relations between old and young, male and female, the conflict between good and evil that might be found anywhere at any time.

She admired idealists and tried to dramatise them. In 1937 she wrote a three-act play, *Akhnaten*, an idealist if ever there was one. She was attracted by the characters – Horemheb the betrayer, the Queen Mother Tyi, the Queen Nefertiti, Tutankhaten, who promises to restore the old gods, and the High Priest. Although she was pleased with the play, with which she had been helped by Sir Max, it proved too difficult and too expensive to stage. However, many years later, in 1972, she sent the manuscript to her agent Edmund Cook, deeming it apposite in view of the exhibition at the Royal Academy:

> It seems to me to be particularly applicable just at this time, that is if anyone was willing to put some money into staging it – and it would no doubt be an expensive production – but there is such a furore over the Egyptian Tutankhamun ... I like the play very much, though I am quite prepared to accept the fact that there is no one who will put it on stage. If that does turn out to be the case, I would like to have it published.

It was, by Collins, in 1973.

Evelyn Waugh was another writer who was not enchanted by the country, particularly its hotels, when visiting in the 1920s. He has this to say of them:

> All the hotels in Egypt are bad but they excuse themselves upon two contrary principles. Some maintain, legitimately, that it does not matter how bad they are if they are cheap enough: the others,

that it does not really matter how bad they are if they are expensive enough. Both classes do pretty well. We sought out one of the former, a large, old-fashioned establishment under Greek management in the Midan el-Khaznedar, called the Hotel Bristol et du Nil, where rooms even in the high season are only eighty piastres a night. My room had three double beds in it under high canopies of dusty mosquito netting, and two derelict rocking chairs. The windows opened on a tram terminus. None of the servants spoke a word of any European language, but this was a negligible defect since they never answered a bell.[66]

Of the several journalists who have written books on the country following their connection with it as foreign or war correspondents, during and after the First and Second World Wars, one was Gordon Waterfield, who, as we have remarked earlier, was the great-grandson of Lady Lucie Duff Gordon. Like her, he lived in Egypt for seven years. After the First World War he worked for a cotton exporting firm in Alexandria for a while before joining the editorial staff of the *Egyptian Gazette* in Cairo, leaving it in 1928 to become *The Times* correspondent there. He left Egypt when he joined Reuters and was posted to Paris. His connection with the country reopened when he was responsible for expanding the Arabic Service of the BBC after the Suez Canal fiasco in 1956. Of the various books written in his long life – he died at the age of 84 in 1987 – most were published after his retirement from the BBC but the biography of his great-grandmother was written in 1937 and it was in the inter-war years that his connection with Egypt was closest. Both the edition of Lucie Duff Gordon's letters (1969) and *Egypt* were published during his retirement when he was busy writing other books as well.

Let us look again at what is revealed by the *Oriental Spotlight*[58] switched on by Major Jarvis in the 1930s and view Egypt through his humorous eye:

> Cairo is Egypt and Egypt is Cairo. No other place in the Nile Valley is in the picture at all, but it is just as well not to stress this fact too much with the Alexandrians who pretend that Cairo does not exist.
>
> Cairo has a population of one million, of whom 955,000 are Government officials, and the odd 45,000 are servants, taxi-drivers, shop-keepers and sweepers. The city consists of some shops and hotels, the Turf and Gezira Clubs, and about 10,000 Government

offices. To the north is Abbassia where the soldiers live, and north again is Heliopolis where enormously wealthy retired Egyptian officials have palaces, and the Royal Air Force small flats, and south is Maadi where some highbrows addicted to gardening dwell. They also read poetry and write books.

Sport was still of paramount importance to the British:

> Gezira Club provides facilities for every sport and pastime, from the plutocratic racing and aristocratic polo to mid-Victorian frivolities like croquet and plebeian pursuits such as bowls and hockey. It is on Gezira polo grounds that the officers of the Cavalry Brigade are tested for military efficiency and fitness for command, and on Gezira tennis courts that examinations are held to decide as to the desirability or otherwise of retaining in the service the British officials of the Government.

Finally, John Cromer cannot resist the inclusion of a reference to his own wartime service as an Intelligence Officer in Egypt with this description by Jarvis:

> The section of the British Army that takes itself more seriously than any other is the Intelligence Service . . . It is an intelligence that sent two divisions into the unoccupied town of Gaza in 1917 where they were decimated by non-existent Turks; whilst the same intelligence kept 25,000 troops waiting to repel an attack by 100,000 Senussi Arabs, who were marching across the desert to attack Cairo, and as nobody ever saw these Senussi except Intelligence it goes to prove how discerning and keen-visioned they were. This also happened in 1917, which suggests that this must have been a vintage for Army brains.
>
> The Egyptians are a marvellous and adaptable nation, and if there is a sudden demand for a commodity that is temporarily out of stock they will not fail to rise to the occasion and deliver a supply of something that resembles the real article. If information is required of, say, the Western Desert and that which lies beyond, there is no need to ask the man on the spot, for both Cairo and Alexandria can produce wall-eyed and verminous romancers, who for reasons closely connected with public security have not been allowed to dwell near the frontier for fifteen years, and who will for adequate compensation supply any information required. The bigger the pay the better the story.[58]

At the outbreak of the Second World War, Cairo had many of the characteristics of a foreign colonial enclave. Out of a total population of 16.5 million, foreigners numbered 250,000, of whom nearly half were Greeks. There were about 60,000 British, who included about 50,000 Maltese, Cypriots, Indians, etc. with British passports. For a strictly clinical summary of the political background against which the drama was to be played, we can do little better than quote the official *History of the Second World War – Vol. II*:[67]

> By the Treaty of 1936 Egypt was pledged as an ally to come to the aid of Britain if the latter became unavoidably engaged in war. The Cairo Government had evaded a declaration of war on Germany in September 1939, but had broken off diplomatic relations with her and had in fact taken all the practical measures required by the British. In June 1940 they were still reluctant to declare war, but unlike the Turks they broke off relations with Italy and they agreed to fulfil their treaty obligations. Egyptian troops did, moreover, play some part in the defence of their country. Strong pressure was needed, however, to induce King Farouk to send away the Italian diplomatic staff and to appoint a Prime Minister in whose cooperation the British authorities could feel confidence.

As to the military position, the account runs:

> In January 1940 the [British] Cabinet had approved the Chief of Staff's proposals for building up in the Middle East a reserve of land and air forces, including nine divisions in Egypt and Palestine and some 22 bomber and fighter squadrons. This programme was naturally far from accomplishment in June, and on the naval side too, there were grave difficulties. Our land forces in the Middle East at the end of May comprised some 36,000 men in Egypt, including New Zealand and Indian contingents. They were not, however, organised in complete formations, and equipment was short throughout, especially artillery of all sorts, ammunition, fighting vehicles and transport. In Palestine there were about 27,500 troops, including two Australian brigades and an incomplete horsed cavalry division; the greater part, however, were not fully equipped and trained, and one brigade might be required for service in Iraq. In the Sudan were three British battalions and the Sudan Defence Force, in Kenya two East African brigades and two light batteries. A brigade from the Union of South Africa arrived in June 1940.

The ebb and flow of the fighting which followed, although not so regular as the tides of the sea, had something of a tidal quality, the desert itself being like some vast, restless ocean. But we will not anticipate, or be sidetracked into military history. At this point we are seeking merely to set the scene for our personal participation in the cultural life which went on behind the fighting.

The English poets and novelists who lived and served in Egypt in the immediate pre-war period and during the Second World War itself left an indelible mark on a whole generation of scholars. Some of the individuals to whom we shall refer in succeeding chapters had established their literary reputations when the war started. The younger ones had perhaps published a few poems, short stories, even a juvenile book; the older ones had done more. There were not many who were actually in Egypt at the beginning and nearly all were civilians. Terence Tiller, leaving Cambridge in 1939, taught English literature and history at Fouad el Awal (now Cairo) University, soon to be joined by Robin Fedden who, in that year, had resigned as Cultural Attaché at the British Legation in Athens. Other lecturers were John Speirs, Bernard Spencer and P. H. Newby. In this capacity they were able to impart English thought directly to their students. They introduced them, not only to the English classics, but also to what were then such modern writers as D. H. Lawrence, T. S. Eliot, Virginia Woolf, Graham Greene, Louis MacNeice and others.

For the eager and enthusiastic Egyptians their four-year studies were a time of discovery and learning. Their teachers spared no effort. Their guidance was not just in the academic life but through the method of tutorials they were able to create a bond between teacher and student, listening to the students' problems, whether they were emotional, financial or social, helping them in many ways.

More than that, the English staff of the University encouraged dormant talents to surface and to become active. A sonnet competition was organised every year and the best sonnet was given an accolade in the form of a valuable book. Incidentally, Mursi won four years in succession and he still has his prizes. One of them in particular is very close to him, *The Knapsack*, an anthology of poetry and prose edited by Herbert Read.

There were many other extra-curricular activities which contributed greatly to the development of what one may call the 'English school of criticism'. A particular activity, which was organised by both the British Institute which opened in Cairo in 1938 under C. A. F. Dundas, and the University, was the Shakespearean Group, led by H. R. Edwards. The group met once a week, either at the Institute or the Graduates Club, a club for graduates of the English Department of the University. Every week the group went together to see a play – English or Arabic – or a film, then met and discussed the performance.

Members of that group included some of Egypt's best present-day critics and playwrights: Aly el Rai, Mahmoud el Manzalawi, Louis Awad, Nooman Ashour and many others, including Mursi Saad el Din.

This group has continued to hold literary sway in Egypt until today. What is more, they have been able to produce a new generation of creative writers who were strongly influenced by English writing. One clear example is the influence of T. S. Eliot on a whole generation of Egyptian poets, led by the late Salah Abdel Sabour. Eliot's influence reflected itself in the breaking away from classical forms of versification, the use of symbolism and the introduction of English poetic forms.

This point needs an explanation. The unit of classical Arabic poetry is the line and not the poem. One can shuffle the lines in any way and the meaning does not change. There is no one idea that runs through a poem, and no division into stanzas or quartets. The modern Egyptian poets changed all this and their poems acquired well-constructed forms, similar to the English poetic formulae. That was a great revolution which created strong opposition from the classicists. This controversy still goes on at the present time.

There were other figures on the literary scene. Keith Bullen, with much of his Baudelaire translations completed, divided his time between his Headmastership of the Gezira Preparatory School and the Turf Club. J. S. Blake-Reed, when not adjudicating in the Mixed Courts of Appeal in Alexandria, was working on his translations of Horace. Colin Baly worked at the British Council. Raoul Parme, a Maltese teaching at Victoria College, wrote primarily in French and had translated into this language German and English poetry. He had been writing since 1926 and his slim volumes – all out of print – comprised a first collection of poems published in 1926, then more poems, *L'Emoi possible* (1929), a one-act verse play, *Maître Urion* (1929), *Suite antique*, poems (1930), *La Prométhée* of Goethe (1932) and an *Anthologie des poètes allemands* (1935).

Of the non-British writers, Arsène Yergath, the Armenian poet, was perhaps the best known. His work had been published in Paris: *Les Cyprès embrasés*, *Les Yeux limpides* and *Scarabées*; in Brussels: *Le Tisseur de soies*; in Marseilles: *La Maison des images*; in Tunis: *Liens*, and in Cairo *Scarabées II* and *Le Cantique d'hiver*. Ahmed Rassim, a modest belle-lettriste, had printed collections of his prose poems for private circulation among his friends. Edgar de Knevett, quiet and courtly, was also a translator of poems and a minor poet himself.

As the armies gathered and the naval and air forces deployed around them, there came in their ranks writers of many talents, who were soon to find common ground in Egypt. As Europe fell, country by country, to the Fascist forces, more civilian writers were forced to flee and they, too, were welcomed on Egyptian soil.

4

The Second World War –
The Cairo Scene

Once again, Egypt had become one of the focal points of a world war. This time it was different. Only Great Britain and the neutral countries remained free from the Fascist invasion of Europe, while Spain and Portugal were free of hostilities. Turkey, a protagonist in the First World War, remained on the brink, likely to go either way. As before, troops poured in from Britain and the Commonwealth countries, supported by those Europeans who had been able to escape from the invading armies. Among the armed forces were writers, artists and musicians, known and unknown, while civilian refugees arrived from all parts of stricken Europe.

In some ways it was the old story all over again, and the same places were to become the rendezvous of leisure hours. Gezira Sporting Club was one of the magnets, still providing the same wide range of sports as it did when Major Jarvis was there. The Turf Club, too, flourished. It was then in Adly Pasha Street, at the back of the Metro Cinema. It was a typical example of a colonialist club, where Egyptians were strictly forbidden, even as guests. It was mainly a drinking and eating place, its membership mostly British businessmen, supplemented by staff officers as the war progressed. Alan Moorehead described Cairo at war in 1939 in his *African Trilogy*[68] thus:

We had French wines, grapes, melons, steaks, cigarettes, beer, whisky, and abundance of all things that belonged to rich, idle peace. Officers were taking modern flats in Gezira's big buildings looking over the golf course and the Nile. Polo continued with the same extraordinary frenzy in the roasting afternoon heat. No one worked from one till five-thirty or six, and even then work trickled through the comfortable offices borne along on a tide of gossip and Turkish coffee and pungent cigarettes.

James Aldridge takes up the story in his book *Cairo*:

History was laughing at itself, and once more Clot Bey's brothels filled to overflowing with British Tommies. Once again Shepheard's and the Continental were jammed with staff officers with suede boots, fly whisks and swagger sticks . . . But Cairo blossomed. British soldiers seeing sun and desert and clean air for the first time in their lives looked hungrily at the first beautiful European girls who swished their pretty legs in the streets and on trams and in the cafés. Many of these soldiers had come from appalling conditions in the black and grimy back streets of British cities not yet recovered from the depression. Many of them had never seen before what they now enjoyed every day in Cairo, and Cairo's Europeans were generous with friendship and help. But it was not long before the relationship between the British soldiers and officers and European girls in Cairo became an intricate and complicated entanglement which very few escaped, and many good British marriages foundered in those soft Cairo evenings when love rushed through the city on the wings of an exotic escape.[55]

But what about the Egyptians themselves? And the foreigners living in the country, including the thousands of Italians? Freya Stark's assessment of Egyptian views appears in *Dust in the Lion's Paw*,[69] in which she wrote, in 1960:

Of the fifteen million Egyptians, most thought we would lose the war. The gap before we had any trump card in the way of a military success was a very long one, and the atmosphere remained friendly chiefly, I believe, because of a personal trust and liking for individual Englishmen in the Egyptian Service of the past. People like Russell Pasha, Walter Smart, Reginald Davies, John Hamilton and many others are still remembered, and twenty years ago their influence carried over the sticky summer and all Mussolini's intrigue. Yet, with many exceptions, sentiment was unfavourable as one reached the richer society. 'We are getting ready here,' I wrote to a friend in the summer of 1940, 'without a united country behind us. If we took to leaning against anything it would turn out to be a fifth column no doubt.'

Freya Stark also describes the position of the Italians within the country:

80,000 Italians, nearly all tied to Fascism by their purses if not by their hearts, were loose in the capital and even more so in Alexandria. Their Party chief had transferred himself into a Swiss diplomat for the duration and was therefore unassailable; he held the schools, hospitals, charities, workmen's clubs, etc. open to Fascists only, and these walked about with an exuberant confidence in the streets dimmed with blue lights against their bombers, and bought up all stocks of green, red and white material suitable for the making of flags to greet their advancing troops. A small, devoted but disunited band of anti-Fascist Italians struggled against them.

Yet relationships between Egyptians and Italians had long been friendly. But whether for or against Mussolini, many Italians were interned by the Egyptians because they were on Egyptian soil. It was a tolerant regime, allowing for the occasional weekend visit by internees to their wives and families. From time to time, however, as the war progressed, the British military authorities protested, particularly when escaped Italian prisoners of war were being harboured. John Cromer well remembers being spat upon by angry Italian wives when hauling away errant internees in security sweeps. But of all the foreigners in Cairo, the Italians were probably the most popular.

It was against this background that the creative impulse bubbled up. The country which had inspired so many travellers, visitors, government servants, soldiers and others to express themselves in writing, continued to exert its influence on the thousands of newcomers. Not only was the urge to write excited by the exotic nature of an unfamiliar scene but the need to provide reading material for a voracious clientele added impetus to the budding literary skills which began to flourish. With the closing of the Mediterranean sea lanes, books, papers and magazines from the various homelands had to come the long way round the Cape or be squeezed into the very restricted space in aircraft that could be spared from military requirements.

It did not take long for this germination to flourish, either with the help of official backing in media provided by officialdom itself, or by the publication of works in the newspapers and journals being published regularly in Egypt, Palestine and elsewhere. There was no shortage of material, authorship or readership – only the rationing of paper and the occasional exercise of censorship, and that for security reasons, would act as a brake on the burgeoning talent.

The base camps, like the Infantry Base Depot at Geneifa, and the barracks of Kasr el Nil, Abbassia and other parts were great training and transit centres, breeding grounds of boredom. Not only entertainment had to be provided, as will be chronicled later, but education could not be neglected, the Army Education Corps being active in filling the gap. The actual fighting time in the desert, throughout the whole campaign, was not very long. Between the bursts of action, there were lengthy periods of tedium, relieved by reading and writing by those who were so inclined. The same was true of the other forces, both naval and Air Force personnel having to face similar stretches of inaction. John Cromer recalls his own experience in the October days of 1940. A lance-corporal then, in the Hampshire Regiment, he was with the battalion Headquarters staff, working from an abandoned garage in Mersa Matruh, keeping a dozen books of regimental accounts – Indian Army style – hammering away on an old Oliver typewriter and relying on what he could scrounge to read, his copy of D. H. Lawrence's *The Rainbow* having been ripped in two by a piece of shrapnel from an Italian bomb that had come too close for comfort. Odd pieces of mail filtered through after a two- to three-month journey, including the first of a regular supply of *Horizon*. The sand-blown roneoed sheets which comprised *Slit Trench News* did not provide much stimulation for the mind and it was not long before the lowly lance-corporal had been entrusted to organise a system whereby the NAAFI rebates could be pulled in from the dispersed companies (to the chagrin of the Company Quartermaster Sergeants, who lost some of their perks thereby) to provide a fund from which supplies of paperbacks could be brought up from Alexandria (together with fresh fruit and vegetables) for distribution among the troops. This is quoted merely to show the kind of personal initiative that was allowed to develop in the somewhat free and easy life in the desert, where units were scattered far and wide.

Back in Cairo, the networks of writers, war correspondents, teachers, lecturers, broadcasters and entertainers were forming, and city life was broadening from its peace-time pattern into a livelier, more hectic kaleidoscope of activity. The military headquarters staff grew, sucking in civilians of both sexes, while the Embassy, British Council, commercial concerns and others added to the social whirl. Freya Stark saw it thus:

> Cairo was the centre of our world during the first three years of war, the stage on which all glances south of the Alps were focused. It was the goal of the pincer movement of the Axis, the artery of our oil and communications, the keystone of our Middle Eastern arch. It had returned to the days of the Ptolemys when Egypt was the gate to Parthia and India and all the spice trade. You would hear every European language (except German) in its streets. In the wartime epilepsy, people travelling from everywhere to anywhere

would have to pass through Cairo: they would come from Scandinavia or Chungking, and salute you unexpectedly on the terrace of Shepheard's or the Continental. Exhausted as we all were at the end, the threat was an enhancement and no one can forget the gaiety and glitter of Cairo while the desert war went on.

The army magazine which was welcomed when it first appeared in August 1940 was a professional, well-illustrated weekly called *Parade*, published under the auspices of GHQ (ME) and printed by Al-Hilal on their photogravure press in Cairo. Edited by Captain H. L. Ruston, it contained news from Britain, the Commonwealth and all parts of the world, keeping the troops in touch with their home news and containing interesting illustrated articles – a three-page, well-photographed article on the Gayer-Anderson house in Cairo comes vividly to mind – short stories and some humorous bits and pieces. It maintained a high standard and in mid-1941 G. S. Fraser was posted to it. He says of his arrival there, in his autobiography, *A Stranger and Afraid*:[70] 'Like a Fury I began to write for it, and from then on my army fortunes started to look up.' George Fraser might have added that his literary output, but perhaps not his fortune, started to look up also, for he was soon engaged in writing of various kinds for different media. Let us use him as our guide to places and people for the next part of our story, for his peregrinations are typical of the writers of the time. He fell easily (perhaps 'uneasily' is the *mot juste*) between the two categories, as Mursi puts it, the civilian writers or writers in mufti as they were called and the military writers in khaki. He also distinguishes between those writers who were the product of war, that is soldiers and officers who were never in print before the war, who were all poets, and those who had already been established and were inspired by the events of the war. Mursi knew them all as a group of writers who found themselves thrown together in Egypt as a result of the war. The common denominator is that they were in Egypt prior to, during and after the war. They were all influenced by Egypt to a greater or lesser degree and, in their turn, they left an indelible mark on the intellectual and cultural life of the country. 'I joined them,' says Mursi, 'in literary meetings, poetry readings, drama groups and critical discussions about literature.'

George Fraser, too, knew them all. He bracketed his contemporaries and the city together when he wrote in his autobiography:

Against the background of Cairo, about so many of my friends as
I remember them, there was a garishness – a flourish and ostentation
of every eccentric quality, that had often a deadness about it, exactly
like that of posed waxwork figures. That inner exhaustion from
which we all suffered affected that side of each of us that can be
called the actor – the side of critical self-awareness – rather than
the other side, that can be called the character. We were all too
much 'in character', predictable in our responses; and these tended
to be violent and shallow. Cairo was a place of quarrels and the
making up of quarrels, of rows at parties, of little rival gangs, not
a matter of these quiet and steady dislikes, and settled loyalties,
that are a normal part of the British character. Partly this was due
to the climate, partly to the intimacy of the small community, where
everybody knew everybody else's weaknesses and a passion for
gossip, shared by us all, sooner or later brought to one's ears every
unkind remark that had ever been made about one. Between rows,
one might meet one's enemies over a drink, and seem to be getting
on well; a gathering, on the other hand, consisting of one's friends
of the moment, would often break up (when the heavy drinking
had broken down too many reticences) in bickering; so there was
a constant shifting of alliances, and every friendship had its background of resentments and reconciliations. These tendencies were
general, but they were accentuated in the circle in which I chiefly
moved, one of journalists, writers, each anxious to be admired and
liked. Inner anxiety or boredom led to extravagant behaviour which
aroused malicious comment; malicious comment led to quarrels
which made a man shift from one group to another, leaving him,
for a short time, in a state of isolation; in its turn, isolation conduced
to anxiety and boredom, and the wheel had come full circle.

This is so apt a description of the scene and period that it
requires little comment to enlarge upon it. Wartime Cairo
seemed no different from the literary cliques and circles of
earlier days – Bloomsbury, Fitzrovia, Paris in the 1920s, with
its 'lost generation' of expatriate Americans. The pattern was
all too familiar. Yet it was a very productive time and the
stream of words flowed as steadily as the Nile along whose
banks so much was written.

Let us stay with our guide for a further insight into off-duty
Cairo and what it offered to the livelier minds and seekers after
culture. Fraser continues:

When my daily work was over I was to be found mostly at soldiers'
clubs, helping to edit an unofficial magazine (very dull it was, too),
taking part in debates, or giving talks, across a great gulf, about

modern poetry. A soldier would get up and ask me why modern poets did not write something simple and moving, like 'Underneath the Arches'. A fat, pink officer (with a rather sheeplike baa and moustaches like the Golden Fleece) would read out long passages of Rupert Brooke, as an example of how to do it, and short passages of Mr Eliot, as an example of how not to. Communist soldiers would make, very briskly, the point that the poems I was reading reflected the culture of our present society, and that the masses did not want to acquire that culture, since it merely reflected the balance of pressures that held them down. They would create their own new culture, springing from a social order not based on the oppression of one class by another. I would shrug my shoulders at that and say, 'You are fools if you think you can break quite clean away from the past.' But the past, they would say, was surely just what had landed us in our present fix – years of insecurity and mass unemployment, followed by a great war. The argument would continue amiably enough, afterwards, over cups of coffee, but I had the feeling of offering them something they did not want.

Mention of Rupert Brooke has a dual connotation – the gulf that exists between First and Second World War poets and the placing of Fraser by H. K. Gudenian, in peacetime a Fleet Street journalist with *World's Press News* and in wartime, among other things an associate editor of *Orientations*, the Middle East monthly (making its apologies to Sir Ronald Storrs) which was first published in March 1942 from the Victory Club, Cairo, one of the soldiers' clubs referred to by Fraser. Gudenian wrote in the first issue of the magazine:

> To paint a picture to oneself of exile has an unreal facility about it that makes tennis at Gezira, where officers play in Wimbledon white, sergeants in Streatham Common grey flannels, and 'men' in exotic deshabille, the only possible alternative to melancholia. Romanticism of this war is patently imitative [of the last war]. That is why that spring doesn't play now. That's why instead of Rupert Brooke we have G. S. Fraser, who, instead of wallowing in a trench in a Byronic dream, has the good sense, though possibly the bad taste, to envisage such things as totalitarian democracy.

The Victory Club was one of the first venues to provide serious entertainment, relaxation and education for the troops in Cairo. It was in the solidly-built block numbered 7 Sharia Soliman Pasha and boasted two telephones, one for the library and information about events and the other for that all-important facility, the tea-rooms. It provided a good meeting place for anyone in the services with literary pretensions and it was not long before a magazine entitled *Victory* appeared. This was a mixture of poems, jokey presentations, articles and some not very good illustrations. But it was an effort to sustain an interest in literature and provide a forum for the talent which was beginning to emerge. John Cromer, who by then had left the desert and the Hampshire Regiment to join the Field Security Service, looks back on it with a certain affection because it was one of the first vehicles to publish his poems in Egypt. 'Reverie' and 'Asleep in War' appeared in February 1942, by which time he had been commissioned into the Intelligence Corps and was working in Security Intelligence Middle East (SIME). He was not pleased to find that one word had been omitted from the first line of 'Reverie'. The italic typeface used for printing the poems was then changed to an eccentric bold for the issue of 21 May 1942 in which the title of his 'March Winds in Egypt' was made up from three totally different faces. This magazine was soon to be replaced by *Orientations*, of which more anon.

George Fraser was despondent about his own efforts at the Victory Club. In his *Passages from a Cairo Notebook*, he reflects:

Every culture is fundamentally based on an *assent* of some sort; in the sense in which liberalism is a merely negative doctrine, and is not a disguised form of the doctrine of aristocracy, there is no liberal culture. In that sense I am one of the most negative people I know; in that sense I have no culture. That explains, I think, my total failure, while in Cairo, to interest my fellow soldiers in poetry. They could be made to take an interest in poetry as standing for something; but why should they be interested, as I am, in the mere mechanics of an art? When I give talks or take part in debates at the Victory Club, I find that there is a group which cannot use me, and therefore wishes to discredit me; a group of Marxists. 'Poetry' is a general term and therefore must stand for a general idea; and the general idea of the average soldier is based on a few pieces he did at school; I think roughly he believes that poetry is something written in an unnatural but lofty language, and expressing sentiments which, like those of a sermon, have as little as possible to do with everyday life . . . Discussions about poetry or about any art soon resolve themselves into discussions about value; and the most obvious point of view, and the most popular, particularly backed by this vigorous and intelligent Marxist group, is that what the mass of the people like most must be good, and what they do not like bad.

The other main centre for the troops was 'Music for All' at 3 Sharia Maarouf, off Soliman Pasha between the National Hotel and the YMCA. This had a more serious purpose and was, indeed, true to its name, providing a remarkable range of music both live and on gramophone, throughout the whole of its existence. It was started by Lady Russell Pasha and provided not only good music but poetry readings, talks, discussions, debates, bridge, chess and other pursuits. Its scope was described in the *Services Guide to Cairo, 1940* as follows:

'Music for All' provides a recreation centre primarily for music and talks. It is for all ranks, men and women, anyone in uniform is admitted. There are 4 entertainments every night in the 'Air Conditioned' Music Room. Four nights a week there are concerts, including a military band; one night a week, a gramophone recital (symphonies and operas), one night a talk, and the other night varies from week to week. First-class artists only appear, and all the distinguished visiting artists in Egypt can be heard here.

In addition to this, the Centre's own Trio plays from 12 to 1 and from 4.30 to 6.30 p.m. every day, and there is also something going on every evening from 6 to 6.30, talks, bridge, chess or a gramophone recital or concert. Teas and light refreshments can be obtained in the Music Room during the day. The Restaurant serves fixed luncheons and dinners as well as meals a la carte, all served at usual city prices. The catering is by Groppi.

This somewhat detailed description is valuable because it shows the range of interest, the inducement both to relax and be stimulated, and the opportunity to meet and to chat with others of like mind. Professor Worth Howard of the American University of Cairo was the Director and he saw to it that there was always variety of entertainment and plenty to keep the mind occupied.

Here it was that most of the poets in uniform would meet each other and their friends, while the musicians made music or listened to the works of others. John Cromer was a regular frequenter throughout his sojourn in Cairo and recalls with pleasure the hours of talk and musical appreciation. He led a poetry group one evening on the subject 'Russia Has Poets Too', later to appear in print. His talk 'Grandeur and Gusto' on the writings of Thomas Wolfe and William Saroyan was also later incorporated into radio talks. More on this medium will appear later.

The story of 'Oasis' is also still to come but 'Music for All' was the venue where the three non-commissioned editors, Victor Selwyn, David Burk and the South African, Denis Saunders, met to plan the anthology which was to be published in 1943. Many of the contributors to that book have paid tribute to the time they spent in both 'Music for All' and the Victory Club.

Mursi Saad el Din confirms that the two clubs, with the places still to be described, played a large part in his formative years, when he was working at the *Egyptian Gazette* and writing for some of the English magazines. It was one of the joys of both places that there were virtually no restrictions as to guests, and local civilians were as welcome as all ranks of the forces, those working in Cairo, in transit or on leave from the desert or elsewhere. The atmosphere of informality and free exchange of ideas was an important ingredient in the literary mix and development of understanding between Egyptians and the assorted foreigners in their midst. It was a two-way movement of influence from which the collaborating writers of this book conceived mutual respect and friendship, a relationship which thrived throughout the literary scene, despite the tiffs and quirks referred to earlier by George Fraser.

Mursi and others frequented other venues, including the British Institute and the Anglo-Egyptian Union. The former, situated at 5 Sikket el Maghrabi, was also a centre for literary and study groups, where the university lecturers and freelance writers would spread their knowledge among soldiers and civilians alike.

The Anglo-Egyptian Union at Zamalek was originally the residence of the Sirdar, the Commander-in-Chief of the Egyptian Army. It had beautiful lawns with tables scattered over them, a well-stocked library and, needless to say, a gourmet kitchen. It was only because of its name that Egyptians were allowed to join, and their membership was so limited that they had to be proposed by one of the more prominent British members. The British membership itself was also restricted to university professors, lecturers, diplomats and certain high-ranking officers. Mursi, who was proposed by Bryn Davies, avers that he was elected more on the strength of his extra-curricular activities than on his academic performance. He was one of the few locals who had access to places that were out of bounds to Egyptians or which were difficult to join, and at the Union he was able to meet and mix with his professors and their friends, as well as British Council staff. In this way he became a member of many a group, both civilian and military, which gave him a rare insight into a world that few of his compatriots were able to penetrate.

Let us now meet the characters in the literary pageant that was beginning to spread across the Cairo scene. The war had gathered momentum, Greece had been evacuated and refugee writers were congregating in Egypt from different parts of Europe. In *Return to Oasis*,[71] John Cromer has told how he greeted Lawrence Durrell on his arrival from Alexandria. The bar of the Anglo-Egyptian Union was the spot where most of the poets would meet at one time or another and it was here that G. S. Fraser met Durrell as he so describes:

> Durrell was by no means unaffected by the melancholy of our time, that did not express itself in him, as it does in so many of us, as sag and hesitation. I fancy that my own sag and hesitation were wearisome to him when we first met; and though he liked some of my poems, he hated my journalism, especially when I tried to introduce his work and that of such friends as Bernard Spencer and Terence Tiller to the wide army audience for which I was writing. He found my anxiousness to bridge cultural gaps dreary, and my 'personal touches' exasperating. 'The trouble with you, George,' he once wrote to me, 'is your vulgar sub-editor's interest in whether the poet picks his nose or not.' He once tore up something I had written about him, with the remark, 'Little poetasters making publicity for themselves out of their acquaintances with *great poets*!' I felt drawn to him, and also that I was a nuisance to him; this kept our relationship on a certain level of awkwardness, though when we did meet he was kind. He was a small, burly man, with a round, comedian's face, and a light voice that fluted away in unexpected malicious phrases; monopolising every conversation, without appearing to do so, he could make an evening magically entertaining. He, for his part, can hardly have found me entertaining; he got angry with the gaps in my experience that made me behave in a juvenile way. On the whole, he showed as much patience with me as I deserved. He occasionally rapped my knuckles, even in print; but he exuded a kind of well-being that made me forget, when I met him, my resentments. It is not very common to meet a person of rare gifts who is in harmony with himself.

Durrell's own recollection of Fraser at that time is recalled in the introduction he wrote for *Return to Oasis*:

I recall George Fraser visiting me in the press department of the Embassy. I was horrified to see that, though in uniform, he was wearing tennis shoes and a dirty scarf while his trousers were fastened with string. I asked with concern whether he wasn't reprimanded for such wear and he said that he never had been, probably because his boss was a writer too.

Mursi also recalls:

This is how I remember George too, but also with steel-rimmed glasses and the way he used literally to grope his way, being very short-sighted. He and I shared the same room with John Waller in the British Ministry of Information, where he was working with *Parade*, and I was then head of the Arabic department. We became good friends and Fraser showed great interest in the poems I used to write and often corrected their metre and rhyme . . . He was always writing something and was never seen without being crouched over his portable typewriter, enfolding his left arm around it, as if fondling a lover, and with one finger he typed at such speed that would put professional typists to shame. Apart from writing for *Parade*, broadcasting for the Forces' Programme and publishing books of poems, Fraser used to sit at his desk and concoct stories of the bravery and valour of the resistance movement in Europe. From his small office trains were made to be derailed by French Maquis, Nazi military cars overturned by Greek guerillas and bridges blown up by Norwegian resistance groups. He always did this with a permanent sarcastic smile that never vanished from his lips.

To return to the bar of the Anglo-Egyptian Union, two regular patrons were Bernard Spencer and Terence Tiller. Spencer had had to leave his British Council post in Salonika and was teaching at Fuad University. He had contributed to *New Verse* in London, had written some poems in Greece and was writing more in Egypt. Terence Tiller, also at the University, was writing, as was Robin Fedden, another frequenter of the Union. They were to be joined by R(eggie) D. Smith and his wife, the novelist Olivia Manning, in from the Balkans. G. S. Fraser describes Reggie as 'a great, brawny, black-browed man' for whom 'there had not really been a poet worth talking about since Auden and MacNeice, and he felt that poetry had gone off the rails since it had ceased to concern itself primarily with the social situation and the political struggle'. Fraser continued: 'Reggie's kindness to me was all the more admirable in that, if he was no enthusiast for Durrell's poems, he was even less so for mine. He thought I had a minor, imitative talent and in an article in *Horizon* his wife described me as writing "pleasant Georgian verses".'

This mention of *Horizon* calls for a brief diversion from our main theme because it points up one of the continuing rifts between those writers in uniform and those in mufti which went on not only in Egypt and London but no doubt in whatever theatre of war was allowed the luxury of a base with facilities for literary expression. The particular row to which Fraser refers started in the introduction written by Keidrych Rhys, editor of *Wales* but then serving in an A A battery in East Anglia, to *Poems from the Forces*.[72] This anthology was published in 1941 and of the 32 contributors only three – John Cromer, G. S. Fraser and John Waller – were there in the Middle East. In his introduction, Rhys had first vented his spleen on Cyril Connolly, the editor, by declaring:

> The pre-war, editorial-chair attitude of *Horizon*'s editor is almost typical; and has much to do with the same journalistic-values that still govern the unflourishing, unchanging state of letters in liberal England. Here are some of his gems: 'War is the enemy of creative activity and writers and painters are right and wise to ignore it.'

The other 'gems' are not reproduced here but Rhys carried on:

> However, I am glad to say not all literary editors despised the man in uniform. But, as you can see, I can hardly say our fighting men were exactly encouraged by these icy liberals: the appearance of one of us in print was always a bit of a wonder: and in the meantime, the gossip-writers and feature-scribblers had no option but decide overnight, as it were, that this was an unpoetic war.

He goes on to relate how he collected the poems for his anthology and after an apologia on the difficulties of writing faced by the poet in uniform, he bursts out with his champion's cry:

> The time has surely come for someone to write a defence of The Poet in Democracy and in War: so that his rare gifts of generosity, of spirituality, of feeling and of leadership might be more widely understood and recognised. The poet in uniform in particular finds himself in a thankless position, born into the wrong times, accepting conscription with grace, with a bunch of tame versifiers on one side and an older generation whose views he does not wholly support on the other. The intellectuals of the depression have betrayed him. The culture side has been left to people so limited in their grasp as

to, consciously or unconsciously, oppose the war. The culture of the country has been left to two magazines, neither of which poets respect or feel it is any honour to be in.

It was this last attack that was picked up by Robert Hewison, writing in 1977 in *Under Siege*.[73] He identified the two magazines: 'There is nothing exclusively "service" in this attack on *Horizon* and *New Writing*; the fact of being in uniform only heightened the tension felt by the poet between his personal needs and the society in which he lived.' Looking towards the Middle East, he wrote later:

> Military circumstance created a chance culture in Egypt that is a near microcosm of literary life in London, complete with its mixture of soldiers and civilians, factions and decadence . . . The accidental culture of Egypt involved a small group of people, a group of exiles thrown together by little more than the fact of their exile, and inevitably self-referring; Olivia Manning defended them against *Horizon*'s accusations of having lost touch: 'Whether willingly or not, they have become cosmopolitan; they have met and been influenced by refugee writers of other countries; they have learnt foreign languages not commonly learnt by English people and so absorbed new literatures. The character of poetry written out here may suffer from being outbred as that written in England during the same period may suffer from being inbred.'

Which brings us back again to the Union bar. Fraser admits that although he felt at ease with Reggie Smith, 'liking his boxer's burliness, his pleasant, asymmetrical face, the eyes that saw so much behind their thick glasses, and his habit of singing folk songs to himself', he was not so much at ease with his wife Olivia . . . 'nor was she so patient with me. She, too, had a fascinating appearance; slim and tubular, with a face at once oval and birdlike, whose pattern she completed with a turban, so that an artist of the school of Wyndham Lewis might have drawn her as a swathed, beaked egg balanced on a cylinder.'

Fraser came to meet Reggie and Olivia through John Waller, who, as Fraser says,

> was a link between the world of the civilian intellectuals in Cairo, in which I always felt an intruder, and my own shabby and harassed barrack-room existence . . . John, in those days, at first glance looked pink, hot, vague, slightly crumpled; with pebbly blue eyes and fluffy fair hair. Then one noticed that he had an unusually handsome face, marred by certain lines of indecision – as if he found it hard to decide whether he was enjoying himself or not –

and by the faintly fretful and abstracted look that goes with the
serious pursuit of pleasure . . . He hated conversation on general
topics but loved the sort of gossip in which people display not only
their victims but themselves comically in character . . . It was not
easy for him to be quietly intimate; as he told his long, elaborate,
and often bawdy stories – interpreted with coarse sniggers – I
watched his long, graceful hands with gnawed nails, moving around
nervously, touching things, expressing thoughts and feelings he did
not put into words . . . There were for him two worlds, a practical
and a real one. The real one was that of friendship and poetry.
About the practical world, he was cynically realistic: one got what
one wanted by making the right contacts and pulling the right
strings . . .

   About the real world he was sensitive, and it was in this world
that he was always getting hurt. He would go out of his way to
do things for people whose writing he admired; but often he
would find that instead of increasing the circle of his friends, he had
added to his reputation as a clever and unscrupulous wirepuller.
To add to the complication, John, who had a strong sense of
the comic aspects of the role he was playing in Cairo, enjoyed this
reputation.

John Waller was also the link between this group at the
Anglo-Egyptian Union and the last place one would expect to
find a hive of buzzing poets – Gezira Preparatory School, where
Keith Bullen was the urbane Headmaster. But more than that,
he was a true poet, a first-rate translator of French poems, a
liberal host and a steadfast friend. His first book of poems,
Bells on the Breeze,[74] was published in Cairo in November
1940 and bears the worthy dedication: 'To the memory of my
kinsman – A. H. Bullen – (1857–1920) a true Elizabethan
whose works first led me to the quest of "Visionary Gold".'
This was his theme and he helped many a young poet, and older
ones too, in search of it. He held court on Sunday morning, in
the drawing room above the schoolroom, entertaining anyone
who came along in search of the company of writers. His great
friend Raoul Parme was an expert in printing and layout who
helped in setting out the pages of *Bells on the Breeze*.
   Let us turn to G. S. Fraser once more for his description of
Keith:

[He] received us in a great white room, full of sunshine, and on
low tables there were large, flat bowls full of the snipped heads of
dark roses. Keith, dark and red, often liverish on a Sunday morning,
sprawled in an armchair in his dressing-gown, was himself like a

great blown rose. He was enormously stout; his pebbly blue eyes seemed strange mineral intrusions in his rosy flesh . . . When he stood on the stone steps of his house, in a white panama and a floppy white jacket that fluttered in the breeze, he looked like a big captive balloon that the stick had moored to the ground.

Sunday morning in Keith's room, talking about poetry, or the fourth dimension – Ouspensky's book was on the shelves in the corner, beside the first editions of Swinburne – or the odds on the races and social feuds in which we found ourselves involved, was a soothing time in a fretful week. One drank brandy, there, too, but it was better brandy; one talked, but not to pay with clever talk for the drinks one could not buy. The chairs were deep and comfortable, the room at once cool and sunny.

To this friendly room came Edgar de Knevett, a man of great culture and an authority on French verse, John Cromer and, soon afterwards, John Waller, and on one of those warm Sunday mornings in 1941 the Salamander Society was born, as Cromer writes in the preface to *Salamander*:[75]

> to provide a meeting place for literary expatriates and a source of encouragement and assistance for amateurs of the arts. It aimed at breaking down through a common interest in poetry some of the more artificial barriers that divide men. Not then or at any subsequent period did it consider itself a formal group, competing with other groups, but rather as a point of contact for independent individuals. It has never been a clique of the pretentious, the petulant and the petty and has excluded nobody; individuals have been left to exclude themselves.

Further on in that preface, Cromer wrote:

> The fundamental belief of the group has always been that art is international and above ideologies and that the free intellectual intercourse of individuals with different backgrounds is useful both to themselves and to the societies to which they belong. As a result, a platform was provided on which men of all ages could meet and express themselves. All shades of opinion were given full rein and every aspect of literary theory and poetic belief allowed a means of expression.

It was not long before the Salamander Sunday mornings began to attract poets in uniform and non-academic civilian poets who found this haven of culture a congenial meeting place for the exchange of ideas. The latter were personal friends of Bullen, Parme and de Knevett and as time went on they heightened the continental/oriental atmosphere of some of the gatherings. With a welcome extended to all, irrespective of nationality, colour, religious or political creed, Cromer saw, and still sees, Salamander as being truly representative of its colophon, the significance of which is 'the spirit of fire'. He concluded his preface to the miscellany with these words: 'Created in the midst of war, flourishing in the rear of a combat area, remaining steadfast in its belief in art and poetry as a keynote to international understanding, Salamander is indeed a microcosm of world literature.' That statement he stands by today.

In the early days, the talk was primarily about poetry, with some philosophy. The novel, as such, was of little interest, the dying art of language and translation took up most of the time of these blissful Sundays. The art of poetry translation was paramount and it was in this sphere that the first Salamander trio predominated. Keith Bullen's forte was translating from the French – Baudelaire, de Musset, Samain, Aragon, he was master of them all. Edgar de Knevett's favourites were Corneille, Gautier and, a specialist field, Felix Arvers. Raoul Parme's interest worked in reverse, translating into French from the English of A. E. Housman, Lionel Johnson, W. B. Yeats and Keith's kinsman, A. H. Bullen. John Cromer remembers vividly an agonising hour when he, Keith and Raoul paced the floor, arguing over the exact translation, as mitigated by nuances of metre and sense, of two lines of de Musset. The fact that France had fallen, England was battling it out alone and, in the Middle East, Wavell was fighting single-handed, or so it seemed, was of secondary interest for that brief period. Those lines had to be right.

Freya Stark was there, in Cairo, and caught the moment thus:

> In 1941 the desert victories held the early spring. Then came the Greek defeat and the Libyan pendulum swung against us: between March and June General Wavell had five fronts on his hands. While this went on, Cairo became more anxious, more cosmopolitan, more brilliant than ever before, with the flight from Greece and the added impact of European royalties and diplomats, officers, commandos and agents showed like bits of glass in a kaleidoscope, to change and dissolve.

As time went on, the atmosphere changed. The poets in uniform began to arrive as word went round of the Sunday mornings. Among the new arrivals was Erik de Mauny, a former journalist with *The Dominion* and the *New Zealand Listener*, serving with the NZ Expeditionary Force. He brings back a whiff of Cairo life at that time in this extract from one of the vignettes in *Return to Oasis*:

> The images that return are not all of violence, of squalor and discomfort. There were also nights of music at the Victory Club in Cairo; memorable drinking sessions in congenial company in a certain Greek bar off Sharia Kasr-el-Nil, where a boy in a soiled galabieh would offer us feqafiq, baby quail, roasting on a red-hot brazier; long walks along the escarpment above Maadi where I would try in imagination to project myself back into the Egypt of the Pharaohs; Sunday sessions of poetry and pink gin with Keith Bullen at the Gezira Preparatory School and the Anglo-Egyptian Union.

He was writing poetry at this time, as we shall see, and was also struggling with a novel, as his diary for 1942 records in *Leaves in a Storm*:

> February 18th – Typed furiously fast at lunch time several more pages to Chapter 10 (of a novel called 'The Brief Spring' which I subsequently burned during the Alamein period: it was about the retreat from Greece, and it failed to come off). During the afternoon, reviewing the chapter, it seemed very bleak and skeletonic, and the old doubts arose: what's the use of writing at all? Why spend all this effort on something that can't possibly be good enough for any intelligent person to read? I don't know.

And the following month:

> March 6th – Poetry is in me, and truth and beauty, but can I ever deliver them as I feel them – can I say anything out of this welter of life, out of these strange, arid, nerve-pained, joyless flats?

Max Bowden, a Captain in the Royal Artillery, was writing sharply turned out poems from his experience in the desert and in convoy on the way there. His work was published in *Salamander, Oasis* and *More Poems from the Forces*[76] but he was one of those whom diligent research failed to find when details for *Return to Oasis* were being sought. John Cromer retains the envelope of his last letter to Max, marked 'Cannot trace – return to sender'. Round-faced, with a black moustache, he always managed one visit to Zamalek when on leave from the desert.

Events in the battle area had their repercussions in Cairo in July 1942 when the first battle of Alamein was fought and Rommel's advance threatened the whole of the delta and caused waves of panic. Erik de Mauny's diary encompassed that period succinctly:

> June 30th – Heavy cold and black depression. Rommel pushing towards Alexandria and the war in a stinking mess . . . July 1st – Hellish flap on generally in Cairo, and many civilians leaving the country . . . The atmosphere in town is weird. Tonight as I went to see A. there was a big crowd outside His Britannic Majesty's Courts, all applying for visas, I suppose. Many business people have already gone. Mrs S. and her mother off to Suez, to wait for evacuation boat there. The old girl tried to commit suicide by cutting her veins . . .

Then, less than a fortnight later:

> July 13th – The Battle for Egypt continues to rage on the El Alamein front, yet now the abortive crises of a few days ago have faded, I find myself strangely unmoved by the struggle . . .

For a fuller account of this momentous period in the lives of the hitherto relaxed Cairenes, let us turn to Barrie Pitt and volume 2 (Year of Alamein) of *The Crucible of War*:[77]

> What later became known as 'The Flap' was triggered by the evacuation of the Royal Navy from Alexandria during the last days of June . . . Rumours of the imminent arrival of the Afrika Korps fluttered the cosmopolitan hearts of the Levantine populace, for these immediately to be chilled by details of a 'scorched earth' policy to be put into effect by the retiring British as they fled back into the doubtful security of the Sinai Desert – both rumours being unfounded but assiduously cultivated by agents of the Axis Powers, with whom the Delta had been well seeded.
>
> The Egyptian Army and Gendarmerie disappeared from the streets which were patrolled instead by English officers self-consciously wearing their revolvers, and groups of other ranks equally self-conscious because they were headquarters clerks and orderlies suddenly enrolled into emergency units to keep order, and with little idea of how to set about it. Other groups of soldiers on the Cairo streets were also self-conscious – and worried too, for they were from the fighting units which had been overshot at Gazala or one of the intervening battle areas, had during the retreat overshot the stop lines at the frontier, Matruh or El Alamein, and were now anxiously avoiding the eyes of Authority – especially those of the Military Police – as they had for the moment no wish or intention to return 'up the Blue'.
>
> And above both cities during that epochal day, especially over the centre of Cairo where the main Allied Military Headquarters

lay, towered a black cloud from which drifted down to the streets a perpetual rain of charred paper, from the bonfires of official and confidential documents which a worried Command had ordered to be destroyed. For months afterwards chaos existed at such ordinary levels of military life as pay, equipment returns, and acting, unpaid promotions, and one South African officer was able to boast afterwards that during the holocaust he had put all the documents relating to nineteen Courts of Inquiry to the flame, thus bringing relief to a few doubtless undeserving wrong-doers.

Having been responsible for the burning of documents in the incinerator on the roof of Red Pillars (GHQ in Kasr el Aini), Major A. W. Sansom was chagrined to find that:

> this operation was hardly over when one of my NCOs bought some peanuts from a street vendor and found that they were wrapped up in a paper marked MOST SECRET. Asked where he had got it, the vendor said he had picked it up in the street. It turned out that it was one of many papers that had gone up in smoke, but unburnt, from the open incinerators at GHQ. A strong wind had ensured that they were scattered over a wide area of the city. We could not have done a better job distributing secret documents round Cairo if we had tried.[78]

Warren Tute comments on the effect in Alexandria in *The North African War*:

> In Alexandria, with one or two honourable exceptions, the civilian population had written off the British, and were taking what steps they could to remove, sell or otherwise dispose of their property in anticipation of the Axis take-over which was almost hourly expected. Rommel had even broadcast the name of the house he intended to use as his headquarters in Alexandria. (One of the honourable exceptions to this general panic mounted a machine-gun on the reception desk of his Alexandria hotel so as to give the Germans a proper welcome.) Altogether it was touch and go.

Olivia Manning caught the scene at Alexandria station in *The Danger Tree*:[79]

> The train was sighted and a groan went through the crowd. The train came at a snail's pace towards the platform. The groan died out and a tense silence came down on the passengers who, gripping bags and babies, prepared for the battle to come. As the first carriages drew abreast of the platform, hysteria set in. The men now flung themselves forward, regardless of women and children and began tugging at the carriage doors. The women, suffering the usual disadvantage of having to protect families as well as themselves,

were shrill in protest, but the protest became more general. The carriages were locked. The train, slow and inexorable as time, slid on till it touched the buffers at the end of the line.

John Cromer, jerked out of the pleasant Sunday-morning routine, had two main tasks allotted to him as one of the Security Intelligence team – one, to get the security records on to a three-ton truck to the safety of Palestine, which was done with expedition and a minimum of fuss; the other, potentially more difficult, to stand by to escort the 'compromised personnel' ('cps'), a motley collection of 'agents', real and imaginary, to a place of safety in the Sudan. In retrospect, what had a touch of drama at the time seems little less than hilarious. The briefing was simple – to be present at Abbassia station with kit (confined to one kitbag), pistol, together with a limited number of rounds of ammunition, and a compass, to take command of the train-load of 'cps', who would be kitted out for the occasion with British uniforms and paybooks, irrespective of their real nationality. Cromer knew what was in store and had a glimpse of the pantomime cast, all in varying degrees of funk. He had packed up his books and papers, leaving them in the care of his kindly Syrian landlady in his room overlooking the barbed-wire fence of GHQ (ME), and prepared to go through the motions of standby. The last briefing was at 24 hours' notice to leave. His Colonel had not been encouraging:

You are in charge of train 'A'. Get your people down to the Sudan and go on southwards. You have a compass. This first train will probably be a prime target, so be prepared for bombing attacks on it at any time. They may even start before you leave the station.

Twenty-four hours' notice was reduced to 12 hours, then to eight. It looked serious. They would soon have to go. On four hours' notice the whole venture was called off and never referred to again.

Barrie Pitt remarks on the brevity of this extraordinary period:

Ash Wednesday, as the day inevitably became known, was to live for many a day in the memory of those who were present, and time has done little to diminish a remarkable legend. But even more remarkable was the speed with which the panic ended. By the evening of July 3rd the packed exits had emptied, the crowds of refugees returned – shamefacedly in many cases – and the somewhat meretricious life of the Delta was resumed.

For John Cromer it was back to normal. The kitbag was unpacked, the books put back in their places, the security records came back from Palestine and the next few weeks were spent busily answering queries from the British Embassy because many of their archives were among the ashes. It was a relief to get back to Sunday mornings with Salamander, where discussion had given place to great activity.

This centred upon publications. For the past few months, before 'The Flap', there had been a move, urged on by Raoul Parme, to put the unstructured ideas which floated round on a Sunday morning into more tangible form. The first issue of *Salamander*, and six separate books of poems by its members, three by Keith Bullen, one by Raoul Parme, one by J. S. Blake-Reid and one by John Cromer, appeared in 1942. More details of these will appear in the next chapter.

It was almost as if the momentous events in the desert had sparked off an outburst of creative activity. Many hands have chronicled the second and decisive battle of Alamein and it is not proposed to vie with them by attempting yet another version. Auchinleck had come and gone, Alexander and Montgomery were firmly in their respective commands, high-level conferences under Churchill had taken place and on 23 October 1942 the battle commenced.

From then on, the issue of the war was never in doubt. The importance of this battle has been summed up in a few words by the incomparable pen of Winston Churchill in Volume IV of *The Second World War*:[80]

> The Battle of Alamein will ever make a glorious page in British military annals. There is another reason why it will survive. It marked in fact the turning of 'the Hinge of Fate'. It may almost be said, 'Before Alamein we never had a victory. After Alamein we never had a defeat.'

The same volume contains a pull-out with facsimiles of the two most telling documents of the campaign, which we cannot resist repeating here. Upon a sheet of notepaper headed 'British Embassy, Cairo' 'Most Secret', there follows in Churchill's own hand, this Directive to General Alexander, Commander in Chief in the Middle East:

1. Yr prime main duty will be to take or destroy at the earliest opportunity the German-Italian Army commanded by Field Mar-

shal Rommel together with all its supplies & establishments in Egypt & Libya.

2. You will discharge or cause to be discharged such other duties as pertain to your command without prejudice to the task described in paragraph 1, wh must be considered paramount in His Majesty's interests. WSC. 10.viii.42.

Beneath this directive is a facsimile of the field telegram addressed to the Prime Minister from General Alexander:

Sir, the orders you gave me on AUG 15th 1942 have been fulfilled. His Majesty's enemies together with their impediments have been completely eliminated from EGYPT, CYRENAICA, LIBYA and TRIPOLITANIA. I now await your further instructions.

The turn of the year marked the nadir of the Salamander Society. After the burst of publications, the Sundays flagged. The only year of the war in which John Cromer kept fragments of a diary was 1943, and this record is sufficient to show that the Sundays in Zamalek were atrophied by illness of the principals and the absence of military presence. One after another the original civilian trio were struck down, Bullen and Parme with colds and minor ailments, de Knevett more seriously with a stroke. Cromer held things together. In January Ruth Speirs, acknowledging assistance from John Speirs, Bernard Spencer and Terence Tiller, had published *Selected Poems of Rainer Maria Rilke*[81] which she had translated. In the note preceding the poems, she had written that she had aimed at giving as exact a translation of Rilke as possible:

I have tried in the case of each poem to keep to the original metre, but I have made no attempt at rhymed verse because a rhyme coming naturally and necessarily in the one language would have to be forced into the translation – and much of the original text would have to be sacrificed or mutilated merely for the sake of rhyme. Rilke's abundance of meaning does not *depend* on rhyme for its transmission, but bursts upon us in some degrees even through a 'prose' translation if only we let him speak in words that, in the kindred language, are as closely equivalent to his own as it is possible to render them.

Such an approach was too much for Parme. He urged Cromer to buy the book so that they could write a critical review together. They analysed the work, read through the original Rilke, re-read the translations and fumed. Where had the poetry gone? It was all very well to talk about abundance of meaning but with a poet so musical as Rilke, it was essential to recapture the music of rhyme in the translation. Bullen could do it with the French poets, so could de Knevett.

With the spring came a revival of spirits and activity. Fraser was now in Asmara but Denis Saunders, the South African corporal-poet writing under the name of 'Almendro', brought a fresh sound of youthful poetry. He also brought news of an anthology of Allied Forces' poetry which he was collecting with two other NCOs, Victor Selwyn and David Burk. As the Sundays slipped by, washed down in bottles of Clos Mariut and Clos Matamir, the wines of the country, the corpus of work built up as preparations went ahead for the second number of *Salamander*. Cromer's diary records a meeting in Tommy's Bar to read the proofs and a fortnight later the publication of the magazine, which was a disappointment: 'Raoul has slipped, the Anatole France quotation ("One must be a philosopher to see a salamander") being poorly set, the advertisement page for Salamander books slipshod and he cruelly omitted the colophon from my poem ("Death over Europe").'

Life in Cairo was changing as the war moved away from it. Freya Stark was alive to the change:

> When I last came through Cairo, on one of my temporary visits in the summer of 1943, Alamein and the danger were over. It was as if a dust had settled on the town. Athena's grey eyes that cheer the matadors and soldiers, the tang of life and death which belong to the bull ring or the battle, had disappeared.

John Waller would bring his friends along to the Salamander meetings, which would inevitably end with the usual trek across the road to the Anglo-Egyptian Union in response to John's call, 'Let's go over to the Union and have a lot of drinks.' There the party would break up, some remaining together to carry on discussions which had started earlier, others to mix with the other poets who were already there as part of the *Personal Landscape* group.

Meanwhile the collection of poems for the anthology had grown considerably and the task of weeding them out and making a selection was entrusted to the Salamander Society with Denis Saunders, whose two colleagues had been posted away. In early May, Cromer records:

> Another Salamander meeting with Keith, Raoul and Saunders. An argument arose as to the ingredients for the anthology. Raoul and

I were agreed that the first consideration was quality, that it was better to have fewer poets and several good poems than a great number of contributors with no more than one poem apiece. Saunders thought it better to be representative with a heterogeneous collection. I still think this is the wrong policy to adopt and told him so.

Cromer lost the argument. A fortnight later his diary reads:

I have not read through about 60 of the poems submitted for the anthology and think that only about a third of them are really good. Nevertheless, I shall be overruled on most of them and do not mind. So long as the book is brought out.

And brought out it was, on 18 September 1943.

Autumn came, a period chronicled by Norman Craig in *The Broken Plume*:[82]

Now that the tide of war had receded along the coast of North Africa, and through Sicily into Italy, Cairo no longer had the vital military importance of a year or so before. Yet the city still dominated the Middle East, with an air of permanence and immutability far transcending its cursory involvement in our own vulgar and ephemeral brawl ... We pressed through the milling crowd to a waiting taxi, drawn, as if by a magnet, to Shepheard's Hotel ... Shepheard's was quite unlike any other hotel. It had the cloistered dignity of a cathedral, with its enormous domed ceiling, rich stained glass windows, sumptuously tapestried armchairs and glittering displays of glassware. There was no trace of anything cheap or gaudy or flashy; just an impression of solid, unornamented wealth. Nothing could compare with the somnolent peace of the lounge that afternoon as we sank into the depths of those enormous easy chairs. In the evening the hotel sprang into throbbing activity. Through it was filled at the time with numbers of Europeans, it remained essentially Eastern and was the focal point of Cairo Society ... [and] continued to be the spiritual home of the Middle East Force.

Craig's description of his leave epitomised that of most officers passing through the city and, indeed, many who were stationed there:

After a leisurely round of drinks at Shepheard's or the more garish Continental Hotel, and a meal at the Auberge du Turf, or the Petit Coin de France, we normally finished up for a night at Doll's Cabaret. At Doll's you sat at the bar or danced with the artistes who hovered round. After a dance it was customary to repay your partner with a drink, the 'artiste's special', which was twice the normal price and little more than coloured water. When the bar closed at ten o'clock you could only buy 'champagne' at three pounds a bottle, or cider at ten shillings a glass.

In terms of Salamander publications 1944 was, perhaps, less productive, Bullen's Samain translations[83] and Waller's *Spring Legend*[84] having appeared the previous year, but it was a high point in good fellowship and in the number of poets meeting to talk and drink on a Sunday morning. The third number of *Salamander* came out in January and included some first appearances – a prose piece by Colin Baly and poems by Evan John, better known as a novelist and the author of *Crippled Splendour*, who was then working in the SIME headquarters, down the passage from John Cromer; John Towers, a Turf Club pal of Keith Bullen, whose poem was entitled simply 'To J.S.B-R.'; and Frank Elliot, who had died only a few weeks after sending in his nicely turned sonnet for publication.

There were new faces from the forces, and more civilians put in an appearance at the Sunday gatherings. Darrell Wilkinson, then a Surgeon-Lieutenant in the RNVR, would drop in when he wasn't being dropped by parachute into the enemy-occupied Greek islands to give medical help to the SOE operators in the region. He collected walking sticks on these clandestine visits and would usually arrive with a different one each time. Dudley Charles made one or two appearances and was off again with his unit to an unidentified destination. Victor Musgrave, although the son of an army officer, was himself a Leading Aircraftman in the RAF, editing one of the service magazines. Although he was more interested in art and was an artist himself, his poetry, of the surrealist school he embraced, was another facet of his talent. Although he was not published in *Salamander*, his 'Song of Egypt' later appeared in *Return to Oasis*. John Cromer was able to perform a particular service for him when he was married to Ida Kar, the photographer. One of Cromer's duties was the security vetting of marriages between members of the British forces and foreign nationals. This marriage having been approved, Victor and Ida wanted to go to Palestine for their honeymoon but did not know whether Ida would have her British passport in time, as she was obviously not entitled to it until after the wedding. The ceremony over, Cromer went forward to congratulate the happy pair and from his pocket took a British passport which he offered to Ida as a wedding gift. The couple caught their train as planned. They did not, unfortunately, live happily together for ever afterwards as the marriage was dissolved some time after their return to London.

Among the civilians, more was seen of Ahmed Rassim, Arsène Yergath and Ivo Barbitch, all of whom wrote in French and were strongly supported by Raoul Parme in their efforts. Salamander added greatly to the cultural life of Jean Moscatelli, poet and philosopher, because being an Italian, he had been interned by the Egyptians and his movements even then were restricted as the war in Italy was not yet over. Fortunately, John Cromer was able to use his influence to allow Moscatelli to have time out on Sundays in order to take part in the Salamander mornings.

The most colourful addition to the poetic ranks was, however, John Gawsworth, who seemed to fly from battlefront to battlefront, or rather in the wake of the advances in North Africa and Italy, finding local poets and printing presses and writing ceaselessly his poems, prose and bibliographical notes. He is best described by G. S. Fraser as:

> a very untidy RAF sergeant with a long, thin, saturnine face, drooping eyelids, and a twisted nose. A cigarette hung slackly from one corner of his pliable mouth. Occasionally one eyebrow would cock upwards, sardonically, and simultaneously the corner of the mouth would move and the cigarette would point upwards towards the raised eyebrow. The RAF tunic was stained and short of buttons; but there was a little coloured button in the lapel, that of a Chevalier of the Court of the Bey of Tunis.

There are four vivid pages on Gawsworth in *A Stranger and Afraid* and it is all vintage stuff, not least the glimpse of John writing poems at a bar, glass at elbow, passing them on to George for comment: ' "Stow it away, George, stow it away. I got millions of 'em. Millions of poems at home. Write 'em on little scraps of piper (*sic*) and stow 'em in an old tin trunk." Another sip of brandy and more concentrated scribbling.'

Lawrence Durrell, too, had similar memories as he set them down in his introduction to *Return to Oasis*:

> Inevitably the King of Redonda, the Bard, John Gawsworth, arrived and set up shop in a sort of underground Arab café near GHQ. Here he caused considerable alarm by his flamboyant conversation. He was only an Aircraftman, and thus denied access to the hotels

and cafés reserved for officers. But he carried his lowly rank off with an air, protesting that he had only accepted it to honour the memory of T. E. Lawrence. He had given my name as a reference and in next to no time I had a heavily breathing Security Officer sitting in front of me in the office showing the whites of his eyes and expatiating on my friend.

No, this time the Security Officer was not John Cromer, who was unable to prevent the posting away of the colourful Gawsworth, who, before he left, had given him a copy of *Legacy to Love*,[85] which had been published in England the previous year. Even this little courtesy was exploded into a typical Gawsworth firework. At the time, the inscription ran: 'John Cromer's copy "certified" by his friend the writer John Gawsworth, Cairo 1944.' When the two Johns met later in London, JC had the book with him. With the brandy flowing, JG grabbed it, inserted a comma after 'certified' and wrote above 'my foot!' and below: 'I apologise, my dear John, for the utter and completely unwarranted "chill" of the horrible inscription above. Forgive me; I repeat, I am your friend and sympatico to a common ideal.'

By the time Gawsworth had descended, 'like glittering Phaeton' upon the Salamander scene, enough material had been collected for another issue of the magazine to be published, including a poem written in Arabic and English (and so printed) by Mursi, on the poet El Mutanabby. It seemed that by publishing regularly, although its appearance was anything but regular, *Salamander* ran the risk of having to obtain a licence as a periodical, which meant time and money, lobbying, innumerable coffees and more than a modicum of baksheesh. As one of the two lawyers of the group, John Cromer – as well as serving His Majesty and writing poetry, he was also a solicitor – was given the task of sorting out this legal nicety. Having tracked down the source of the threat, he discovered a loophole which was confirmed by fellow Salamander Judge Blake-Reed. No. 227 of the *Journal Officiel* of 24 December 1944 contained arrêté No. 162/42 which governed the law relating to publications, but in a list of exemptions (4–7) in para. 158 of the decree, it was found that no licence was necessary if the particular publication was part of a continuing work and not a periodical as such. Hence the next issue of *Salamander* appeared in the autumn of 1944 as 'Folio IV'.

The year ended with a virtual takeover of the Christmas

number of *The Sphinx* by regular or intermittent participants in the Salamander gatherings. Seasonal articles by G. S. Fraser, John Waller, John Gawsworth, Erik de Mauny and Alan Arnold, a poem by Keith Bullen and another by Fraser, and theatre reviews by Waller and Fraser Sutherland, one of George's many *noms de plume*, were all squibs to adorn the festive season, one of a succession of drinking parties.

With 1945 came the break-up of the group. 'Folio V' was the last of the *Salamander* magazines to appear, as the actors in this long-running wartime piece began drifting home. Fraser has recorded the dying fall by quoting a letter from John Waller to Erik de Mauny:

> John Cromer leaves for England this week. The Salamanders had a farewell dinner for him at that peculiar place known as Parme's bistro at the Cairo end of the Bulac bridge. There came to it John Cromer, Keith Bullen, Raoul Parme, Jean Moscatelli, George Hepburn, Alan Arnold, Nicholas de Watteville, G. S. Fraser and myself. Really it cannot be described as altogether a success, since it ended up with everybody quarrelling with each other furiously . . . Keith and Cromer made very sentimental speeches. Parme could scarcely talk for emotion and most of what he said was to the effect: 'I have supported French literature for forty years – ask my friend Moscatelli' . . . Parme accused everybody of trying to bilk the bill. Nicholas was rude to him. I was then rude to Nicholas, Cromer and Alan started up a quarrel about effeminate young men in Cairo and Jean Moscatelli just looked on wonderingly . . . Anyway, so it all went on till about half an hour after midnight, when I found myself back in my flat, having had a hearty quarrel on the way with G. S. F., about which neither of us could remember anything the next morning.

This was a typical Waller rendering of an event and, give or take a little seasoning, not far from the truth. This was not the end of Salamander, but the party was over, and whatever activity there was, continued not in Cairo but in London, where the echoes of these heady days rang on before being lost with the years.

Meanwhile, throughout the same period, the other writing group had flourished across the road at its habitat, the Anglo-Egyptian Union. The mufti poets and writers came to be known as the Personal Landscape group, the name being taken from the quarterly which they published, the first issue appearing about the same time as the first *Salamander*. Robin Fedden, one of the editors, recapitulated the apologia of these writers in his introduction to the 'anthology of exile', as *Personal Landscape*,[86] published in London in 1945, was subtitled. 'The writers share no common outlook and subscribe to no common policy; in spite of the efforts of well-meaning and misguided critics who see flocks and shepherds everywhere, they remain united only in exile.' From that point on, Fedden's anatomy of an exile deepens the separateness by stressing the strangeness:

> For a variety of reasons many people find exile in Egypt difficult out of all proportion to the trials which at first appear to be tangibly involved . . . First of all there are the difficulties of climate. Egypt was designed for Northern Europeans to visit, not to live in. The winter is incontestably perfect, like an ideal English summer; but when one outstays what was once the tourist season and drags on for three or four years, as is inevitable in war-time, the disadvantages of having no real winter become all too apparent . . . The landscape too, though beautiful in its own relaxed way, is as flaccid as the year. Except for the deserts where only the soldiers have lived, it is boneless and unarticulated . . . Not the least curious thing about a country with so much 'past', is that the stranger finds no historical continuity . . . What is missed and missing is the middle distance; where there should be an eighteenth century, there is the Turkish hiatus. Saladin is juxtaposed to cinemas, and Today, having no ancestry, is ridiculously isolated and uncertain of itself . . . There is another sort of isolation, cultural rather than temporal, which many people in Egypt find an exhausting business in the long run. It is possible to travel almost anywhere in Europe without getting quite off a familiar cultural beat; whatever the country, Christianity – whether the inhabitants like it or not – is at the back of the way they think and act. Once you cross to Islamic Africa it is a different story; nothing is to be taken for granted and you don't even know the general shape and outline of things . . . Finally, the war, which elsewhere would probably have given meaning to a banishment for which it was directly responsible, has in the Middle East lacked poetic, if not practical urgency for all but the minority who actually fought through the desert . . . War in a neutral country like Egypt is war at its most sterile; expatriates of all nations have felt here the length and inconvenience rather than the inspiration of the struggle.

One of the differences between the Personal Landscape coterie and Salamander was that the former felt their sense of exile keenly whereas the latter were a more mixed group of the uniformed poets, making the most of their fate, and the civilians who had chosen to live in Egypt or, even more than that, had been born there, so that the tragic sense of exile did not exist. Furthermore, the interplay between the English and French languages helped to break down barriers between the different nationalities and backgrounds of the Salamanders themselves, between the foreigners and the land which was their host. The writing from the two groups reflects the difference. That from Salamander was more directly influenced by Egypt and, with the prose pieces on Sir Richard Burton (by Colin Baly), John Lewis Burckhardt (by Herbert Addison) and Lady Hester Stanhope (also by Colin Baly) had an oriental bias whereas Personal Landscape looked towards Europe and was more influenced by Greece, particularly the poems by Bernard Spencer, Lawrence Durrell and Robin Fedden, although the later work reflected the inevitable hold that Egypt had upon all who sojourned there. One could feel a warmer, more human and, it may be said, sunnier atmosphere and spirit at the Gezira Preparatory School than round the bar at the Union. If Salamander was the spirit of fire, Personal Landscape was the spirit of water.

In terms of value judgement, it is probably true to say that Personal Landscape had the better writers and Salamander the broader scope. Since neither group claimed exclusivity, it was not surprising to find their work overlapping in other journals. As for cross-fertilisation, G. S. Fraser was as happy to appear in *Personal Landscape* as in *Salamander*. Terence Tiller, on the other hand, probably regretted that he had allowed his 'Birthday Poem' to appear in the same issue of *Salamander* as John Cromer's 'Death over Europe'. The differences between these two came to the surface on an evening in October 1943 on the lawn which the Anglo-Egyptian Union shared with the Egyptian Officers' Club, when, well supported by a good proportion of Egyptian members, Cromer gave a talk, reported thus in *The Sphinx*:

> On Tuesday night last an appreciative audience listened to an interesting talk by John Cromer on the subject of 'War Poetry in the Middle East' . . . The lecture itself was thoughtful and sincere and was punctuated by the reading of selected poems. These were excellently rendered by Raf de la Torre . . . Mr Arthur Delany thanked the lecturer in purposeful, aptly-chosen words which formed a fitting climax to a well-proportioned and illuminative talk.

Terence Tiller pointedly walked out.

In her two post-war novels *The Battle Lost and Won*[87] and *The Sum of Things*,[88] Olivia Manning caught much of the atmosphere of the Anglo-Egyptian Union (although there was no swimming pool as she avers). The later stages of the war and the characters in these novels came straight from the *Personal Landscape* contributors. In the latter book, she sets the scene:

> It was a pleasant time of the year. Winter in Egypt was no more than a temperate interval between one summer and the next. It did not last long and there was no spring though a few deciduous trees that dropped their leaves from habit, were now breaking into bud again. They went unnoticed in Garden City, lost as they were among the evergreens and palms and the dense, glossy foliage of the mango trees. The evenings were limpid and in the mornings a little mist hung like a delicate veil over the riverside walks.

She also described her husband, the Guy Pringle of the book being a thinly-disguised Reggie Smith:

> Now, no longer challenged by the nearness of war, he could see the futility of a reserved occupation. Lecturing on English literature, teaching the English language, he had been peddling the idea of empire to a country that only wanted one thing: to be rid of the British for good and all. And, to add to the absurdity of the situation, he himself had no belief in empire.

Olivia Manning had come on from the Balkans and seemed able to absorb the atmosphere of whatever country she was obliged to pass through or remain in, either from choice or force of circumstance. One last quotation from *The Sum of Things* shows her skill in portraying the already run-down centre of Cairo as it was in the mid-1940s. The central figure in this passage is herself:

> The Esbekiya, she said, still had the sunken look of a lake bed and in the old days, when the Nile rose, it used to be filled with water. Now the square was a turn-around for the tramcars but a few of the old houses remained with trees dripping over the garden wall as though to reach the water that was no longer there. Napoleon had lodged in the mansion that had been turned into Shepheard's Hotel. She thought there was still a hint of the oriental, pre-Napoleonic richness about the square but it had become a centre for raffish life and raffish medicine. On the seedy terrace houses that had displaced most of the mansions, there were advertisements for doctors who cured 'all diseases of love' and promised to the impotant 'horse-like vigour'. Gigantic wooden teeth, bloody at the roots, were hung out as a sign that cheap dentists were at work.

'Why has this become so run-down?' She pointed to the small, dry garden in the centre and told him that the assassin of General Kléber had been impaled there, taking three days to die. 'After that, who would want to live here?'

As with Salamander, so with Personal Landscape. The actors were gradually leaving the stage, most to return to England. Bernard Spencer went back to Greece but, alas, did not live long. Lawrence Durrell went to France, to embark on his *Alexandria Quartet*. Terence Tiller and Reggie Smith found a haven in the BBC and the other writers went their various ways.

Before we ring down the curtain on the cast and turn our attention to the play – the literature of the time – we should say a word or two about the café-society effect of Egypt on writers, both strangers in the land and inhabitants of it. Just as the coffee-houses provided a breeding ground for the wits and poets of eighteenth-century London, and the St Germain cafés a debating place for those of nineteenth-century Paris, so the bars bubbled with chatter in wartime Cairo. When the writers were not in one of the meeting places we have mentioned, they would foregather in less formalised groups in this or that bar or restaurant, one at least to be found in every street in the city centre. None of them was out of bounds and it was common to find both officers and other ranks there. Restaurant Rex was more sophisticated than the rest and its clientele was mostly officers with their girlfriends. The restaurant is still there, just as it used to be, the same tables, the same tablecloths, and judging by their age, the same waiters.

Then there were the parties, organised at different houses. Guests were invited to bring friends and sometimes a party originally for a dozen invitees would end up with a hundred. All had fun and got drunk on good NAAFI Scotch whisky, or local third-class brandy or wine, but a good time was enjoyed by all. Some of those parties became scenes of limerick competitions, usually led by John Waller, who was always the initiator of such events. Most of these limericks were new, composed either on the spur of the moment or during the war years. Some were decent enough for the ears of the very few women who were present, while others, like the famous 'There was a young girl of Tobruk' were definitely not. After each limerick there followed the inevitable, 'That was a cute little rhyme, sing us another one, do'. Another of John Waller's specialities was the shaggy-dog story. He managed to produce at least one new one whenever he appeared. Some of the best parties were given at the house of Colin Baly, a lecturer at the British Council, who lived in Shubra, the district famous for its Italian and Jewish communities.

5

The Second World War –
The Publications

Looking back over the last chapter, one will be struck by the fact that a very small number of people were writing a large amount of words. As an example, G. S. Fraser is recorded as having used about 40 pseudonyms throughout his army career in Cairo and Asmara. The writers we have been considering spent a great deal of their writing time on the smaller change of journalism. Those in uniform were mostly engaged in writing for service papers or propaganda for the Ministry of Information. The civilians were teaching the English language or literature in the universities, schools, the British Institute and the British Council or were moonlighting from the British Embassy. The American University was much more modest in its English-language output although it had support from the cultural section of the American Embassy. There was more than a little literary incest as most of the writers we have mentioned reviewed each other's books and discussed each other's works in the local periodicals and in lectures. In a closed society, such as wartime Cairo had to be, this was well-nigh inevitable. The ephemerae of newspaper and magazine articles took as little time to write as many of the poems which were published. There was not a great deal of sustained work and virtually no novels. It was as Fraser said: 'I knew dozens of people who said they were going to write a great novel about their experiences in the desert – and of course they never did. We talked away the rest of the 1940s, instead of writing our great novels.' The longer works by Lawrence Durrell and Olivia Manning were yet to come.

This train of thought was the inspiration of an article in the August 1943 issue of *Citadel*, 'Where is the War Novel?' by W. J. Makin. He opens with the sentence, 'To saunter through the bookshops of Cairo is to discover that many books are being published but few real writers are writing.' He develops his theme as follows:

> The rare writers appear to have adopted an asceticism suitable to the times. To the public anxious for good literature it would seem that these authors have abandoned their ivory towers to sulk in their dug-outs . . . Poets perhaps are silent because verse that is worth while needs cerebration in quietude. At the moment this is a very noisy world, tumultuous with events. True, many men in uniform are writing verse which will pass muster . . . The gestation of genius in war novels is as shy and slow as that of the elephant. It may take many years. All the better, for the public today asks only for great events to be reported and recorded, to be trumpeted by the voice of some unknown god through the microphone, or headlined by some hidden priest of the craft in a newspaper office . . . So the recording of these great events is left to these journeymen of letters, the reporters. In the main, they make a good job of it . . . Some of these reporters of events have produced books, often in the shape of hurriedly written diaries, full of hero-worship both objective and subjective. Most readable, and likely to be the stuff out of which the writer of genius will unhesitatingly and unashamedly help himself.

Citadel was first edited by Reggie Smith, assisted by David Hicks, a lecturer at the British Institute, who later took over the editorship. It was a literary magazine, open to all, civilians and military. A great deal of the content came from England but the major part was produced in Egypt. The October 1942 issue contained a manifesto, in which the following appeared:

> We have been making a survey of *Citadel* during the first seven months of publication in 1942 . . . and produced the following totals: most of the writers were English, including quite a number of Scottish, Welsh and Irish. There were 21 civilians writing in Egypt, one in Turkey, one in Iraq, one in Cyprus and three in England. Many contributions came from the British Forces, mainly in Egypt. There were fifteen writers from the Army and only three from the RAF – perhaps four, but at all events not as many as we should like . . . and we forgot to mention one war correspondent and one American fighting with the Free French. Six of the contributors were Egyptian, which is not so high a proportion as we should like to see in a magazine published in Egypt. Three were Palestinian, one a free Italian and four Greeks. There were 21 articles specifically about literature, one about language, one on war, two on education. Six articles were about England and its social affairs, four about Egypt, two Turkey, two Yugoslavia, one Palestine. We published

seven stories and five pieces of reportage. Finally, our readers had a full measure of poetry, for there were four and a half poems in every number of *Citadel* from January to July.

Citadel helped in supplying the avid seekers of books with reading material. The variety of content gave it its unique character and resulted in its continuation longer than any of the other literary magazines. It was a specific medium for the dissemination of culture. It published poems and stories by Lawrence Durrell, Robin Fedden, Olivia Manning, John Waller, G. S. Fraser, Keith Douglas, John Sykes, Ian Fletcher, Ruth Speirs, Max Kenyon and others. *Citadel* differed from the other literary magazines in its encouragement to Egyptian writers. Mursi was one of its regular contributors and was also editor-in-chief of *ESFAM*, the English section faculty of arts magazine, for four years.

ESFAM was published once a year and managed to publish 'Beggar' by Terence Tiller, 'Feluccas on the Nile' by Bernard Spencer as well as articles by Robin Fedden, John Speirs and a number of Egyptians who, later on, distinguished themselves in the literary field.

We have already mentioned *Orientations* and despite George Fraser's depreciatory comments, it did provide a forum for writers in the Middle East War Zone. The first sentence of that first issue in March 1942, written by Haig Gudenian, one of three associate editors under Fraser's editorship, summed up the feelings of those early drafts to the Middle East who saw the rising numbers of new arrivals as diminishing their own self-importance: 'As there are more of us, so do we feel less in Egypt.' That first paragraph ends: 'We are too many for distinction now, and that realisation is distasteful.'

Although most of the contributors to that issue were journalists, there was a short story by the Egyptian writer Mahmoud Taymour, poems by John Waller and William Mangan Campion and a nostalgic look at Corfu by Lawrence Durrell, using for almost the last time the pseudonym under which he had written *Panic Spring* – Charles Norden.

Although Fraser was one of the originators of *Orientations*, he did not stay long as editor. In his 'Passages from a Cairo Notebook' in *Leaves in the Storm*,[89] he attributes what he refers to as the failure of the magazine to his 'negative liberalism'. He says:

The things I have written in it myself are not good, because they lack not only any general assent, but my usual self-confidence . . . Yet *Orientations* was a sound idea; somebody else would have made a success of it; never, I think, a literary success . . . which is where the jeers of civilian poets like Reggie Smith and Bernard Spencer are irrelevant.

Perhaps the original structure was too top-heavy with journalists, with three associate editors and an editorial board of four. By November 1942, the board had gone and there were four editors, only Haig Gudenian remaining from the original team, having been joined by Neville Armstrong, William Wells and D. J. S. Thomson. The number of editors went up to five when Erik de Mauny was added in March 1943. The pattern of a single editor, Thompson, with assistants, was restored in May and continued thereafter, although the personnel changed from time to time.

The early days were the best for the regular contributors, or so they chose to think. John Cromer saw the magazine as a means of letting down hair and sounding off, creating controversy and enjoying the consequences. He launched a series of polemics under the pseudonym 'Intrepidus', beginning in the first issue with 'Manifesto', which for him was a continuation of a form of writing which was all youth and enthusiasm but lacking in specifics.

> Youth must ensure that the lead which it follows does not degenerate into the misleading which has been so great a failing in the past. It is not enough to follow blindly . . . We have the right to question and criticise. That right must never be allowed to lapse. It is the right to know to what end we are fighting – what planned world is envisaged by the men who now direct our destinies.

The articles which followed were much in the same vein, looking to the future, and they received some support from the correspondence columns. The voice was, however, too strident and Cromer's diary for 22 March 1943 records the dénouement:

> I had an editorial meeting at *Orientations* HQ at the Victory Club – I always like talking to the lads there. Gudenian, the Editor, has a slow, appraising way with him and is a good restraining influence. William Wells, vague and floating in the background as usual, had odd suggestions and ideas. I was greatly pleased with Erik de Mauny from New Zealand. I like his poetry and his ideas are fresh and impulsive. We debated the 'Intrepidus' idea and I could see that

they think my rhetorical heaviness is somewhat overdone. Although it was not directly suggested, I think it was assumed I should either stop or change the style. My own suggestion, which was immediately adopted, was to run a 'reform' series, starting with the Law, which I should write, which could be followed by Health, Agriculture, Education, Public Services etc. and should prove a success.

This series went ahead, with Cromer leading off under his surname Braun with an article in the May issue, 'Light on the Law'.

The other field of controversy was poetry. Making a different, less engaged, approach to the problem of 'selling' poetry to the troops and reading public at large, Cromer's belief in the simplicity of the word and his antipathy to the direction poetry was taking, caused him to strike out with an article on modern poetry entitled, 'The New Hieroglyphics', which appeared in the January 1943 issue of *Orientations*. Egypt was already exerting its influence on his pen, both in the title and text, which began:

> The history of ancient Egypt is carved upon stone in many places, for all to see and few to appreciate. The pictorial figures and alphabetical cuneiform stand open for discovery and interpretation by the archaeologist and historian, remaining to the layman little more than a mysterious and fascinating tableau of the past . . . One comes, one sees, one wonders . . . So it is with poetry.

After some tongue-in-cheek side swipes at Eliot, Auden, Dylan Thomas, the Surrealists and the New Apocalyptics, of whom Fraser was one, he concludes, with the voice of 'Intrepidus': 'Roll up the papyri, seal the bamboos, bury the tablets. Preserve the poetry of these generations for another thousand years, then uncover it as the new hieroglyphics. Maybe somebody will be able to understand it. Maybe.'

This was, of course, too much for the intellectual writers who took it seriously. Max Kenyon was quick off the mark with his riposte in the next issue, 'Fair Play for the Poets'. He seemed particularly hurt at the slighting of Eliot and hit back:

> Mr Cromer has been so taken with his pretty analogy between modern verse and Pharaonic hieroglyphics that he has stretched his argument a good deal, perhaps more than he intended. But that does not mean, I think, that we can allow what he says to pass unchallenged. Whatever the temptation an idea may have to make

us talk rot, I think we should try to diminish the rot, even at the expense of the idea. But we cannot leave this subject, Mr Cromer, until I have accused you of deliberately shutting off your intelligence and knowledge in order to score a debating point.

Next into the arena was G. S. Fraser, riposting with 'New Simplification' and drawing upon Egypt to support his powerful lunge:

No modern poem is half as obscure as a stroll down Soliman Pasha. Indeed, though I do not think he has chosen his examples well, I would, in fact, agree with Mr Cromer that modern poetry is often more difficult than the poetry of some, though not of all, previous ages. The reasons are not very far to seek. The streets of Cairo are more confusing in their impact than those of Birmingham or Edinburgh. What gives the cities of the Middle East their peculiar fascination is that in the Mediterranean, and in Egypt particularly, so many streams of life from so many directions have come together and mingled their bitter waters. And Egypt is a good metaphor for our age. Every religion, every philosophy of the past affects us, and yet none can command a general assent . . . The hieroglyphics of 'The Waste Land', embodying its jetsam and flotsam of all cultures, ending in its eclectic yet desperate cry of faith are, for him who can decipher them, a precise reflection of the historical situation in which we find ourselves.

Although Cromer was later to be involved in the advertising business, he was at that time innocent of all such connections and avers that in this pseudo-controversy, the case he was making was an unreal one and it was not his intention to attract publicity for his book of poems, *In Battle*,[90] which came out shortly afterwards under the Salamander imprint. Nevertheless, it soon sold out. From the timing, it would seem, in retrospect, that the event had been well orchestrated by the editors.

Mursi Saad el Din was not involved in these capers but his poems were published later in *Orientations*, which had then become a helpful medium for civilians as well as service men and women, providing a hungry readership with a wide range of material of all kinds, and adding in some measure to the appreciation of the host country. The many illustrations – paintings, drawings, photographs – gave an idea of the many facets of the local scene, when sent home to families to show them the exotic life behind the lines. A four-page spread in the Christmas 1943 number entitled, 'Morning at the Victory' deserves a place in the archives of immortality if only because the last of the series of photographs shows a smart (!) George Fraser emerging from the door with cap straight and khaki belt instead of string – and the brass is shining. Contributors and readers look back at the Victory Club and *Orientations* with a great deal of affection.

We have already introduced readers to the Salamander Society and referred to its publications, more in connection with the writers than with the written word. Now we wish to put together the published works as part of the history of the time. Salamander embraced several activities. Starting as a meeting place for writers, primarily poets, it was inevitable that the expression of their output should be given effect by publishing a journal. Individual members of the group were enabled to publish their own poems under the Salamander imprint. Another achievement was the overseeing of the publication of *Oasis*. In sum, the output was not great but it continued through the war period and it was purely literary.

Five issues of *Salamander* appeared between September 1942 and early 1945. Twenty-three writers were given the freedom of its pages, 11 of them in the services, and 12 civilians, most of whom had been living in Cairo or Alexandria when war broke out. Fifty poems appeared, 29 English originals and the rest translations – two from English into Latin; two from Latin into English; eight from French into English; seven from English into French; one from Arabic into English; and one original French. There were seven prose pieces. Only two of the original poems showed any direct connection with Egypt – G. S. Fraser's 'Streets of Cairo' and John Gawsworth's 'Cleopatra'. Yet these years were to be the seedbeds from which later flowers would bloom.

We have already referred to the group of civilian poets who contributed to *Personal Landscape*. In 1942, Lawrence Durrell and Bernard Spencer suggested to Robin Fedden that they should all produce what the first-named referred to as 'a little chapbook of verse printed among friends' and the last-named as 'something in the nature of a private publication'. Fedden saw the venture as 'for all three of us in some degree the extension of moods and relationships shaped in a country to which from our exile we often looked back'. That country was, of course, Greece. From this thought developed a quarterly magazine, eight issues of which were published between 1942 and 1945. The first number consisted of poems by the three editors plus Terence Tiller. As a result of the interest roused, they decided to go public. As Fedden wrote subsequently:

> The success of our first number showed that there were many people in the Middle East who wished to read live verse, and the contributions which subsequently came in proved that there were also more people writing it than we imagined. Further, the absence of any other serious verse publication, and the lamentable level of various Middle East anthologies of 'war poetry', directed the best of this interest and this practice towards *Personal Landscape*.

At that time, the other verse publication, *Salamander*, had not yet appeared and although most of the Personal Landscape group held a jaundiced view of war poetry, such a view was probably not directed against *Oasis* which was not to come for another year. It also produced one piece of irony. One of its contributors was Keith Douglas, who was probably the most outstanding of the Second World War poets. He and Sidney Keyes were the two who most closely revived memories of the First World War poets by their individualism, their heroism and the power of their writing. Douglas had a wayward streak but as well as being a fine poet he was a fearless officer, a Captain in the Royal Armoured Corps. He was also something of an artist, as appears from *Alamein to Zem Zem*,[91] published with great care by Poetry London and made up of poems, prose, drawings and watercolours, one of which, 'Cairo Street Scene' provides the back cover for *Return to Oasis*. In that book, Tambimuttu has written 'Last Lunch with Keith Douglas', a most valuable account of his meeting with the poet only a few days before the latter departed for D-Day and his early death. It tells much of the vicissitudes of his work:

> That morning Keith had also brought all the poems he wished to preserve, in a folder. The several editors he has had (there are three editions of his two books, the first from Editions Poetry London Ltd, the second from Faber and Faber and the third from Oxford) speak of emendations and alterations by other hands than the author's. I feel quite sure this statement is correct since as he hovered, tall over my shoulder at the desk, making suggestions for alternative readings, deletion of entire passages, the welding of several poems into one unit, I had taken the precaution of initialling each suggestion Keith made, after making a note of it. There was a sense of hurry and urgency and after a recital of the names of people who had read his poems, Keith said (I must record, quite

immodestly, in view of the present terrible muddle over his poems), 'You are the only editor I can trust.'

The biography, *Keith Douglas*[92] by Desmond Graham, tells the story of his life but the editing of his poems has always been a difficulty. One small example is the poem 'Vergissmeinicht', one of the four Douglas poems published in *Personal Landscape*. Written in Tripolitania in 1943, it appeared in *Return to Oasis* as 'Elegy for an 88 Gunner', the title given to it by the poet himself, so authentic. There are a number of changes in the text although the rhyme form of the six stanzas remains unchanged. This is typical of many of his poems. He could not bear being away from any fighting that was going and disobeyed orders in order to take a tank into action at Alamein where he was wounded. On sick leave in Cairo, as on his regular leaves from the desert, commemorated in his poem 'Cairo Jag', he made his way to the Anglo-Egyptian Union, hence his inclusion in *Personal Landscape*. His best friend there was Bernard Spencer, who wrote his obituary note in the last number of the magazine, after Douglas had been killed in Normandy.

Another friend was John Waller, who wrote in *The Collected Poems of Keith Douglas*,[93] which he edited with G. S. Fraser:

I myself was privileged to know Keith Douglas both in Oxford where he struck me as slightly sombre and reserved, though with expressive dark eyes, and again in Cairo, in September 1943, after he had returned from his desert campaigns and was kicking his heels in boredom at a base camp outside the city. He visited me at my office and later we had a lunch with G. S. Fraser at the Anglo-Egyptian Union in the garden and spent an evening or two in the garish Egyptian bars. He seemed to me then an unaffected person and a natural poet, modest sometimes to the point of seeming shy, but shrewd in judgement and understanding. Perhaps in those last meetings I felt him also to be a little depressed and cynical. 'Once you have been in one battle, you have been in all,' I remember him saying. He disapproved of what he considered to be the pseudo-heroics exhibited by a number of war writers; his fundamental sense of realism prevented him from indulging in attitudes of this kind, and moreover he hated anything that could be used as propaganda. Our last meeting (though of course we did not realise at the time it was to be our last) was in the bar of Gamache, the Taverne Française, in the Sharia Elfi Bey, a well-known cosmopolitan rendez-vous during the first half of the war. G. S. Fraser was also with us. But, as we had exhausted our money and the evening was late, we parted gloomily after a few drinks, instead of dining together to mark the occasion as we had planned. Shortly afterwards I heard that his unit had moved away and Douglas with it.

The works contained in the various issues of *Personal Landscapes* were put together as an anthology under the same title, as mentioned earlier, and published by Tambimuttu in 1945. We have already quoted extensively from Robin Fedden's introduction but the book contained besides a good cross-section of poetry and prose. A most interesting collection of notes appears under the heading 'Ideas about Poems', prefaced by the statement:

> These notes on poetry do not present a manifesto, and will often be found diametrically opposite in standpoint one to another. Personal and private, they do not even present a series of individual manifestoes. An attitude is not a permanent belief, and these notes are the expressions of attitudes, of moods, which need not be more permanent than the mood from which an individual poem is born. It is, indeed, in this sense that they are presented: as backgrounds only to sections of their author's work.

The authors referred to are Lawrence Durrell, Terence Tiller, Gwyn Williams, Bernard Spencer and George Seferis.

Although not strictly in the category of literary magazines, *The Sphinx*, published weekly, contained a great deal of the poetry and prose output of all the writers we have mentioned. They also provided music and book reviews, social snippets and other marginalia under a variety of pseudonyms. The editor, Philip Taylor and his daughter, Paula, were good friends to the many service men and women in the area and through them the network of contributors kept a constant supply of material flowing into the magazine's offices in Sharia Galal. John Cromer was able to publish several poems, all on the subject of Egypt, his fable 'The Jacaranda and the Flamboyant' and reviews of books, stage shows and music.

Another popular weekly which also provided an outlet for writing was *Cairo Calling*, the 'Radio Times' of the Egyptian State Broadcasting Service. At this distance in time it is easy to overlook the important part which radio played in the fields of information, education and entertainment but there was, of course, no television then in the Middle East. Since there would have been no magazine without the medium, it seems permissible to digress a little from publications to say a little about radio, as it covered so wide a field and performed an invaluable service.

As today, the BBC news service provided the world with the best factual coverage, whatever may have had to be added during wartime for propaganda – very discreet, naturally – counter-propaganda and coded messages for underground movements. In Egypt, regular BBC news broadcasts could be received direct on the appropriate wavelengths in a wide range of languages in addition to English and Arabic – most European languages, including German but not Scandinavian, all the main Balkan languages, Turkish, Persian, Afrikaans and Hindustani. The Egyptian State Broadcasting programmes were the Main Cairo I, the alternative Cairo II and Alexandria, and a short-wave service with daily Arabic and European programmes. In addition to four daily news broadcasts in English and French, there were daily news bulletins in Polish, Italian, Greek, Rumanian, Bulgarian, Czecho-Slovak and Serbo-Croat. A time-pip signal was radiated hourly except where this might interfere with Koran or other religious readings and the Fuad I University clock could be heard each day at 11 a.m. and 8.30 and 11.30 p.m. All services closed down at 11.30 p.m.

The studios and offices of ESB were at Radio House, 5 Sharia Elui, Cairo and this is where the administrative and broadcasting staff were to be found. The man at the top was the General Manager, Ronald Ferguson, whose radio work had started in 1908, following Sir Oliver Lodge's wireless experiments by 'broadcasting' from his bedroom to the greenhouse, with a third 'station' in the potting shed. Radio was his life and he had been working on it in the USA and with the Marconi and other companies before coming to Egypt in 1934 for the post he then occupied.

The Engineer-in-Chief was Herbert John Russell, who also arrived in Egypt in 1934, shortly before the first ESB programme was broadcast. He, too, had a well-based career in wireless telegraphy and was an old Marconi hand. The third Brit in the hierarchy was Frederick George Stewart, known within the system as 'Freddy', who was the General Secretary and Chief Accountant. He started his working life as a telegraph boy with the Marconi Company in 1918 and worked his way up from there. He was the first member of the ESB to arrive in Egypt in 1933, and was largely responsible for building up the organisation.

Two key Egyptian members complete this brief run down of the top echelon. Mohammed Said Bey Loutfy was Controller of the Arabic programmes, a man of wide culture and no political affiliations. Having obtained an Honours degree at Oxford, he spent a lifetime in the Egyptian Administration and on retirement was appointed to his job at the ESB in 1933. A lover of poetry and an eminent Arab historian, he was known to have given over a hundred talks on Moslem history. Mostafa Bey Rida was Director of Oriental Music at the ESB as well as being Director of the Royal Institute of Arab Music in Cairo. He had done much to raise the status of the musical profession in Egypt, where until the 1930s it was not greatly esteemed. He had formed the first Oriental Music Club, which led to recognition by King Fuad and the first Arab Music Congress in 1932.

These, then, were the men who had established a state broadcasting service in Egypt and who were at the helm when the audiences were increased so dramatically by the arrival of armed forces from many nations. Radio House became the hub of a very considerable amount of locally-made programmes. While it is true that much of the insatiable demand for entertainment was made up of recorded programmes, little thought is given today to the production of music, drama, variety and talks by performers and artists from the services and local entertainers. We shall have more to say later about the live shows and concerts, many of which were relayed on radio but our present purpose is to concentrate on literature.

Cairo Calling was, of course, well established when the wave of new listeners flooded into the country, but reinforcements had to be brought in from the services to provide the editorial skills as a back-up for the widely varied programme material. We should like to single out one unsung hero for the versatility, knowledge and unfailing humour which he brought to the journal. Staff Sergeant Leslie S. Barnard who, as it happened, had journeyed out with the same Hampshire Regiment draft as John Cromer, performed an outstanding service for music and literature in many ways, not only as a critic and contributor but in his unfailing assistance to illustrators, performers and artists all along the line. Putting aside for the moment the musical aspect, his devotion to literature was almost as great. With weekly snippets in 'Forces Forecast' on coming events under the pseudonym 'The D. R.', he would also write on Shaw,

Dickens, Joyce, introductory articles on particular programmes, and all that he wrote was eminently readable. As the greater part of all programme notes from 1941 until 1943 (when they hardly appeared at all) were written by him – mostly anonymously, it may be realised what a gap in knowledge there would have been without his contributions. We would call attention in particular to that cheerful Christmas issue of 20 December 1941 in which Barnard scooped the pool under various pseudonyms. L. S. B. provided a page 'It's all right in Screenland!' where everything is so well arranged and it all comes right in the end; Leslie S. Barnard had managed a page and a half on 'O. B. from Dingley Dell' in true Dickensian style; Stephen John had another page, 'Christmas Music'; 'Cairo Calling' wrote an Open Letter to the Editor of *Radio Times* after filling a missing column with an A. A. Thomson piece from the 1939 Christmas number of the BBC journal – 'We searched, we selected, we stole'; and unattributed programme notes were provided for a piano recital, the radio trailer for the Cairo Amateur Dramatic Society's production 'Revue Order', an adaptation of 'A Christmas Carol', a programme of theatre organ music, a classical programme of Listeners' Requests, and a note on 'Rhythm on the Air', featuring the Dug-Out Ramblers relayed from the Metropolitan Hotel. This last was of special interest to Cromer because he had his security eye on the double bass player.

Thumbing through yellowing copies of *Cairo Calling*, Cromer was surprised to find that in 1943–4 he had taken up more airtime in the cause of literature than any other single writer in or out of the services, with an equal quota of the columns of the journal. His first series of three talks, 'Writing Now' in the spring of 1942, covered Thomas Wolfe, James Joyce and T. S. Eliot. Extracts from the first and third of these were reprinted in *Cairo Calling*, while Leslie Barnard provided a note on Joyce. In the autumn there followed a series of three talks on writers of the English countryside – Richard Jefferies, Edward Thomas and Henry Williamson, each of which was reprinted in full in the journal. In the winter came Keith Bullen's series 'Visionary Gold' on English poetry, for which Cromer provided introductory articles on Roy Campbell and Rupert Brooke. A longer series of six talks was presented in the summer of 1943, with the title 'Spotlight on Literature'. In these, Cromer spread himself over the master of style, Charles Morgan; the Americans

Christopher Morley and William Saroyan; the Welsh Ambassadors, John Cowper Powys, T. F. Powys and Llewellyn Powys; the American realists Sinclair Lewis and John Steinbeck; two English writers, J. B. Priestley and A. J. Cronin; and to round off in style, 'The Democratic Tradition in American Verse', dealing with Archibald Macleish, William Rose Benet, ee cummings and Carl Sandburg. Cromer also contributed articles to *Cairo Calling* on Browning, to introduce the poems to be read by Raf de la Torre and other sundries, one of which was 'Conversation Piece'. In this he was able to pass on this thought about that dying art and the role of radio:

> The broadcast word has already had a great influence upon our speech and diction, and it seems not unreasonable to hope that it may also assist in reviving the art of conversation . . . We are all eavesdroppers at heart and like to overhear snatches of conversation. That is the role we play when we listen to radio, our activity being a conscious accentuation of natural curiosity. Let us take a lead from radio and give our friends, our neighbours and ourselves a little pleasure by talking more about things worth listening to, and taking more care how we say them.

Lawrence Durrell had one series of six talks, on humour, at the beginning of 1942, starting with Sidney Smith. The series was introduced by a substantial article by Leslie Barnard, 'Humour and Humorists' and he also wrote 'The Importance of not being Earnest', for Durrell's talk 'Utter Nonsense'. A good time was had by all, speaker, writer and, above all, the listeners. Robin Fedden's contribution was a talk, 'Pirates in the Mediterranean', given in November 1941. We have no knowledge of any talks which may have been given anonymously. It is worth recording that all the talks given by servicemen were subject to the usual censorship rules but at no time was there anything but benevolent co-operation from the authorities.

Keith Bullen led the 1942 list of poetry publications with his *Charles Baudelaire*, subtitled 'Un poète maudit', published by Les Amis du Livre Français en Orient for Horus Editions.[94] It was well printed in French and English with a helpful foreword by Léon Guichard and a perceptive note on the poet by the translator. Bullen says in his introduction to the reader:

> Translation always fails; the only consolation in the present case lies in the fact that it is easier to translate French Verse into English Verse than vice-versa . . . The form must sometimes change as well

as the idiom and syntax. Many of the poems of 'Les Fleurs du Mal' are sonnets, and in these I have kept to his rhyming scheme as far as possible.

This was by no means easy but the result was admirable.

In the autumn of that year there was a small spate of 'slim volumes' of poetry. Keith Bullen's *We Stand Alone* and nine other war sonnets was published as a collection in August by the Sphinx Publishing Company.[95] They had already earned interest and respect when they had first appeared in the daily newspaper, the *Egyptian Gazette*. The company's own weekly periodical, *The Sphinx*, also permitted John Cromer to use its columns for a sympathetic review. Apart from the title poem and its succeeding three sonnets, which covered that critical period when England's fate was in the balance, he singled out 'Malta' as 'a fitting tribute to that battered but unconquered island' adding later in the review, 'The spirit of these poems is one of homage to true fighting stock and exhortation to further effort.'

It would be remiss of us if we did not chronicle here a ceremony which had taken place in Malta the previous May to mark the close of the island's Dramatic Festival Week. Keith's sonnet was presented to the Government by an officer serving in the Middle East. The sonnet had been beautifully illuminated by a soldier artist in Cairo from an original design by J. H. Rowntree, an old Cairo hand, and was decorated with the arms of St John and St George as well as La Vallette and L'Isle Adam, surmounted by the George Cross. It was offered to the people of Malta by the Salamander Society as 'a small token from a few British citizens of Cairo in recognition and admiration of a very gallant feat of arms'.

In September 1942, the same month which saw the appearance of the first issue of *Salamander*, one of its members, J. S. Blake-Reed, brought out his *Twentyfive Odes of Horace Rendered into English*, under the imprint of Whitehead Morris of Alexandria.[96] These polished little gems were the answer to a question which the translator had put to himself and which he poses in his foreword: 'If you were sent into exile and allowed to take with you only one book, what book would you choose? The answer came at once and spontaneously: "Horace".' The poems were attractively illustrated by the line drawings of Blake-Reed's fellow Judge in the Mixed Court of Appeal, E. S.

Lemass. It should be remembered that this book was published between the panic days of 'The Flap' and the thundering barrage of Alamein, which was within earshot of Alexandria.

Ten days before the attack, Raoul Parme's *Poèmes d'Angleterre* were collected into the first individual volume to appear under the auspices of the Salamander Society, being the translator's seventh book.[97] The English poets whose works he had rendered so felicitously into French were Walter Savage Landor, Elizabeth Barrett Browning, William Johnson Cory's unforgettable 'Heraclitus', A. E. Housman, W. B. Yeats. G. K. Chesterton, John Masefield, Joseph Plunkett and Francis Ledwige – an interesting and catholic choice.

John Cromer was fortunate in his timing for, in November, with the Germans now on the run in the desert and a triumph of British arms in the offing, the Salamander Society published his own volume, *In Battle*, 11 poems of war, which included, not surprisingly in the light of the prose works mentioned earlier, 'A Call to Youth'. The poems were not remarkable but 'Asleep in War' appeared later in several anthologies. Cromer's pen had not been idle in other directions, as he had contributed a preface to Keith Bullen's translation of Alfred de Musset's long poem, *Souvenir*, published a fortnight later.[98] Reflecting on that preface, Cromer would like to take this present opportunity to reiterate the view there stated:

> The art of poetry translation is akin to that of perfumery. Just as the apothecary must know and appreciate not only the rare and fleeting charm of essential fragrance, but also the physical quantitative scent of the flower or sensation he is seeking to produce, so also must the translator be not only skilled in the languages he is handling but also in the writing of poetry. He must be a poet to recognise the value and form of the work he is translating and also to re-create that work into a fresh poem in another language.

He called Bullen's translation 'an education and a delight'. It still is.

The last of the Salamander productions in this eventful year, both in military and Cairo literary terms, was John Waller's *Spring Legend*, 17 poems, all of which had been previously published but which, brought together in this form, provided a neat conspectus of the poet's early work. The poems reflect his Oxford days, early army life and the voyage out. John Cromer remembers the waving hands, the slight stutter and flourish of the poem as the other John dashed off his dedication, adding, 'despite all arguments', which summed up their relationship.

This seems a fitting place to pay tribute to the printer of all these books of poetry – F. E. Noury et Fils, who not only worked with remarkable speed but also with equally remarkable accuracy. Raoul Parme masterminded the production and agreed the layouts and although the typefaces were not always immaculate, the bold characters in particular suffering at times from an excess of ink, the number of literals was next to nothing. Noury did not know English and was obviously at home with the French texts, but sight-setting as his staff did, the result was a triumph of typography. It was the speed with which the authors were able to correct the near-immaculate proofs that enabled the Salamander Society to produce such a creditable list in so short a time. The runs were, alas, short and all copies were soon sold out, never to be reprinted.

The same care and skill was applied by Noury and his firm when it came to the publication of *Oasis*[99] which, as has been stated earlier, started with its three original editors meeting together in 'Music for All'. As the story of how this anthology of poetry developed has already been told by the editors themselves in a preface to *Oasis* and again by Victor Selwyn in *Return to Oasis*, which reprinted the original preface, we would direct readers to those texts. Two short paragraphs by Selwyn sum up the achievement:

> When we launched our appeal to the troops for poetry the highest rank amongst us was corporal. We had no official backing. Yet three thousand poems descended on us, the editors, from eight hundred contributors. We would only have space for one hundred and twenty-one! Paper was rationed.

That was the beginning.

> The troops' own NAAFI (equivalent to US PX) finally distributed and sold the 5,000 paperback edition to make £250 profit (under US $500) for the Red Cross. *Oasis* sold at 25 piastres a copy (25p or less than 50 cents US).

Between these two events came the intervention of the Salamander Society which has also been recorded earlier in this book. Before the poems came the editors' introduction; a preface by Worth Howard, Acting Dean of the Faculty of Arts and Sciences at the American University of Cairo and Director of

Literary Activities at 'Music for All'; an article, 'Poetry Today' by John Cromer; and a special foreword in the shape of a facsimile letter from the C-in-C Middle East, General Sir Henry Maitland Wilson. Howard's preface contained two apt comments:

> Perhaps no record relating to the war in the Middle East will be closer to the spirit of the men who have served than this volume of poems. This is true because poetry has the quality of engaging our emotions so directly and so powerfully. By a word rightly chosen or by a phrase rightly coined, a poet opens vistas or captures the heart as no other artificer may.

And the concluding words:

> We are told not to expect great art in the midst of great conflict. No matter what the verdict of time is upon the rank of these poems, there is certainly assurance that the creative springs have not been choked by this awful sport of Mars.

Cromer's five-page article concluded:

> It should be a matter of some pride for the peoples of the United Nations that the men and women of those forces who have achieved victories by armed assault on foreign soil should at the same time be maintaining the victory of culture over the horror and ugliness of the time.

The poems had been written under all kinds of conditions at times of stress and times of reflection. They were mostly of war experiences and thoughts, recapturing feelings and scenes of home, convoys, the desert and various places in the Middle East. They were all gathered together in that oasis of culture – Cairo. Today Cromer can still feel the damp paper of those proof sheets and can see again the good work of Noury as the memory returns of the taxi ride from the Boulac to Zamalek for final revision before the proofs were passed for press.

Oasis had a good critical reception throughout the Middle East. George Bishop reviewed it for the *Egyptian Gazette* under the banner headlines 'Fifty-one Middle East Poets Wrote This Book'. He congratulated the editors on having eliminated the out-and-out trash, the literary garbage which he put under three heads:

> First, there is doggerel unadorned, traced out by the man with something to say and no language in which to say it . . . Equally infuriating – and prolific – is the man bitten by the Jingo bug, who

must wave outsize flags and beat the biggest of drums . . . Third, and not unknown in the Middle East, are the 'Precious' school, writing a language of their own – mercifully for the consumption of their own circle.

Having said that, he continued:

These are out. What is to be found? Some excellent imagery, some fine, live similes, some strong emotional feeling, and themes worthy of poetic treatment.

The *Egyptian Gazette*'s reviewer reproduced the whole of General Wilson's foreword, much of which, in itself, bears repeating:

I consider *Oasis* very aptly named, because of the pleasure that it will give to many who have found War an aesthetic desert; and because most of us in the Middle East will always remember the feeling of excitement and anticipation on approaching those patches of greenness and water in the Western Desert; not knowing whether they would turn out to be real or mirage – I feel in the case of *Oasis* it will prove to be the former.

La Bourse Egyptienne gave two good columns, rightly stressing the Egyptian input: 'L'Egypte, les paysages égyptiens, le désert, la vie et les moeurs égyptiennes y sont partout présents.' This review concludes:

Oasis est un petit livre plein de substance et de musique, d'une musique pas toujors joyeuse et pour cause, qu'on doit lire si l'on veut connaître l'âme britannique, l'âme des soldats dont la vie d'héroïsme et de sacrifices a été pour nous tous en Orient un facteur primordial de salut.

The *Eastern Times* of Syria saw the anthology as serving a dual purpose: 'Not only has it given a chance for unknown poets to have their works published, but it has also killed the illusion that the present generation in the Forces lacks culture.' The *Palestine Post* was not lacking in generosity: 'By any standard, there are fine poems in this anthology. Some of them, while lacking technical accomplishment, show great promise. Almost all have the stamp and ring of complete sincerity . . . The anthologists have done a very difficult job very well indeed.' Jan Bielatowicz of the Polish *Orzel Biaky* (in English, 'White Eagle') went sadly astray with his figures: '*Oasis* – small in size but rich in contents – has been sold in nearly a million copies. Surely a record for any book of verse! It is the companion of almost every soldier, forming part of his kit no less than his arms and equipment.' Alas, this is one piece of fiction which is a long way removed from fact.

At the end of the month after the publication of *Oasis*, Salamander Productions published Keith Bullen's *Albert Samain, un pastelliste exquis*,[83] which was a selection of poems and prose rendered into English. The translator said in his foreword:

> I have chosen poems which appeal to me personally, but I have also tried to make the contents of the book representative . . . Although I have tried to keep as close to the French text as possible, there are occasions when either sense or imagery must suffer slight distortion if a poem is to be preserved as a whole. On the other hand, I am unrepentant over the preservation of well-worn rhymes and circumlocutions as traditional French verse by its very rules abounds in these . . . The tribute I have attempted to pay to the greatness of French Literature is frail but purposeful, for with it goes the conviction that the mutual understanding and appreciation of each other's literature are essential contributions to a permanent liaison between the English and French speaking peoples. They breed friendship of the heart.

The brief biographical note preceding the poems is enough to throw light on the man who is described as probably the least romantic of French poets. When asked about his own life for the provision of details to go with his own work, Samain is said to have replied, 'There is no story attached to my life.' He was a minor government official and had one odd correspondence with the English civil servant/poet, Humbert Wolfe. Bullen points out in a footnote that Samain confessed that when feeling pessimistic, he contemplated a rose. Wolfe's finest sonnet begins: 'Rose, be a parable when love's afraid . . .' The Samain poems are taken from 'Au Jardin de l'Infante', 'Le Chariot d'or' and 'Aux Flancs du Vase' and Bullen has done a great service in reviving the art of this gentle man.

Francis Jammes described Samain as 'a swan who floated idly past the scenes that he had sung, listening only for the sound of bells chiming from a church in Flanders, the church where an old lady knelt to pray'. Bullen considered this to be over-sentimental, his own appraisal being:

> He is the pastellist of French verse, exquisite in theme, in colour and design. He excels in portraiture as well as in landscape . . . He is the poet of the half-light, the dawn and crespuscule, the moonlit sky . . . He is the poet of lingering eventide, when distant skies are

faintly luminous, when flowers dream, and the angelus is softly ringing. He is the poet of the season's end, when autumn mists forget the burning rose and memorise the fallen, faded leaf instead . . . His is the deathless voice of all regret.

The year 1943 saw other publications. Denis Saunders, writing as Almendro, had contributed to some of the publications already mentioned and this year published two small volumes on his own account. *Heaven's Tramp*[100] came out in April, R. Schindler of Cairo being the publisher. The desert fighting and the two sides of Cairo, reflected in 'Egyptian Dancer' and 'Beggar', were already having their effect on the young South African and his poetry was maturing apace. The little slip of a book, with its 12 poems, was enhanced by the delicate but expressive line drawings of Eric de Nemes. G. S. Fraser said in his *Passages from a Cairo Notebook* that the best thing in *Orientations* had been Nemes's covers – the scavenger hawk and the Sassanid bull – and continued:

> Eric has a wonderful library, and enjoys hearing me read Edward Lear while swiftly, deftly, and in utter boredom, he does neat drawings for advertisements. He had been offered a job as a political cartoonist but turned it down. 'I would be afraid of being sent to jail if I gave Nahas Pasha the wrong sort of squint.'

But we digress from Almendro, whose other little book, no more than a pamphlet, appearing in May, was a single poem entitled *Jan Christian Smuts, Field Marshal*,[101] a panegyric in eight sections, eulogising the South African leader, whose uniformed head and shoulders appeared uncompromisingly on the front cover.

Another front cover of a very different kind, 'The Belle of Shubra Village' looked out from a little book entitled *Egypt Now*,[102] a miscellany edited by Hilary Wayment, another of Mursi's professors at the University. It was published by Horus, another of the enterprising bookshops, whose interest in books extended beyond mere selling, taking them into the publishing business. This book really was little – 12cm × 17cm – but it is a gem, containing three main sections – stories, sketches and poems; history and monuments; people and problems. The foreword by the anonymous 'X' sets out the aim of the book:

> This book is intended for the Forces, but that need discourage no one . . . It is not sentimental, contains no pin-ups and is not particularly suitable for reading in a tent with five other occupants during

a sandstorm. It is a book for intelligent visitors to Egypt. There are many thousands of intelligent visitors in Egypt just now and most of them are in the Forces. So it is their book . . . And there is a certain amount of guidance. After his first fears of Egyptian diseases have subsided, the new arrival in this country would do well to digest the article 'Eat Egyptian'. The photographs will say different things to different people. To some they may provide the first intimation that a contemporary school of Egyptian painting exists . . . For most of us, when we first arrive, Egypt has always seemed a land of tombs and departed glory. In the minds of some it cannot but remain inextricably associated with death, destruction and disease. But others have pleasanter memories – of town life after weeks at sea or the first green after months in the desert. A bath first, of course, and a cable home, and a dance for those who are lucky. But on the fifth evening, perhaps, you might read this book.

There are pieces from the Egyptians Tewfik el Hakim, Taha Hussein and Ahmed Rassim (on the painter Mahmoud Said), a knowledgeable article on the mosques of Cairo by H. Devonshire and an equally good one on the Mulid el-Naby by Bertha Gaster among the many treasures. We cannot leave this delightful book without quoting two of the local proverbs contained in it: 'My husband lies to me, so I lie to the neighbours', and, 'If they hadn't dragged me from under him, I'd have killed him'.

In 1944 Denis Saunders published his third small book, *Tomorrow is Soon*,[103] this time adding the forename Juan to his adopted Almendro, and changing publishers from Schindler to the Anglo-Egyptian Bookshop. Keith Bullen contributed a sympathetic foreword which was as symbolic of Keith's generosity as it was a tribute to the poetry:

> I find in Juan Almendro the sincerity that springs from a natural poetic sense, and in this alone he holds an advantage over many would-be poets. His thoughts are not harshly coloured with the past nor tangled in the web of modern intricacy. He is too honest to deal in the chicanery of words . . . So once again a younger poet joins the endless cavalcade of those who have seen visions and dreamed dreams. After the nightmare of protracted death he starts his pilgrimage and makes the golden journey. He, too, I think, has heard the vanguard's shout that echoes down the ages: 'Courage and Truth are our abiding stars.'

Forty poems covered a wide range, subject matter including geography, recalling the desert, Italy, Sicily, Malta, Jerusalem and, inevitably, 'In Cairo's Streets'; persons, including a homage to Benedetto Croce; the seasons and the weather; and a range of emotions. 'The Pen is Silent' was reprinted from *Salamander, Folio IV.*

In Alexandria, Judge Blake-Reed had continued his devoted Latin translations and published a further 50 under the title *More Odes of Horace*,[104] with illustrations by his old friend and colleague Judge Lemass, his friend E. St Leger Hill of Victoria College, and his wife. His foreword contains such an understanding of the old poet, distilled from his works, that it seems almost as if he were a personal friend:

> It is really as the prophet of an unambitious, quietly dutiful and humbly contented life that Horace most completely claims our affection. And in him it is comforting to find an outstanding example of a man, born in a humble station and exalted by sheer genius to the friendship and familiarity of the great and powerful, yet preserving his modesty, his dignity and his human kindliness to the end. They were a wise generation of statesmen who could win the trust and affection of such a man.

In December of that same year (1944), Raoul Parme and Ivo Barbitch produced a special issue of their magazine *Calligrammes*, a nice little centenary homage to Paul Verlaine, who had been born in Metz in 1844. The homage was made jointly to Keith Bullen, whose nine translations were the subject matter of the book, which had an evocative head of Verlaine on the front cover, another example of the versatility of Eric de Nemes. In his dedication, Barbitch paid this tribute to Bullen:

> Par delà les Nations et leurs langages différents, par delà tout ce qui peut parfois séparer des peuples faits pour se comprendre, un poète anglais a compris et aimé deux grands poètes français et leur a consacré une partie de sa vie. Il continue dans cette voie avec cette émouvante sollicitude et cette profonde compréhension qui font l'admiration de tous ceux qui suivent ce précieux labeur, si propice au développement de l'amitié franco-britannique, à un moment crucial de la destinée humaine, alors que la France et la Grande Bretagne, ayant mis en jeu toutes les richesses de leur passé, luttent aujourd'hui, avec leurs Alliés pour la liberté du monde.

As a *bonne bouche*, the devoted editors inserted a slip-page containing four Bullen original English poems, two from *We Stand Alone* and two from *Bells on the Breeze*.

It was not a time for writing novels and too early for the

prose accounts of war experience and the written-up diaries which began to appear when the war was over. Yet one enterprising New Zealander did get off the mark quickly. Martyn Uren's *Kiwi Saga*[105] was published by the Anglo-Egyptian Bookshop in 1943 and gave a straightforward account of his journey from his home country and his subsequent experiences. His remarks on the fly strike a chord in the hearts of those who have suffered from its torments:

> The fly, in itself, deserves a paragraph too. For the Egyptian fly is a fierce, persistent, energetic and hungry insect who seems to live on men and beasts. He is a prolific breeder, and at times in the hot months a thousand can be seen round a beast's head, or a hundred may be counted on a man, especially on a native who does not bother to remove them from his face, eyes or mouth. They are naturally worse around native quarters and about camps. We have found to our disgust that whereas, at first, upon going to a new place in the desert, there were no flies, after a day or two have elapsed there are swarms of them.

Uren sums up the way in which so many of the troops from the UK and other parts of the Commonwealth came to look upon the country in which they spent so vital a part of their formative lives:

> Gradually, almost imperceptibly, I began to acquire a liking for Cairo and some other parts of Egypt. And, looking back upon it now, I can practically date the real commencement of this new affection for the place as from the return from Greece. Perhaps it is because one feels like enjoying quiet and rest after action – for I began to know Cairo well about this time and know just where these essential conditions could be found. Or perhaps it was just the effect of the anti-climax. But I knew that it was with renewed interest that I regarded Egypt.

It so happened that a moment such as this was recorded by John Cromer in that brief period in 1943 when he kept a diary. On Sunday 18 April of that year, he wrote: 'Today I made peace with Egypt. Yes, I felt within me a consonance with the country for the first time, a feeling that I could settle down here and appreciate the real beauties which lie beneath the pall of dirt.'

Among the interesting local writers in French was Albert Cossery. In 1944 'Masses' Publishing House brought out his book of short stories, *The Men God Forgot*,[106] translated into

English by the anonymous 'H.E.' The translator's note, which introduces the book, makes two good points. First:

> Egypt's literary role in the west has not been a happy one. She is known by two symbols: Shepheard's and the Sheikh. The former is a cosy little European island cut off from all that is Egypt by the cliffs of caste; the latter is about as characteristic of her inhabitants as the Sphinx. It is time the English-speaking public met an Egyptian they could believe in. And in the pages of M. Albert Cossery they will do so. *The Men God Forgot* is not comfortable reading.

And second:

> If his picture is a brutal one, it has the brutality that springs from a flaming sympathy with wretchedness in all its forms. His characters are the despised and the rejected: out-of-work actors, tinkers, beggars and drug-addicts. In summer they move under the 'murderous rays' of a tropic sun; in winter they 'offer to the cold and damp their bodies of the newly condemned'. We are at rock-bottom; a submarine world where poverty looms gigantic and real.

The titles of these searing tales give clues to the sub-society in which Cossery's seamy characters move: 'The Postman Gets His Own Back', 'The Girl and the Hashish-smoker', 'The Barber Has Killed His Wife', 'The Danger of Fantasy' and 'The Hungry Only Want Bread'. In these stories we get a true glimpse of the under-side of Cairo.

Herbert Howarth was another of the pre-war lecturers at Fuad I University who moved north to Palestine to work in the British Information Office in Jerusalem. His scholarship was aired when, with Ibrahim Shukrullah, he was joint author of a collection of pieces entitled *Images of the Arab World*,[107] and subtitled 'Fragments of Arab literature translated and paraphrased with variations and comments'. Published in London in 1944, this insight into the literary Arab world found its way back into the bookshops of Cairo and was quickly snapped up by the curious. Its origin is described by the compilers in the preface:

> The season of writing was an Egyptian winter, which imposed hurry before the hot days came back. The background was Montgomery's advance from Alamein, which, by removing the threat to Egypt, made one ready to attempt creative writing again in the odd moments that could be spared from work. Work was still intense, however, and did not leave the leisure which would have been necessary for accurate, as against creative, translation.

Their statement on methodology is illuminating:

> We called in three guides. The first was negative. The greater mass of translation into English from Arabic or like languages suffered, as it seemed to us, from the effort to reproduce the spirit and terminology of the original . . . We decided, while seeking specimens of very varied levels of writing and attitude, to refrain from trying to bring over to our English versions of them anything that was not susceptible of interesting the English reader. Of our two positive guides, one was the direct corollary of the above. In the generation immediately preceding our own, English creative writing has drawn handsomely on the legacies of other tongues and ages, by means ranging from close translation to remote allusion. Pound and Eliot unified the arts of creation and translation. They operated by eliciting from their sources what was relevant to contemporary events and emotions and omitting the rest. We wanted, if we could, to adapt this procedure in earnest contexts. At the same time, another criterion was brought to bear, a reference to the definition of poetry offered in the preface to the *Poet's Tongue*. 'Memorable words' was a sanction on certain pieces, which might have been cut out by overstrict application of the contemporary relevance criterion.

An analysis and catalogue of the images was to have been drawn up but just as the three editors of *Oasis* had been split up, so the two collaborators were posted to places three thousand miles apart and the poems, comments, folk songs, nursery rhymes, proverbs and traditions of the Prophet are left to speak for themselves. Readers are told in the preface that they will find 'in a fairly overt and preserved condition the disjecta membra of the modern Egyptian concern with the devil, the creation, original sin, woman physical, and the more vapid forms of philosophy'.

Charles Madge adds a commentary on translation in a foreword to the book:

> The problem of translation varies with the nearness of the time and language to our own . . . The present volume is an attempt to convey the quality of the Arab world in terms of the language and ideas of recent western poetry. These versions are not afraid of being literal if that helps to give a striking effect; nor do they hesitate to paraphrase, to expand or to condense, if that will bring relief from flatness. The whole principle of selection and translation is to avoid boredom . . . Of the Howarth and Shukrullah method of translation as a whole, one feels that if it departs from the accuracy which in any case may be impossible, it does not superimpose an alien poem like the versions of Carlyle, and that it has a speed and compression

which perhaps conveys a special quality in the original, hitherto unrendered.

Also in 1944, Tambimuttu published G. S. Fraser's first book of poems, *Home Town Elegy*,[108] a collection of his earlier work. John Cromer reviewed the book in the *The Sphinx* and made the point, 'Hardly any of the poetry written overseas appears in the book, but "Nilotic Elegy" is an earnest of the more mature, more sensitively moulded poetry which has placed Mr Fraser in the forefront of those poets now in the Middle East.' He shared a love for two other poets with members of the Salamander Society. Like Keith Bullen, Fraser had also been attracted to Albert Samain and had translated 'Elegy', which does not appear in the older poet's collection. And as Blake-Reed had fallen under the spell of Horace, so had Fraser, two translations being included in his book. One glance at the very different treatment of 'Fons Bandusiae' will show how greatly they differ in their approach, the spare, clipped stanzas of the lawyer-translator contrasting with the flowing, freer version by the poet.

When V-E Day and V-J Day had come and gone and most of the troops had been demobilised and the world was beginning to adjust to the new order of things, those who cared enough strove to publish what they had been unable to print in the war years or anthologised the ephemerae, as we have seen with *Personal Landscape*. Paper was still rationed and for the English language London had regained its place as a publishing capital. The former groups, military and civilian, had scattered and a number of the leading figures had died. For the Salamander Society, the greatest loss was Keith Bullen who, after a stroke and a short illness, died in Cairo on 30 July 1946. He had been back in England in 1945 and had many plans – more translations, the publication in England of those already done in Cairo, a biography of A. H. Bullen, a poetry bookshop, perhaps with Sunday mornings in the upstairs room as they had been in Zamalek, a miscellany of Salamander works, published and unpublished. Cromer recalls the meetings they had together at the Royal Court Hotel in Sloane Square. The two of them had been through the manuscripts and, as joint editors, had agreed the format for the miscellany. Cromer had the task of finding a publisher and gathering the photographs together. Back in Cairo, Raoul Parme was chafing at the bit, anxious for news. In November 1945, he wrote to Cromer: 'Here in Cairo all intellectual and artistic activities are as well as dead. Some of our friends have left Egypt, Fraser for instance as you probably know. Waller, too, will leave in January. So what about our poor Salamander Society meetings?'

What indeed? The loss of Bullen signalled the effective end of a group which had existed almost solely on the generosity and hospitality of that Chestertonian figure who had provided a meeting place of culture in a foreign land. We have eschewed the quotation of poems, whole or in part, for a number of reasons, but there is one that cannot be denied, for it captures the man and the moment. It is the finest epitaph that could be made and was written by G. S. Fraser.

An Elegy for Keith Bullen

(Headmaster of Gezira Preparatory School, Cairo
and a friend to English poetry and poets)

A great room and a bowl full of roses,
Red roses, a man as round as a ripe rose,
Lying in a bowl of sun. And who supposes
Such a sad weight could support such a gay pose.

Flying his sad weight like a round baby's
Petulant balloon! He has blue pebbles for eyes,
Petulant, bewildered, innocent eyes like a baby's;
Like a great baby or a clipped rose he lies

In a white bowl of light in my memory;
And expands his tenuous sweetness like a balloon;
I shall die of feeling his dear absurdity
So near me now, if I cannot cry soon.

Keith was particularly Sunday morning,
Red roses, old brandy, was unharrying Time,
Was that white light, our youth; or was the fawning
Zephyr that bobs the gay balloon of rhyme,

He bobbed incredibly in our modern air;
With his loose jacket, his white panama hat,
As he leaned on his walking stick on the stone stair
He seemed a balloon, moored down to the ground by that.

As he leaned at the bar and ordered us pink gin
Or arranged a flutter on the three-fifteen
He seemed a child, incapable of sin:
We never knew him prudent, cold or mean.

Or tied to the way the world works at all
(Not even tied enough for poetry);
All that he was we only may recall,
An innocent that guilt would wish to be,

A kind, a careless, and a generous,
An unselfseeking in his love of art,
A jolly in his great explosive fuss;
O plethora of roses, O great heart!

On 21 September 1946, a reunion of the Salamander Society
was held in the Kensington home of John Gawsworth. A good
number of the Cairene group were there: John Cromer, George
Fraser, John Waller, Erik de Mauny, John Gawsworth, Alan
Arnold, Victor Musgrave and Ida Kar, George Hepburn, and
Ian Fletcher. Cromer and Waller paid tribute to their devoted
Keith but it was left to Fraser to make the main speech, which
still exists in his own handwriting. Among the things he said
were:

> To every young writer, of any promise, who passed through Cairo,
> Keith Bullen showed the kindness of a father. He was a man
> incapable of pettiness, meanness or malice, a man who had a more
> disinterested love of poetry, a more boyish zest in life and a greater
> gentleness of spirit than, I think, any other man I have known . . .
> To the original Salamanders, to John Cromer – one of the first –
> John Gawsworth, John Waller and myself it has seemed a proper
> thing that the Salamander Group and what it stood for should be
> perpetuated; partly as a tribute to Keith's memory; partly to keep
> alive those links of service comradeship which we all, I think, now
> recognise as one of the most valuable things of our lives; partly
> so that the spirit of a warm and large-minded humanism, which
> Salamanders of Cairo stood for, can be kept also.

John Cromer was elected President of the Society in England
and Raoul Parme in Egypt. With the prompting of John Gaws-
worth and John Waller 11 new writing members were elected.
The list was widely drawn for it comprised Cyril des Baux,
Albert Cossery, Ian Fletcher, Hugh MacDiarmid, Dylan
Thomas, James Walker, Harry Kilner, A. S. J. Tessimond,
Bernard Gutteridge, Geoffrey Moore and Tambimuttu. It was
an empty gesture, for the Salamander Society never met again.
Spirit of fire it may have been but the fire had gone out.

In Cairo, desolate Raoul Parme wept alone. His letters to
Cromer, in purple ink, reflected his sadness and loneliness.
Before the reunion, he had written of Keith's last days and his

own latest publication: 'My Petrarch has come out indeed. Oh! irony, alas! As the last Salamander Production in Egypt, as this work too has been published under the auspices of our Society.' These were translations from Italian into French, printed in blue and black gothic type (one for each language) and they were sufficiently appreciated to run to two small editions. There was news of the other poets: 'Rassim is still Press-Director at the Ministry of the Interior. Moscatelli is now a regular contributor to *Images*, a weekly magazine. Barbitch left Egypt definitely and is at present in Belgrade, Secretary in the Ministry of Foreign Affairs. As for Yergath, I hear that he is leaving Egypt for his country, Armenia.'

The next and last letter to be received by Cromer was sent after the reunion. The ink was as violet as some of the text was violent, stressed by double underlining. He was happy about the proposed new structure of Salamander — 'Congratulations, my dear President, and beloved friend. So much for the principles of organisation which I quite agree.' He was, however, most unhappy about some of the new members — here came the double lines — and imposed his veto as a founder-member. He had questions to ask about administration, finance and publications. He was worried about the legal permission to publish in Egypt, recalling, 'You know that we were "more or less clandestine" if I may say so and that we were not allowed to sell it as a periodical.' Alas, the times had changed, Cromer was back in his legal practice and immersed in local politics and the other poets were going their separate ways alone.

Two of them, John Waller and Erik de Mauny, had teamed up as editors of *Middle East Anthology*[109] which appeared in the autumn of 1946. The rationale of their selection, which was both poetry and prose, was set out in their joint preface:

Although selected at the end of a war this should not necessarily, we feel, be either directly concerned with war or about the Middle East. For writers have not proved automatons, immediately reacting to their surroundings or completely conditioned by them ... Fighting is to some extent automatic, but writing is not; it has therefore been easier to fight than to write in the Middle East. Some of the prose in this selection has no direct connection with the war at all, some of the poems are directly conditioned by it. That probably is because poetry is the more sensitive instrument ... Survival at least is something, whether for writers in uniform or literary exiles from Europe. And we feel that these writers, through their forced separation from their own countries and through their survival, have found a difference from their contemporaries that may later become more marked and perhaps splendid.

It is a catholic mixture, with Salamander and Personal Landscape writers cheek by jowl, and among other contributors are Uys Krige, Pennethorne Hughes, John Jarmain, Sidney Keyes, Herbert Howarth, John Pudney, and two of Raoul Parme's *bêtes noires*, Cyril des Baux and Albert Cossery, whose short story 'The Postman Gets His Own Back' reappears.

Earlier in the year, Evan John had come up with *Time in the East*,[110] lightly subtitled 'An Entertainment' with some amusing coloured illustrations by the author. There was a serious dedication: 'Dedicated on my return to England to those who went East to fight and not to write and will not now return.' The book, a curious mix of prose pieces and poems, was written at odd intervals during military service and has all the ingredients of quirkiness, classicism, mediaevalism, descriptions of places and people that one had come to expect of Evan John. His apologia, written Transjordan in 1943, is honest:

> It was said of the late and much-lamented Humbert Wolfe, by a friend no less witty than himself, that by working as a Civil Servant in Whitehall and writing his verses in Government time, he conferred a double benefit on the public; we got some excellent poetry, and, during that time, we were not governed. I am not so conceited as to think my own literary products of the same vintage as his; but I can at least boast that in collecting materials for this book I have consumed much time which would otherwise have been devoted to clogging the Wheels of War with more and more of that paper which at times threatens to bring them to a standstill . . . I would like to share with you some of the things which I have found most absorbing during my Time in the East. I would like to re-tell a few tales from the Past of those countries in which I have been a wanderer, and submit to your judgement a few thoughts about the action of historic Time in the East. We may be able to discuss a few books and poems that are relevant to the main theme. You may like to examine such few scraps of wisdom as I may imagine myself to have picked up in forty checkered years. I will put all this into such good English as a classic-bred pedant can contrive to write. Above all – and I trust I shall never forget my principal duty – I will do my best to keep you entertained. Shakespeare could say no more.

A chapter on Cairo introduces the reader to some of the undertones of SIME which has been mentioned earlier, a French home in the city and some reflections on the Pyramids. It is sad to relate that Evan John took his own life.

Bernard Spencer, who was also destined not to survive many years after leaving Cairo, also saw the publication of his book of poems, *Aegean Islands*,[111] another of Tambimuttu's acts of faith in the poetic ideal. The poems, nearly all previously published elsewhere, are in two sections, the first half from 1940 to 1942 and the second, those written before 1940. While the title poem and most others in the first section are about Greece, 'Libyan Front', 'Egyptian Delta', 'Cairo Restaurant', 'Yachts on the Nile', 'Egyptian Dancer at Shubra' and 'Sarcophagi' reflect the mark made by Egypt on the poet.

For two years more the aftermath of those Cairo war years spilled over into the publication of poetry and prose for which London publishers felt there was a public, although the bloom was already beginning to fade and the multi-volume novels had yet to germinate. In 1947 the *Salamander Poetry Miscellany*[75] finally appeared, a year later than the surviving editor would have wished but, as we have recorded, an all-round record of the poetry of the time, with photographs of all the contributors. Enough has been said of the meetings and the characters; the book itself remains as a fading monument to a brave defence of culture, with its mix of peoples and languages being sustained through an anxious time.

Leaves in the Storm[89] was published in the same year, subtitled 'A book of diaries, edited with a running commentary by Stefan Schimanski and Henry Treece'. The editorial preface states its content:

> The excerpts collected in this book are not diaries in the strictest sense of the word. Few of them mention dates; hardly any speak of factual events and none attempts to re-create a pictorially accurate description of actual happenings. They are, in fact, parts of the auras surrounding such events rather than their mirror-like reflections . . . They are, strictly speaking, notebooks, or mental records which try to conjure up the atmosphere of the time and to indicate the actual dates by invoking their corresponding moods . . . These pages are taken from the journals of some twenty-five contemporary poets. For, even though some of them have never actually written verse, their approach is that of the poet and not of a reporter and as such more valuable in relation to the past and the future.

The Middle East contribution was limited to excerpts from G. S. Fraser, also writing from Asmara, and Erik de Mauny, with a second contribution from the Italian campaign. John Waller wrote 'Athens in Spring' but glimpses of his Cairo days appeared here and there in the text.

Also in 1947, the first novel of Albert Cossery was published in England. *The House of Certain Death*,[112] translated from the French by Erik de Mauny, was also delayed in its appearance. It extends the slum base of the earlier short stories into a threnody of degradation. In his introduction, de Mauny says:

> At first, Cossery's technique is purely realistic. His slums are recognised and recorded for what they are. Yet some will perhaps demur; it cannot possibly be as bad as that. After spending several years in Egypt, I would say that it is worse; or so bad that no stroke of the pen can be too vigorous nor too crude. I saw that country through uniformed eyes; it held more disenchantment than a battle. And the reality, one realises on reading further, is transcended by a super or *sur*-reality. If the characters emerge gradually, they end by becoming stock figures of tragedy, figures as much of an inner as an outer landscape.

The story is as much of the tenement house on the verge of collapse (a not infrequent event in some parts of Cairo) as it is of its miserable characters. It is, as the translator puts it, 'a tragedy, in short, which points all the way to violence! For how otherwise would they live, these outcasts like Abdel Al, except for the great, hollow dream of a purifying vengenance on a world grown too cruel to endure.'

The final paragraph of the book demonstrates how well the translator has caught the flavour of the original and the essential hopelessness of the poorest of the Cairo poor:

> 'The house will fall down upon us,' said Abdel Al. 'But we are many. It will not kill all the people. The people will live, and will know how to avenge all the others.' Si Khalil listens to this voice which rises in the night. It is the voice of a people which awakes, which soon will strangle him. Each minute that passes separates him from his former life. The future is full of cries, the future is full of revolts. How can this great river which will submerge whole towns be contained. Si Khalil imagines the house crumbled into the dust of its own ruins. He sees the living appear among the dead. For they will not all be dead. They will have to be counted with when they raise their bloodied faces and their avenging eyes.

We end this chapter with three books of poems from the poets who, in their different ways, brought such a panache and cheerfulness to what might have been a much more sombre period. John Waller's *The Kiss of Stars*,[113] dedicated to Erik de Mauny, includes the 14-sonnet sequence which forms 'The Lovely and the Dead' which won the Greenwood Prize for 1947. The poems, written between 1944 and 1946, reflect memories of the past, Cairo days, Greece and a touch of France, personalities and experiences, all with the Waller touch of magic. He, too, pays his tribute to Keith Bullen in the poem entitled 'Salamander'. In 14 stanzas he brings back the Zamalek days. Let us quote but four:

> So Keith on one eternal Sunday
> Will entertain his friends
> Gathered from the world's ends,
> Wondering what each will say.
>
> Fraser's great boom of speech
> And Erik's quick crystal flow
> Burst over Cromer now
> While Gawsworth in a trice
>
> Springing poets from every land,
> Yergath, Barbitch, Moscatelli,
> Starts a new symphony,
> To a foreign king kisses hand.
>
> A kind soul placidly moving,
> Large moon in a children's night
> Where all simple pleasures were bright
> And the poet's romantic living.

G. S. Fraser's collection, *The Traveller Has Regrets*,[114] ranges over a wide field, including translations from the Italian, particularly some of Gabriele D'Annunzio's versions of the Latin of Catullus, and the French of Pierre Jean Jouve and Mallarmé. He is generous to Cyril des Baux: 'I have included in this selection a French version by my friend Cyril des Baux of an early poem of mine, which I would not wish to preserve in its English version, but which has been very much improved by his translation.' The Egyptian poems stand out among the collection as well as the personalities involved. 'Egypt' is a true picture and 'Three Profiles from Cairo' were surely sketched in the mind at the bar of the Anglo-Egyptian Union. Of the 'Three Characters in a Bar', written in Cairo in 1944, Gawsworth is caught to the life in the lines,

> Charming gentle bohemian
> Last, last of the Jacobites
> Lighting my countless cigarettes.

Finally, to Gawsworth himself. His *Collected Poems*[115] appeared in 1948, the writer's twisted nose at the centre of the T. C. Dugdale portrait opposite the title page. There are 205 poems in the book, reflecting the ceaseless jottings of this lyrical poet's poet. Wherever he was, North Africa, Italy, Greece, India, verses flowed from him, catching the time and the place. We have quoted Fraser's portrait of him at work in a bar, one of his favourite places in which to woo the Muse. Yet, strangely enough, there is practically nothing to recall the Cairo days when, perhaps, the talking and the drinking left too little time for the poetry he wished to preserve.

6

The Second World War – Music, Drama and Other Entertainment

This chapter is something in the nature of a diversion from our main theme but it seems appropriate to place on record some of the other cultural and less cultural activities which made Egypt so lively a theatre, not only of war, but of human accomplishment during the Second World War. The records of the First World War reveal little of the music, drama and other cultural activities which were enjoyed by a small minority of the wealthy Egyptian and European sector but, with some exceptions, were beyond the reaches of the lower orders and other ranks. Government officials, the Diplomatic Corps and senior service officers were able to enjoy such opera and concerts as were available but for the troops there was little except for the concert party and the night clubs. The second time round, it was a very different matter, with a great range of talent, professional and amateur, local and imported, and good places for that talent to be seen and heard. In addition, there was radio and the cinema, media which were barely available in the earlier war and which provided a further dimension to the cultural and entertainment world. The services organisations, NAAFI and many local societies between them catered for practically every taste.

The venues for music were many and varied, ranging from All Saints Cathedral, where choral societies both service and civilian provided the major choral works; and the Royal Opera House for operatic, musical comedy, dramatic and variety programmes; through the university halls such as the Cairo University Hall, the Ewart Memorial and Oriental Halls of the American University; the Entertainment Hall of the Jesuit College and the Ezbekieh Theatre, which became the home of

Garrison Theatre under the management of ENSA/NAAFI; to the live and recorded music concerts at 'Music for All', the Victory, the Empire and other clubs, including the YMCA and YWCA.

There were a number of musical festivals which remain to this day in the memory of those who were there. One of the first of these was the Anglo-Russian Music Festival presented by the NAAFI department of National Service Entertainment during February and March 1943. Four concerts were staged, two at the Ewart Memorial Hall and two at the Guizeh University Concert Hall, a high-class building with ample space and good acoustics. Victor Musgrave provided a preface to the programme, concluding with these paragraphs:

> The spirit of a nation is reflected in music. This is no less so in the case of Russia than in other nations. As announced elsewhere, it has been hoped that the 'Stalingrad Symphony' will arrive in Cairo for its world première. With the epic of Stalingrad still burning so vividly and recently in our memories it would be an unrivalled and thrilling privilege to hear the symphony played in one of these concerts beneath the roof of the beautiful and solemnly appropriate Great Concert Hall of Guizeh.
>
> Egypt, which has always been generously inclined towards the arts, is fortunately a neutral country, and Cairo is one of the few capitals in war-torn Europe or North Africa where fine music can still be heard in an atmosphere reminiscent of the days of peace. Certainly no apology is necessary for not having honoured before so noble an ally with music dedicated to her people.

The score of Shostakovich's 'Stalingrad Symphony' did not, alas, arrive and the first Guizeh concert opened to fanfares from trumpeters from the RAF sounding around the gallery of the hall for the opening piece. Crawford McNair conducted an orchestra composed of players from the Palestine Orchestra, the Cairo Symphony Orchestra, led by Hugo Rignold, the Cairo Area Military Band and the trumpeters. That first piece was the Trumpet Voluntary, then attributed to Purcell but now said to be by Jeremiah Clarke. The soloist in the Trumpet Voluntary was generally a Sergeant Cage, who used to complain bitterly about the number of stairs to the gallery at the Guizeh hall, which he said left him breathless and in no state to play. The concert continued with an all-Tchaikowsky programme, the 6th Symphony (the 'Pathétique') and the Concerto in B flat minor for piano and orchestra which earned the soloist, Pnina Salzman, a resounding ovation, the sound of which was only exceeded by the final item, the almost inevitable 1812 Overture. The second concert at Guizeh, a week later, again began with the Trumpet Voluntary, followed this time by Glinka's overture to *Russlan and Ludmilla*. Pnina Salzman again excelled with Rachmaninoff's Concerto No. 2 in E minor and the evening ended with Tchaikowsky's 5th Symphony. The Ewart Memorial Hall concerts, with the Palestine Orchestra only, were all orchestral.

A more mixed series of programmes of a truly international flavour was provided for the United Nations Music Festival held in November 1943 at the same venues and under the same direction and conductor as the earlier festival. The Palestine Orchestra again played at the two Ewart Memorial Hall Saturday concerts, the first of which began, appropriately enough, with Tchaikowsky's 6th Symphony, for it was the 50th anniversary of the composer's death, which occurred only a few days after its first performance. After the interval, the concert continued with César Franck's Symphonic Variations for Pianoforte and Orchestra, with the indefatigable Pnina Salzman, the Vaughan Williams Fantasia again and a symphonic poem, 'Stalingrad'. If no symphony to commemorate that epic siege could make the journey from Russia for the first festival, Marc Lavry, a young composer from Palestine, had gone some way to fill the breach. The following week, Elgar was the representative of British music, the remainder of this programme consisting of music by Poland's standard-bearer, Chopin, whose Concerto for Piano and Orchestra No. 1 was played most sensitively by Pnina Salzman; and for France, Berlioz's exciting Symphonie fantastique brought the evening to a close.

The Guizeh concerts, again on successive Sundays, were provided by the combined orchestras which had been so successfully welded together for the Anglo-Russian Festival. The first was a special concert in commemoration of the National Independence Day of Czechoslovakia. Once again, 'by almost universal request', the evening started with the Trumpet Voluntary, followed by some Smetana pieces. The second half was filled by Dvořák's Symphony No. 5, 'From the New World'. The final concert of the festival began with a contribution from Italy, described in the programme foreword by Crawford McNair as 'the latest to declare war on the common enemy' who 'is providing a vigorous and high-sounding Aria and March written to inaugurate the Royal Opera House in Cairo – a capital whose generous hospitality to her friends and allies is making no small contribution to the ultimate Liberty and Freedom of all nations'. Ida Bettelheim-Foscolo sang Verdi's 'Aida' aria and the soloist in the following piece, Grieg's Piano Concerto in A, was the very popular and talented Lance Dossor. The festival was rounded off by Tchaikowsky's Symphony No. 4 in F minor, the combined strings sounding very well in the sustained pizzicato of the third movement.

Classical music had been well supported at all times, but by the end of 1944 it had reached a very high standard of performance and appreciation. The Middle East Symphony Orchestra had been formed, with Gerald Gover, primarily a solo pianist, as principal conductor, and Joseph Shadwick as leader. In December, the NAAFI–ENSA management put on a Bach–Mozart festival in three venues. The rationale for this enterprise was set out by Gover in a foreword to the programme:

> The increase of interest in Good Music since the outbreak of War has aroused widespread comment, and those of us who have been in the Middle East for some time have seen it develop and spread amongst the Forces in the most remarkable way. The greatest possible efforts have been made to stimulate and encourage it and, during the last few years at 'Music for All', the Cathedral Hall, the Victory Club and latterly, the ENSA Garrison Theatre, an astonishingly large number of Concerts have been given to ever-increasing audiences. The interest in the works of the great Classical Masters remains predominant, and two local musicians, Dora and Gerhard Willner, have given cycles of Beethoven, Schubert, Brahms and Schumann to give the public ample opportunity to delve deeper into the secrets of these masters. For some reason however the two greatest of all composers, Bach and Mozart, have been comparatively neglected, apart from occasional performances of isolated works by the Palestine Orchestra. It is because of the numerous requests that have been received, and because of our own deep conviction that these two composers possess the qualifications of true greatness more than any others, that we have decided to give this Festival.

The opening Bach concert, on 2 December 1944 at the Ewart Memorial Hall, was given by the MESO conducted by Gerald Gover, and the final Mozart concert was held in the ENSA Garrison Theatre with Albert Jarvis conducting.

Between these two concerts were the two others, both given at 'Music for All'. The first, all Mozart, was performed by the

Percy Coates String Quartet and another Bach concert, the MESO, which was conducted by Clifford Harker.

In April 1945, a Beethoven Festival was held, with three concerts at the ENSA Garrison Theatre, two at 'Music for All' and two at the Oriental Hall. Once again, the scene was set by Gerald Gover in his foreword to the programme:

> In the foreword to the recent Bach–Mozart Festival, I gave as our chief reason for holding it the fact that these composers had been comparatively neglected in Cairo. I made at the same time the rather categorical statement that they were the two greatest composers. This was not done with the intention of belittling Beethoven in any way, but rather to convince the public of their real greatness.
>
> Beethoven's greatness is undoubted, and his popularity immense, and it is this universal demand for more of his music that has led us to arrange a comprehensive Festival of seven concerts. I think I can say that never before in the Middle East have so many works of Beethoven been given in the space of a fortnight, and I am proud to add that, at the completion of the Festival, the Middle East Symphony Orchestra will have played all his symphonies but the Ninth during the last eight months.

Respect must surely be paid to the dedication and expertise of all who made these festivals possible.

In the course of this last festival, the MESO played Symphonies Nos 2, 5, 6 and 7. The Consecration of the House, Leonora No. 3 overture, the 'Emperor' Piano Concerto, with Ignace Tiegerman and the Violin Concerto in D major, with Adolph Menaszes. Gerhard Willner played eight sonatas in his two recitals at the Oriental Hall. At 'Music for All' the Cairo Area Trio – Robert Colman (violin), Cecil Beattie (cello) and Gerald Gover (piano) – played two trios, one being the demanding 'Archduke', and four songs for Beatrice Gibson (contralto) to sing; and the Percy Coates String Quartet played the Quartets in B flat major and F minor.

These festivals have been reported in some detail as the apotheosis of a sustained effort in the musical field which started almost at the beginning of the war in the Middle East theatre. The orchestral music provided by the Palestine Orchestra, the Cairo Symphony Orchestra (an Egyptian State Broadcasting creation), Gerald Gover's New Victoria Orchestra and finally the Middle East Symphony Orchestra ensured a constant flow of the best music of many composers, whatever their nationality. We must restrain ourselves from spreading before our readers

any more of the programmes of the rich fare which was provided throughout the period by chamber groups, soloists in
every field both live and on record, but a selection of some of
the offerings should be sufficient to prove our point that the
breadth and depth of the music provided in Cairo was second
to none. Taking for granted the records which brought world
stars to the hungry music lovers in and out of uniform, let us
pass quickly in review some of the locally produced concerts
and recitals.

Piano recitals by Pnina Salzman, whose generous contribution
has already been recorded, the blind George Themeli, Ella
Goldstein, Gina Bachauer, Betty Matthews, Gerald Gover,
Lance Dosser and many others provided continuing high-
standard performances of the repertoire. Other instrumentalists
were as liberal with their own skills, giving the ever-hungry
programmes a full complement of the works at their command.
The voice was heard as much as the instruments, as we recall
the names of Kay Langford, Barbara Gilmour, Hedy Schack,
Gina Campasse, Tatiana Preston and other sopranos; Laura
Arnstein and Beatrice Gibson among the contraltos; Iowerth
Thomas, trained by the great Norman Allin (bass); Ioan Sissoieff, Albert Messenger, Joseph Prokop (baritones); and Harold
Parkinson, George Wilson and Arthur Rimmer (tenors). It can
be seen that there was an easy mix between service and civilian
singers. Among the more esoteric performances was one which
must be recorded lest it be lost for ever under the sands of time.
This was a rare May Day concert in 1943 at Musica Viva in
the Sikket el Fadl entitled 'Les Rapports entre la Musique orien-
tale et occidentale, Recital Commenté' presented by the Section
de Musique Ancienne under the direction of H. Hickman. There
were 12 items, of the twelfth to the seventeenth centuries, ranging from a Tristan's lament of the fourteenth century, and a
William Byrd piece for flute and drums, to an appropriate Couperin, 'L'Egyptienne'. The make-up of the orchestra was a triumph of musical history over the *zeitgeist*: violins, viola, viola
da gamba, cello, double bass, clavichord, spinet, lutes, flutes,
oboe, trumpets, trombone, cymbals, kettle drum and hand
drum.

The most keenly awaited events were the visits of the great
concert artists, three of whom in particular stand out as examples of the enthusiasm with which they were greeted. The impact
of Solomon, who gave a piano recital at the Ewart Memorial

Hall on 18 October 1943, was recorded in separate reviews. The professional hand of Leslie Barnard, writing for the *Egyptian Mail*, caught the excitement of the occasion. This piece opened in bold type: 'When I arrived at the Ewart Memorial Hall for Solomon's recital, there was a crowd in the street. "Door's not open yet," I said. But I was wrong: these were the people who could not get in.' And it closed with these words: 'Had not Solomon, with an air of finality, sat down and played The King, he would be there playing encores yet, and large numbers of the Forces would be absent without leave.'

John Cromer, allowed more than a column and a half by an indulgent *Sphinx* and with more time to reflect, put the recital into the perspective of world events, seeing, as always, each cultural occasion as part of the heritage for which the war was being fought:

> [Solomon] was not merely gratifying the will-to-pleasure of a mass of uniformed men but re-creating in each single soul a feeling of ulterior value beyond the stress of war days. This aspect of the struggle is every whit as important in the sphere of human endeavour and continuity as that of each fighting man for whom he played. Great men in the arts and in life are few indeed, and when they move they carry with them a full atmosphere of fresh impulse and higher appreciation.

A Rhapsody and two intermezzi of Brahms and his Variations and Fugue on a Handel theme opened the concert. Cromer then related the following pieces thus:

> While Solomon played . . . in other parts of the world the souls of his fellow Jews ached in a long torment . . . And but for the determination and doggedness of the free peoples of the world, and Britain perhaps in particular, Solomon, too, might at this moment have been brutalising those precious hands in some menial and degrading task, if the bulwark of freedom had cracked asunder. Instead, as his sensitive fingers pirouetted immaculately through the Waldstein Sonata of Beethoven there was a challenge and a vindication in every note.

And for another piece:

> While Solomon played . . . the hands of the wounded and dying twitched in agony and pain, some plucking at the sheets of hospital beds, others grimy with the soil on which they lay. As the waters of oblivion rose, the rippling fingers of Solomon, with that insistent

left hand, brought a vivid picture of the waters flowing over 'La Cathédrale engloutie' of Debussy.

Similar reflections developed round the Rachmaninoff Preludes and Chopin's Polonaise.

Pouishnoff paid two visits to Cairo during the winter of 1943/4, one before a tour of the forces in Palestine and one after. On each occasion he played whatever occurred to him on the spur of the moment, announcing his programme as he went along. At the 'Music for All' concert he mixed Mozart, Chopin and Busoni's transcription of the Bach Chaconne with a group of Russian compositions, including Liadov's Barcarolle and a Glazunov Study in C major. He also played two of his own pieces, 'Fairy Tale' and 'Concert Tango' and, as a final encore, Scriabin's 'Tragic Poem'.

The most successful celebrity singer was Lily Pons and her exacting tour of the Persian Gulf, where she gave 28 concerts to the forces in the summer of 1944, concluded with a concert at the Ewart Memorial Hall, supported by the combined orchestras of the RAMC and Cairo Area Military Band, conducted by André Kostelanetz. Great as she was, she upset Leslie Barnard by sacrificing her classical operatic repertoire to popular pap. The heart of his review ran:

> As a popular concert of the lightest kind it was undoubtedly one of the best ever presented in Cairo, but it seems unfortunate that a great singer of the calibre of Lily Pons should be heard in only the slenderest music. As it was, we heard superb singing of innocuous bagatelles: it was like having Benno Moiseiwitsch to play the works of Billy Mayerl. Not until the end of the concert in 'Caro Nome' from Verdi's *Rigoletto* did we have a glimpse of a thrilling voice in its proper element.

As the long tail of repatriation, code-named 'Python' uncoiled, or the troops were redeployed in Europe and the Far East, the entertainment of those remaining was still an important part of the NAAFI remit. Garrison Theatre continued its policy of presenting plays and variety but in each of its seasons through 1945 regular concerts were given by the Middle East Symphony Orchestra, notching up over 20 altogether. Taking the war period as a whole, it is doubtful whether Egypt had ever enjoyed such a wealth of musical fare of such a high general standard. It would be over 45 years before the magnificent spectacle of *Aida* would be brought to Luxor and the Pyramids.

There was more scope for amateur dramatics because the reserve of professional talent was much smaller than in music, largely because of language. Music has no such barriers but the presentation of English on the stage needs much more than just a working knowledge and conversational flow. This barrier was largely overcome by the small band of professional actors in uniform and the visiting companies and, despite some of the criticism which has been made of ENSA, the shows they put on were greatly appreciated by the troops and expatriates, for whom the presence of live actors and actresses was much more acceptable than the flat cinema screen.

The history of ENSA has been recorded elsewhere and although that acronym came to be known as 'Every Night Something Awful', this is an unfair reflection on the many dedicated and hard-working professionals who made their contribution to the war effort by helping the service men and women to relax and enjoy themselves from time to time. In the Middle East, the ENSA standards were probably higher than elsewhere, due to two men, Lt-Col. Greatorex Newman and Lt-Col. F. S. Warren. Leslie Barnard has paid this tribute:

> They proved that you *can* have two captains on a ship, or rather two colonels working in harmony. In charge of production and administration respectively, both were from the world of Theatre, Rex Newman an established producer with the wings of a First World War Flying Corps officer and Bunny Warren a singer of the Lance Fairfax type who had an MC from the earlier war. It was Rex who championed the Good Music parties which were so great a success. From Cairo Rex made a visit to and a tour of India and told the top brass about this success. They all laughed heartily at the idea of 'the troops' liking and wanting Beethoven, Mozart and the like and thought that he was mad. On the return leg of his tour he visited some of the places again and spoke to the same people, by which time some Good Music parties (including Betty Matty Matthews and her lot) had been. They all said how marvellous it was and how they had always known it would be popular.

Both Cairo and Alexandria had flourishing amateur dramatic and musical societies and the CADMS and AADMS geared themselves at an early stage of the war to provide as wide a range of entertainment as their resources permitted. Their success was considerable. Gilbert and Sullivan operas have always been a challenge for this kind of society and *The Gondoliers*, given at the Royal Opera House in April 1942, was the CADMS response. Beautifully costumed and well sung, it was the only full operatic use made of the house and, as with all the society's productions, the profits were devoted to war charities. The musical gem the following year was *The Maid of the Mountains* which also drew good houses.

Between the big shows, the society produced a number of plays, among them being *The Amazing Dr Clitterhouse* and *Badger's Green*, but the biggest money spinners and most popular with audiences of all ranks were the Christmas 'Revue Order' shows. The 1941–2 production at the Opera House by John Ropes and Onslow Tuckley, who wrote the music, had a cast well known to local audiences, as can be judged by the familiarity with which they were described in the publicity (in parenthesis): Jasper Maskelyne ('All done by Mirrors'), for him a welcome break, no doubt, from the more serious camouflage tasks on which he had been engaged in the desert; Leda and Doris ('The Swing-time Pair'), two very attractive local sisters who were in great demand for their vivacious singing; Tommy Thomas ('Cairo's Songmaster'), a title which seems to need no embellishment; and a cast which contained in addition Fred Sparks, Phyllis Pothecary, Dorothy Wadham and Joyce Grew. The following year, the Ropes–Tuckley team put on another 'Revue Order' but John Cromer did not think it as good, for as his diary records: 'although more musical, it was less well presented. One scene, "Checkmate", was really splendid. Leda and Doris were the attractions around whom the show was built and I enjoyed their arrangement of "St Louis Blues". The finale was impressive – three grand pianos at varying height. The repertoire was not brilliant but well played.' Two nights later, he went back-stage for the last-night party, a particular CADMS attraction, which lasted until the whisky ran out at 2.30 a.m. He had volunteered to perform his version of a Russian dance, which he was known to do on any occasion when the alcohol level was high enough, and claims that he was asked to give it on stage at the next show. There was little chance of this ever happening.

The producer, Brigadier John Ropes, was Deputy Assistant Quarter-Master General at GHQ but one would never have imagined it, when meeting him off-duty or hearing and reading his lyrics. Two which drew acclaim were 'Voluntary Ladies of the Town' ('We're voluntary ladies serving voluntary beer to voluntary soldiers compulsorily here') and 'You Mustn't Drop

Your Aitches at GHQ ('You mustn't utter jokes about GHQ, it's only helping Hitler if you do'). Both have been published in *Return to Oasis* as well as in *Middle East Anthology* which also has a third lyric, 'Three Gezira Lovelies' ('We're three Gezira Lovelies, with three Gezira minds, as small as is our talk, as small as our behinds').

Passing from the amateur, and very good it was, too, to the professional stage, there were locally produced shows and touring companies sent out from London. One professional company was the New Vic, among whose productions were *Private Lives* with Arthur Howard, who also produced it. Others from the same company were *The Wind and the Rain*, *The Case of the Frightened Lady* and *The Devil's Disciple*, the last-named with Oliver Burt, a stalwart of the Cairo stage and radio, whose diction was a joy to hear. Among ENSA productions, mostly competent, such as *Love from a Stranger* and *Lover's Leap*, some others were less so, as in the farce reviewed by the anonymous critic in *The Sphinx*:

> In 'A Little Bit of Fluff' at the Opera House this week (9 October 1943) we have had the spectacle of a farce in which practically no one is farcical. It is at best a poor and dated farce and at worst 'A Little Bit of Fluff' becomes a big bit of boredom. It is not a witty play: there is scarcely a witty line in it, wherefore it must depend for its effect on the ability of the cast to infuse humour into every action and bit of stage business. So far from doing anything of the kind, Richard Afton, the lead, plays his part practically straight . . . The vivacious Chili Bouchier, star of the show, seemed wasted on this material.

After Garrison Theatre had been established at the Ezbekieh, the ENSA/NAAFI management settled down to a regular programme and from *No, No, Nanette* in the summer of 1944 onwards, the shows went on. In March 1945 *The Girl Friend*, which had been having a success at the Opera House, was transferred to the Garrison Theatre to make way for the big guns of Donald Wolfit, who had brought his company in for a four-week run of Shakespeare, playing *Hamlet*, *The Merchant of Venice* and *Much Ado about Nothing*. He also included *Volpone* in the season.

Another of the great names in the theatre, Emlyn Williams, came to the Opera House in March 1944. In a short season, he played first in Terence Rattigan's *Flarepath* supported by

Leueen Macgrath, Emrys Jones, Eliot Mason, Leslie Dwyer, Kathleen Harrison, Adrienne Allen and Robert Elson. He followed this with his own play *Night Must Fall* in which he made a deep impression, as he had wherever he played the part, as the psychopathic Danny, after its great opening success at the Duchess Theatre in London. There were many in the audience who had seen the play in the same theatre three years earlier, when the young Anthony Holland was actor/producer in a very competent production.

We should not leave the serious stage without a mention of one particular play which appeared at the Ezbekieh Theatre in March 1944 entitled *Devil's Elbow*, by George Billam, the author of *Spring Tide*. This was being given a world première by the Co-Services Players, produced by Harold Cowan, and introduced at the time as follows:

> Here tonight are a new company and a new play. This alliance is the result of a conversation between two British officers. They found that they were both keenly interested in the theatre. One had just finished a play; the other was an experienced amateur producer. So they decided to present a show on behalf of the British War Fund.

As it seems unlikely that this event is recorded elsewhere, let us pay tribute to the gallant cast now: Joan Carlin (WAAF), Kay Westlake (Embassy), George Cormack (A/c RAF), Matthew Forsyth (S/ldr RAF), Edme Cameron (2nd Officer WRNS), Francis Jeffries (LAC RAF), Pat Cumberbatch (Embassy), S. Farley Robertson (Section Officer RAF), Frank Holloway (Capt.), Peter Sturgess (Sgt), Jack Haskal (Cpl) and Leonard Bailey (Lt-Col.).

Shows which drew the greatest crowds and probably gave the most pleasure to the greatest number were the revues and variety shows. We have already mentioned 'Revue Order' but there were many others. Two which were seen by John Cromer in the spring of 1943 drew very different reactions. The first was 'Acting Unpaid' at the Ezbekieh and the comment was as follows:

> The show was miserably bad. We stuck it until the interval and then walked out. The lyrics were weak, and even if good would have been ruined by the inept singing. The tenor was of the ready-close-my-eyes-while-I-reach-the-top-note kind and effeminate to a degree. The humour was laboured and too much of the soldier's Arabic joke type. The sketches were the weakest I have ever seen,

the dancing was no better than any of my own burlesque pantomime efforts. I have always been at pains to support the local amateur dramatics but the pains were really too great and the accent on the amateur with none left for the dramatics.

Feeling that he had been over-critical, Cromer went once again three weeks later, but his opinion remained unchanged, the second half being no improvement on the first.

The other revue was of a totally different order. Entitled 'Polish Parade' it was first seen by Cromer at Heliopolis. 'Went to Heliopolis 'drome for a performance of "Polish Parade" – the variety show put on by the Poles. I enjoyed every minute of it – music, dancing and humour. I wish our own people would put on something as enterprising.' He was so impressed that he went again, with a fellow-officer and his wife, when the show came to the Ewart Memorial Hall a week later:

> It was even better than last time, for it had a series of excellent backcloths, most beautifully painted in bright colours and treated in that continental style which I like so much and find repeated in the latest American styles. The other new feature was the superb adagio dancer, who was unable to appear before. Her skill is superb and her reckless abandon a new high in adagio dancing.

Cromer was one of a party of four in a further visit to the hall and found the revue 'as excellent as before except that neither the blonde nor the adagio dancer performed'. Later on, when the Garrison Theatre was in full swing, it was always packed for the variety shows such as 'Lucky Dip' (with 'Something for Everyone'), 'Music and Magic' ('an evening of mystery and melody'), 'Café Continental' and 'Double Scotch' ('a Reel Tonic!').

One special visit of the stars stood out in the memory of all who saw the revue *Spring Party* at the Ezbekieh Theatre in July 1943 after its successful tour in North Africa. Cromer, certainly, has never forgotten it, recalling his meeting afterwards with Beatrice Lillie, who had been in sparkling form, Vivien Leigh, tired and seeming a little lost in a corner seat, Dorothy Dickson, belying her age and enjoying the adulation of her elderly admirers, Leslie Henson, as funny off the stage as on, Nicholas Phipps, very much the juvenile in those days, and Mae Craven, who had put in a good performance. This had been a Saturday night of a kind never to be repeated. The stars moved on after the back-stage reception to a fairly heavy drinks party at the Embassy.

Noël Coward was also in Egypt that summer, performing in Cairo and Alexandria. He had been booked for an extended tour throughout the Middle East and to facilitate his travel arrangements he had been granted the privilege of a special travel permit with built-in visas for those countries for which they were needed. This document had recently been negotiated with the governments concerned and was administered by the Security Identification Section in Cairo, of which John Cromer was then second-in-command. Coward was taken to GHQ to meet the Commander-in-Chief and later complained about the lack of security, saying that he had been given this wonderful pass and had not been asked to show it. This was duly reported back to the SIS for investigation. Cromer investigated and was able to report to the C-in-C that Noël Coward had been accompanied the whole time by a Staff Officer who had vouched for him to the corporal at the gate. His arrival and departure times had been logged and his whereabouts known the whole time to those responsible for the security of GHQ.

Coward went on to carry out an exhausting tour of camps and hospitals. It was one thing playing in the theatres of Cairo and Alexandria but quite another travelling from camp to camp, often performing two or three times a day. This was a job that the ENSA concert troupes did magnificently right from the start. Two of the first parties to tour the Middle East were 'Hello Happiness' and 'Spotlights.' Announcing their arrival in its issue of 28 September 1940, *The Sphinx* seemed to be quoting verbatim from a press handout:

The idea is that the 'Spotlights' party will provide entertainment for Egypt while the 'Hello Happiness' party will give similar entertainment throughout Palestine. Each party will service these districts, taking their entertainment wherever the British and Colonial troops are serving. Then they will be transposed and so ensure fresh talent, new songs, dances and sketches at regular intervals. Each company is equipped with a portable stage, lighting, and all the necessary fittings and 'props', so that a show can be quite independently presented anywhere. In order to provide an even more mobile form of entertainment, 'Singsong' vans will tour the Middle East, visiting the canteens and holding informal concerts in which the soldiers themselves will take part. The novelty of these entertainments and their homely atmosphere will ensure their success.

There was no doubt about their success, nor that of other parties, such as 'The Muddle Easters', 'Nomads of the Nile' and 'The Rascals', which were all army concert parties drawn from BTE (British Troops in Egypt). It was not only the army that provided service entertainment. Seven RAF bands sailed from England on the *Queen Mary* in 1942, arriving in Egypt at the end of January 1943. They came under the control of RAF Welfare, Cairo, the officer in charge of bands being Flt-Lt Norman (Nobby) Newman, formerly of the Tower Ballroom, Blackpool. The Big Band (No. 1) was stationed in Cairo under its musical director Frank Cordell. RAF Command Dance Orchestra, Band No. 4 became 'The RAF Mirthmakers', part of the show 'Rise & Shine', with six artistes, including Alfred Marks, then billed as 'The Compère with a Difference'. They opened at the Lycée Française Theatre in February 1943 and toured the Canal Zone, Alexandria, and camps and hospitals in the desert. 'Rise & Shine' was disbanded in July 1943 but a new show, devised by Ralph Reader, 'Best Blue' in September of the same year did not go well and that, too, was disbanded. The band continued playing the camps, touring extensively in their own show 'What's Cookin'?' until going to Italy at the end of June 1944.

It is not until one has seen the programme schedule and movement orders for these parties that one is made aware of the great distances covered, the conditions in which the performances had to be given and the sheer hard work at all times. Let us look for a moment behind the scenes of 'Hello Happiness'. Its members had formerly been entertaining seaside crowds round the coasts of Britain and it was the first concert party to be formed for overseas service in the war, starting in France in September 1939. After travelling with the second company, 'Spotlights', nearly 10,000 miles in France and Belgium, they re-formed to arrive in the Middle East for an even more gruelling stint. The company revolved round Reg Lever, a BBC comedian and popular concert party and pantomime performer, born and bred in show business, and his wife Elsie Winsor, another well-known BBC entertainer. The other members of the company at that time, with their programme descriptions, were: Jack Royce ('Songs of the Southland'), Margaret Scott ('The Personality Girl'), Lois d'Auvergne and Kay Dixon, the dancers, Rex Rashley ('Up to his Tricks, such Fun') and Roma Clarke at the piano.

During their tours of the war zones, 'Hello Happiness' covered thousands of miles and entertained all three of the services, in literally every place where there were any forces, through the whole Middle East, PAIFORCE (comprising Persia and Iraq) and the whole North African war front into Italy. Among the ships on which they gave concerts were HMS *Valiant* and HMS *Eagle* when in port at Alexandria, and they visited Cyprus and Malta while it was under siege. We do not have the itineraries for the whole of Egypt but some idea of what was involved in a comparatively simple tour of the Canal Area alone can be gleaned from a routing sheet for the 1942 tour, with a cast of four males and nine females. They were engaged every weekday from 30 November to 6 January 1943, resting only on Sundays. As the show was on a larger scale than the earlier tour, it could play stands of not less than three nights and, in fact, played 11 venues, some being the Shafto cinemas (see later) and others at transit camps and RAF hangars.

For the North Africa tour, too, the itinerary and attendance sheets for the period 26 January to 31 March 1943 reveal that the company gave 84 shows at 30 different venues, some of them revisited more than once, and including field ambulance and hospital units. Were it not for the fact that we are recording these figures from the actual sheets completed at the time, we would find it difficult to believe that the total number of forces' personnel seeing these shows amounted to 76,800, ranging from a single audience of 1,900 at the Miramar Theatre, Tripoli to a sing-song show for 150 at RAF Martuba. During the shorter period between 19 April and 2 May 1943, there were 17 shows at nine different venues, with one audience totalling 3,000 at one of the five concerts for Sfax Area Mixed Units, the total for that tour, which went right up to the forward areas, being 13,360. Often two shows would be given on one day. There is a note at the bottom of the last set of figures which gives an illuminating account of the full extent of the work done by these artistes:

> In addition to official shows shown above, the company appeared each evening at the 30 Corps Rest Camp in the soldiers' own sing-song at night, giving items concerted and individual. The girls served the men's teas each day and the whole company combined with the local welfare officer in 'Quizzes', 'Spelling Bees' etc. in helping to maintain morale of men just out of the line for a couple of days.

One aspect of culture which has not yet been mentioned is ballet. This art was brought to the Middle East in 1944 by the stars of the Ballet Rambert, who performed in Egypt during their tour. Led by Sally Gilmour and Walter Gore, under the direction of the great Marie Rambert herself, this distinguished company brought with it a full repertoire of the best ballets of the time. The classics, *Giselle* and *Swan Lake*, were represented by the second act of each piece; the original version of William Walton's *Façade* was danced to Frederick Ashton's choreography; the three scenes of *Lady into Fox*, adapted from David Garnett's novel and choreographed by Andrée Howard, had a decor by Nadia Benois; Benjamin Britten's *Simple Symphony* had choreography by Walter Gore himself; Anthony Tudor's *Judgement of Paris*, with music by Kurt Weill, was danced by Pamela Hinton, Margaret Stewart and Joan McLelland as the goddesses Juno, Venus and Minerva respectively; *Death and the Maiden*, with choreography and costumes by Andrée Howard, was danced to the music of Schubert's 'andante cantabile' from the Quartet in D minor; and the series of dances 'Czernyana', based on the composer's familiar piano exercises, completed the collection. John Cromer has a note that a talk, with demonstrations, was given by Walter Terry, the ballet critic of the *New York Times*, entitled 'Modern Expressional Dance'. This was well attended and appreciated and is a further measure of the range of serious programmes which were available throughout the war at 'Music for All'. Cromer's interest was the greater because he had shared a period of leave with Terry in Cyprus earlier in that year (1944) and the two of them, with a companion, had performed a mock ballet in the ancient Greek amphitheatre at Salamis.

One more word should be said about the spoken word before we move on to the next form of entertainment. Radio has been mentioned but its contribution to local efforts outside music and talks has not. This was considerable, for not only were extracts broadcast from the CADMS, ENSA and other musicals, plays and revues, but also many plays were written or adapted for radio by the services unit at the EBS, particularly by the very successful producer Rex Keating, who was well supported by actors in uniform such as Oliver Burt, Raf de la Torre, J. Thornton-Bassett and others. Among their successes were *Outward Bound*, *The Absent Minded Lady*, an adaptation of *49th Parallel*, and many more besides.

above: The Victory Club,
Cairo (1943)

right: Erik de Mauny (left) and
G. S. Fraser (right) (1943)

below right: The Founders of
the Salamander Society (1943)
(left to right) John Waller,
Keith Bullen, Raoul Parme,
John Cromer

below: John Gawsworth,
Cairo (1943)

Saleh Mursi

Youssef Idris

Youssef el Sebai (left) with Mursi Saad el Din (right)

Neguib Mahfouz. The first Egyptian and the first writer in Arabic to win the Nobel Prize for Literature, which was awarded to him in 1988

Mahmoud Teymour

Abbas el Aqqad

Tewfik el Hakim

Like radio, the cinema was something unknown to the troops of the First World War. By 1940, all the young men and women arriving in the Middle East were of an age when the silver screen had brought the glamour and glitter of Hollywood to the High Streets of the Western World and to Egypt as well. There was, in addition, an indigenous film industry which produced its films for an Arab population beyond the boundaries of Egypt. For the thousands of newcomers, however, the cinemas of Cairo and Alexandria added greatly to the amenities and were very well patronised.

There were more than 20 cinemas in Cairo alone, ranging from the air-conditioned Metro, the showpiece of the business (which also claimed that all pictures shown there would not be screened in any other cinema in Cairo until at least 60 days later), to the open-air garden cinemas of varying quality, both in comfort and quality of sound. The Diana Palace was probably No. 2 despite the fact that the Royal had a sliding roof, which gave it an advantage over the Metropole, which always seemed to be very hot. The Opera Cinema (not to be confused with the Royal Opera House) and Studio Misr showed English-language films, although some Egyptian productions also appeared at the latter. The Cosmo and the Kursaal showed the better and most popular locally made films and the Femina and the Lux provided a somewhat lower order of entertainment with second-run films.

The garden cinemas also enjoyed a great popularity, largely because they were cooler, indeed, sometimes distinctly chilly. They usually provided lighter fare than the more expensive first-run 'A' film cinemas but one could pick up some of the better-known 'oldies'. The Parc, Rex, Paradis and La Potinière (showing *Waterloo Bridge* with Vivien Leigh and Robert Taylor in April 1942 after its first appearance at the Metro in September 1941) were the most patronised by the troops and had the best selection. The Regent and St James's were not as good as the restaurants bearing those names and the Ezbekieh and the Empire were more popular with the indigenous fans. The Roxy at Heliopolis provided an opportunity for those living, permanently or temporarily, at that end of town and the Fantazio catered for local tastes at the other end, the Midan Guizeh.

The fare provided ranged from the most prestigious Hollywood films to the abysmal 'B' picture fill-ins, but the wartime population of Cairo could hardly complain that they were not being given the opportunity to receive whatever cultural benefit could be gleaned from this overwhelmingly American export. The Westerns, the musicals, the tragedies, the comedies, the farces, the pseudo-historicals, the block-busters, the war stories and documentaries, the adaptations from novels, the cartoons – all passed in review and were goggled at by an insatiable audience. The programming varied. The best shows would run for a minimum of a week, often longer, as, for example, *Gone with the Wind* at the Metro. Some cinemas split the week into two but not always in the same place, so that one had to be careful to avoid arriving at a cinema with a new film in mind only to find that it had not yet arrived. The newsreels were shown regularly and propaganda films played their part.

It would be tedious and beyond the scope of this book to run through the catalogue of everything that was shown during these years but a dip into some of the programmes may help to show how Egypt was kept abreast of the cinema culture that was being spread throughout the English-speaking world and beyond. The stars were the same everywhere, ranging from the well-established to the new hopefuls. Early in 1941, while Gary Cooper was enacting the life of *Sergeant York* at the Metropole, Barbara Stanwyck and Henry Fonda were performing *Lady Eve* at the Diana Palace, with Bob Hope and Dorothy Lamour at another cinema and Mickey Rooney and Judy Garland elsewhere. At the Cosmo, the local product was *Le Prétendant No. 5*, featuring Assia and an all-Eygptian cast. At the same time, this film was entertaining the local aficionados in Alexandria, Tantah and Mansourah.

Comedy was much in demand as a relief from the fighting in the desert and boredom at the base. It was provided by, among others, the Marx Brothers, Laurel and Hardy, and Abbott and Costello. In November 1941, Geoffrey Household, then a Field Security Officer in Syria, on leave in Cairo, was able to see his novel *Rogue Male* appear on the screen of the Royal Cinema as *Man Hunt*, with Walter Pidgeon, Joan Bennett and George Sanders. There was often a clash of great names such as the week in which the classic *Pride and Prejudice* with Laurence Olivier and Greer Garson competed with *Pimpernel Smith*, one of Leslie Howard's last films. Two months later, in a double bill at the Miami, an unknown Desi Arnaz appeared in the Adolphe Menjou/Gloria Swanson vehicle *Father Takes a Wife*, while the better-known Lucille Ball was sharing the lead with Edgar Bergen and his dummy Charlie McCarthy in *Look Who's*

Laughing. Who was to know then that Desi and Lucille would team up both in marriage and the successful long-running TV series *Living with Lucy?*

Hollywood's best and worst products flowed through the cinemas and the money flowed into the box-offices. Among the 'B' picture players who appeared more than once was Ronald Reagan, whose greatest star part was to be the Presidency of the United States.

John Cromer was an enthusiastic but not very discriminating cinemagoer. During his Field Security days in 1941, one of his duties as an NCO. had been to frequent bars and garden cinemas on the lookout for careless talk and suspicious characters. The garden cinemas were a better patrolling ground than the enclosed regular buildings because of the light, full moonlight in particular, and greater opportunities for identification of doubtful individuals, including escaped prisoners of war and civilian Italian internees. These duties were time-consuming and tiring and by their very nature diminished, and at times destroyed, the enjoyment of the films. But we were not there for enjoyment.

Part of the stock-in-trade of this activity was a supply of visiting cards which would be slipped into the hand of any soldier considered to be indulging in careless talk. One could vary the caution by offering one of the four following texts: 'Please do not talk shop: only enemy agents want to hear it'; 'Katherine Parr never gossiped: she kept her head'; 'Remember what Jonah told the whale, "if you had kept your damn mouth shut, all this would never have happened" '; and the most contrived of all, with the name 'U.R. Requested' in the centre of the card, '2 Refrain from Careless Talk' in the address position, bottom left, and 'Tel. No 1' bottom right.

Cromer made no note of those days in 1941 and it was not until a year after he had been commissioned that he attempted to keep a somewhat sporadic diary. The first half of 1943 provided an opportunity to log some of his cinema visits, sometimes alone, sometimes in the company of army or civilian friends. A few extracts from his unsophisticated critical appraisals record the impact of the films of the time.

January entries show a live interest in the cinema, the first attempted visit ending in failure:

Cairo was absolutely teeming this evening. Geoffrey (West, a SIME colleague) and I had thought of the cinema but for the first time to my knowledge the Miami was full. Metro, of course, was out of the question. We trekked on to the Metropole with the same result. Leave troops and Americans formed a steady milling crowd but everything was perfectly orderly.

Greta Garbo's appearance in *Two-faced Woman* produced a negative reaction: 'It was a complete bastardisation of capability and accomplishment, for great actress as she undoubtedly is, she was called upon to play in yet another of these absurd social comedies which Melvyn Douglas seems to have apportioned to himself.'

The spate of American films with trivial plots and miscast stars increased Cromer's bile. He thought *The Male Animal*, with Henry Fonda and Olivia de Havilland, whose appearance he had anticipated with relish, was 'atrocious':

> I am fairly easy-going and tolerant in film criticism but this was beyond everything. Formless, badly connected, senseless, it was poor propaganda for average college life. God preserve me from another such spectacle.

Nevertheless, the cinemagoing did not abate. Indeed, one February Monday in 1943 Cromer was off duty and went twice to the films. In the afternoon he took Colin Sansom, the son of A. W. Sansom (another Field Security Officer whose book *I Spied Spies*[78] gives a racy account of Intelligence activities) to see *Dumbo* at the Studio Misr: 'Disney's fantasy very well conceived and executed. I am always ready to be amused by cartoons.' In the evening he went with one of the girls from his office to see *Pepe le Moko* with Jean Gabin at the Ewart Memorial Hall. This was primarily a concert hall and not really appropriate for commercial cinemas. Its shortcomings for the purpose are recorded thus:

> Had a certain amount of additional amusement on account of breakdowns etc. First there was a mix-up over seats and we finished up in an exclusive, if draughty, loge. Then the sound failed and we were regaled by recitation and impersonation by one of the students – quite well done as it happened. Then the film *did* start and was mostly through when the sound failed again.

The following month (March) signalled the arrival of a rare British film, *One of Our Aircraft is Missing*, another sell-out, but despite Rosalind Russell appearing in a film with 'wit, extravaganza and good direction' comment continued to be negative, culminating in a broadside against *Once Upon a Honeymoon* with Cary Grant and Ginger Rogers: 'I should like to record its utter fatuity and weakness and the over-acted gestures of Rogers, which were appalling. American films seem to be less and less worth seeing. English films – where are they?'

The cry for more British films must have been heard somewhere, for two appeared in the following month, May, when the diary shows:

> We went to the Metropole (wretchedly hot as always) to see *The Young Mr Pitt*. Robert Donat took the part well and Robert Morley made an excellent Charles James Fox. I quite enjoyed the show and recalled most of the big speeches – which were authentic.

On 21 May *Desert Victory* was shown at the Rex Garden Cinema. Probably too close to home, as it were, to elicit any greater comment than 'very well done'. That was meant to refer to the film but could well be applied to the military achievement.

No story of the cinema in the Middle East theatre of war would be complete without some account of the extraordinary structures and performances provided by Thomas Shafto at army camps and bases. Nobody who has experienced an evening at a Shafto fiasco will ever forget it. Fortunately we are able to provide corroborative testimony from eye-witnesses. The first comes from Norman Craig's *The Broken Plume*: [82]

> There were also the camp cinemas, the property of a notorious contractor. These were large bare tin shacks with rows of wooden benches and a few collapsible chairs at the back for capitalists with fifteen piastres to spare. The projector was worked by Egyptian operators. The film usually began upside down and when this was righted the reels were often shown in the wrong order. The dialogue was American and the film was overprinted in French at the bottom, in Greek down one side, and in Arabic down the other, the picture itself being barely visible beneath the maze of intriguing characters. There were frequent breakdowns and each time the audience cheered wildly, except when the last prolonged and irremediable stoppage occurred; then they would rise as one man, smash the seats and depart in the best of humours. The contractor always accepted this development with the bland, fatalistic, indifference of the Orient. 'Maleesh', he would no doubt say to himself. 'What do a few wooden benches mean anyway? I make a fortune, so why worry?'

Leslie Barnard remembers Thomas Shafto well:

[He] was an Australian so the author of *The Broken Plume* is at fault in implying that he was a local man. It was the bland, fatalistic indifference of a Strine on the make. I met him towards the end of the war. He was into everything including second-hand furniture. I was looking for a particular piece of furniture for a set (I did about five jobs for ENSA simultaneously) and I got it from Shafto. He had the most magnificent Brewer's Pimple I have ever seen. He was spherical and bald. 'They tell me,' he said on our first meeting, 'that I am the most hated man in Egypt.' 'Well,' I said 'I wouldn't say that you were the most popular.'

Martyn Uren reports the Kiwi reaction to broken films and generators:

> For a long time the chaps put up with having to wait while either the projector, the film or the electric plant was mended, but one dark night they lost patience and razed Shafto's Camp Cinema to the ground. I was on guard that night, in our guard room, which was about a hundred yards from the cinema. I was a little bit in sympathy with the whole proceeding, so it was five minutes too late when I arrived on the scene with a file of guardsmen armed to the teeth with empty rifles.[105]

Other forms of entertainment varied from the highly sophisticated to the downright sleazy. As in the First World War, the genteel tea dance, which had continued to flourish through the inter-war years, still drew many patrons, particularly in the 'Officer Only' establishments. All major hotels provided this facility, with Shepheard's and Mena House being top of the swanky league. The exclusive Maxim's Winter Roof Garden in Sharia Soliman Pasha provided lunch with classical music, evening dance music being played by 'The Jazz Baby Almanza, star clarinet player, and his Collegians'; while at the 'Nile' in Elfi Bey, with its restaurant, brasserie and bar, a so-called symphonic orchestra performed, augmented on Saturday and Sunday nights by 'the Nile Swingers'. The dinner-dance was another favourite evening pastime, again provided by the hotels and sometimes given added allure by a floor-show.

In its pre-Christmas euphoria during December 1941, *The Sphinx* waxed lyrical on the attractions of tea:

> Tea as a war-time stimulant is invigorating: tea every day is certainly soothing, but tea on Saturdays and Sundays at the Metropolitan's 'Dug-Out' is peaceful and fascinating. Despite the air-conditioning of the place, the 'Dug-Out' Ramblers know how to make it hot when they add a harmonious touch to the cosy atmosphere of the hall.

And after a detailed description of the 6–8 p.m. dancing session, which included a break for a floor-show, the column concludes: 'Later in the evening, the "Dug-Out" Cabaret is even more popular. It's the place to make merry.' Sault's, in Kasr el Nil, was another restaurant and tea-garden favourite where the dinner-dance was held in the open air and the Hotel des Roses roof garden was almost always full at night.

As for the night clubs and cabarets proper (some may say, improper), they varied with location, the Zamalek clubs and the restaurant/cabarets which opened later in the war along the Pyramids Road, such as the Arizona and the Auberge des Pyramides, were the officer-only, upper end of the market, while the inner-city night clubs were of a different order, particularly along the lower end of Emad el Din. John Cromer is able to provide an anecdotal tour of some of these establishments, rising in tone as he rose in rank. His first hostile encounter with the rough end of the Australian Expeditionary Force was at the 'Sweet Melody' in Emad el Din. He had been detailed with other Field Security NCOs to pick up a man for suspected sales of arms and ammunition. This man was playing the drums and at the end of a particularly noisy number, the band being drowned by shouting and table banging by the Antipodeans, he was taken by two policemen and frogmarched to the exit, which was being secured by the NCOs. Immediately, the incensed troops turned their drunken attention to Authority and bottles were soon flying. Cromer recalls one breaking just above his head before the raiding party got safely away with their quarry.

A somewhat similar episode occurred at the Kit Kat in Zamalek on a stake-out during the run-up to the Eppler spying episode recorded by Major Sansom in *I Spied Spies* and later embellished by Ken Follett in *The Key to Rebecca*. On this occasion, Cromer was in his seedy grey flannel suit, sitting at a table with three other NCOs, including the small Sergeant-Major, who had tippled too freely and mischievously stuck out his foot as a burly Eygptian swaggered past. There was an immediate fracas, with chairs and tables soon in the air. Cromer felt a hand tugging his sleeve and turned to find an attractive redhead from the establishment, leading him to a concealed door, through which he was piloted to find himself in the street with the rest of his party. The giant who had been tripped was an Egyptian wrestling champion.

The Casino Opera in Opera Square opened in the late summer

of 1940 as a music hall and restaurant with roof garden and terraces, giving a fine view over the city. The proprietress was Madame Badia Massabni and the establishment became known as 'Badia's'. It was very popular and Cromer was an occasional patron. One evening in the later years of the war, he went along with a fellow officer to see the cabaret show, when a shooting affray broke out between an Egyptian Army officer and a local Greek magnate over disputed possession of one of the girls. As the shots were fired, Cromer and his friend dived under a table, from where they were able to observe the pandemonium and hear the shrieking as the audience rushed for the doors.

The Auberge des Pyramides was a good place for parties. The food and music were good and the cabaret was usually of a high standard. Cromer recalls one party when the whole of the Security Identification Section officers and secretaries, totalling about a dozen in all, went out for a Christmas party in 1944. It was an evening when King Farouk was bestowing his royal patronage, having driven there in his red Mercedes. He had his eye on an attractive WAAF officer, whose escort had temporarily abandoned her. The office party saw a royal emissary going over to the girl to summon her for the King's pleasure, so Cromer rushed over to the leader of the band, demanding a conga. The music started, the line formed with Cromer's party in the lead. They made for the WAAF's table, hissed at her to join the snaking line, breaking ranks for her to hold on to one of the officers and cheekily encircled the King and his entourage before heading for the exit, where the WAAF was seen into a taxi and the conga line returned to finish the dance.

Both Leslie Barnard and Cromer well recall the jazz pianist Johnny Highsmith, who played at the roof garden of the Hotel des Roses. He played in the Teddy Wilson style and was very popular. His real name was Ali Ali Ahmed Hussein and he was probably Syrian and somewhat suspect. Sansom knew all about him and the security service considered it sufficient to keep him under surveillance. This entailed frequent visits to the roof garden and on one evening when Hussein had been whisked away for some routine questioning, three security officers took his place, 'Bones' Astley at the piano, Stuart Fritsche on drums, with Cromer providing the vocals.

The last contribution Cromer wishes to make on this aspect of Cairo night life relates to Doll's Cabaret in Malika Farida, as it then was, which he visited no fewer than five times between

February and May 1943. Let his diary describe the first of these visits:

> It was the first time I had been there for nearly a year. Always the same, these places – the painted hollow women, the jaded, drink-inflamed officers, the shifty barmen, overdressed pimps, plausible managers, inevitable police, wooden PM [Provost Marshal], the scene never changes – it is only more highly or less gaudily coloured. One can sit and watch and be amused, disgusted or unmoved, according to taste or mood. The manoeuvres, the tricks and the dodges are always so obvious to the observer yet never seen by the dupes, who always wear uniform. So last night there were British officers, American all ranks, Greeks and Yugo-slavs, Poles and Frenchmen. The entertainment level is mediocre except for the Spanish couple, whose dancing is always lively and well executed.

And the last of the May visits:

> The place does not improve at all. Hot as ever, crowded as ever, mediocre as ever. There is no really worth-while cabaret entertainment out here at all. The Bronze Man puts up quite a good show – he is a big fellow painted all over with gold paint and does various exercises with and without accoutrements. His muscle-moving exercises are a little hideous but some of them are pleasantly rhythmical. The rest of the show was down to the usual standard.

Before we leave the low life of night clubs, let us see how it appeared to Olivia Manning, writing in *The Sum of Things*:

> The Extase, one of the largest open-air night clubs, was in a garden beside the Nile. It was always crowded. Angela's party had to wait in a queue composed mostly of officers and their girls. As the suffragi set up makeshift tables in any vacant corner they could find, the queue dwindled steadily. On the stage a man in flannels and striped blazer was imitating the sound of a car changing gear uphill. His imitation was exact and the audience, that would have objected to the sound of a real car, gave him an enthusiastic applause. The Extase served only champagne and some of the officers were hilariously drunk. The arc lights that lit the stage added to the summer heat. The audience seemed a compacted, sweating, shouting, restless, amorous mass of men and girls.

We shall conclude this presentation of aspects of Cairo life during the Second World War with a brief survey of the gastronomic scene. We can imagine the scepticism of some readers at the concept of a Good Food Guide to Egypt of the 1940s but the international and national cuisine in both Cairo and

Alexandria, while varying considerably in range, could be, at its best, of a very high standard. The country has always been very rich agriculturally and the Mediterranean continued to supply the excellent fish which has always been a feature of the table. The hotels maintained as high a standard as could be expected and managed to augment the dwindling stocks of quality wine with imports from Cyprus, Palestine and South Africa. Despite the loss of stores in transit, through enemy action, there always seemed to be a fair supply of whisky, even if, at times, there seemed to be water in it before any was added by hand. Drinkers of brandy could not always recognise the locally distilled version and the back page of the one-off spoof *Gin*, a magazine got up in format and layout to resemble the services' monthly, *Gen*, was thought by some to be not far wide of the mark in the slogan 'Bolanachi's puts years on you – Not a drop is sold till it's five minutes old'.

Even before the British occupation of 1882, Shepheard's Hotel had been the focal point at Christmas for the British community, which was then so small that most of its members knew one another intimately. The hotel was the social rendezvous after morning church and again after the ritual visit to the Pyramids in the afternoon. Throughout the war, Shepheard's maintained its dominance and its cuisine, even if it were not at its peak. In the *Sphinx* hotel list for Christmas 1941, Shepheard's is described as 'The only hotel with a true democratic atmosphere and which is the 100% rendezvous of the Services.' One was urged to visit the long bar and ask for the 'Anti-Axis' mixed drink, 'unique against hangovers'. There was another drink, well known to habitués as a 'Suffering Bastard' but deep research has failed to find its ingredients. Other hotels were in competition for Christmas Eve Gala dinner and dance customers and so great was the demand that tables had to be booked well in advance. Two very tempting menus were published at the time, the Metropolitan Hotel at 100 piastres including crackers, cotillons and cabaret, with dinner dress essential, but the prize for wartime austerity must surely go to the National Hotel, 'the only 100% Swiss hotel in Eygpt', whose 12-course menu at 65 piastres progressed from Caviar en Tartine chez Lucullus to Corbeille de Fruits.

The St James's (Jimmy's) claimed to be the only English table in Egypt, but Captain and Mrs Tommy Bryant, who ran

Tommy's Bar opposite the Turf Club, would probably have disputed that.

John Cromer's interest in food had been stimulated by visits to Paris before the war and memories of a seemingly endless hors d'oeuvres at the Périgorde, at the river end of the Boul' Mich', lived with him through the darkest days. His worst Christmas dinner was that of 1940 in Mersa Matruh when the Hampshire Regiment was in a forward position and the CO decided to redeploy the companies on Christmas Eve, as a result of which all ration distribution was put out of joint, resulting in a failure of supply and general disgruntlement. His next Christmas was a very different affair. Having been commissioned on Pearl Harbor Day, he was invited back by his former Field Security colleagues for Christmas Dinner and still has the menu. Its front cover gives its provenance, 'Intelligence Corps, Field Security Wing, Headquarters and Cairo Sections' and the menu within was:

> Tomato Soup; Roast Turkey, Roast Goose, Roast Beef, Roast Chicken, Roast Potatoes, Green Peas, Apple Sauce, Beer; Christmas Pudding, Custard, Mince Pies, Jam Tarts, Fruit.

The place to meet in Cairo was Groppi's. There were, and still are, three Groppis, one in Heliopolis and two in the city centre. The main Groppi, referred to in the novels, poems and memoirs written in English, is the one in Midan Soliman Pasha. It was there that the world and his wife met, for sumptuous gateaux and cakes, oozing with cream and adorned with pieces of chocolate. That was normally between 10 a.m. and 12, after which the bottles of Stella beer would replace cups of tea and coffee. Apart from serving beer in the tea-shop, there was also a pleasant bar, where the barman Spiro was a Cairo landmark. Groppi was frequented by many Air Force officers on leave, since it was opposite a small pension which was monopolised by the RAF.

The other Groppi, in Adly Pasha, had its own character. It had a beautiful garden, blessed by the warm Egyptian sun. That garden was frequented mainly by British civilians, especially staff of the British Council, which was just round the corner. It, too, had a bar but its clientele normally had their café au lait and English cakes.

Groppi was the place where the twain did meet. Egyptians and British could be seen together, chatting and discussing the development of the war. There were no restrictions on the part of the Egyptian Government, and Egyptians could mix freely with other nationalities.

Sault's had similar attractions. Loques was another tea and ice-cream venue, although the best ices could probably be found at Sourian's. Cromer knew all these and his diary records practically all his restaurant meals, lunch and dinner, between January and May 1943. His favourite was L'Ermitage, on the ground floor of the Immobilia Building which he used a dozen times during this period and up to the time he left Cairo.

A popular pre-cinema restaurant at very reasonable prices and run-of-the-mill but 'safe' food was the Regent, where the service was good, enabling patrons to get away in good time for their evening shows. Cromer used this seven times during that diary period. Another favourite, frequently used as an evening rendezvous for supper before engagements, used only three times in early 1943 but often before and afterwards, was the Carlton. Cromer shared his appreciation of the place with his friends Geoffrey West and Leslie Barnard. The latter and he had struck up a friendly understanding with a cheerful Sudanese waiter, whom they named 'Charlie Chan' because of his resemblance to the cinema portrayal of that role. The restaurant was not the same as the Carlton Hotel.

> We went to the Carlton for dinner – I must again note the service and the food. The barman, Greek waiter and Charlie Chan are always so glad to see me and I appreciate this recognition. Our steak was exquisitely done and we had some fine red wine with it. From the very beginning the place has proved its value.

Another favourite was Le Petit Coin de France. One entry contains a brief round-up of other haunts as well:

> Went for the first time for over a year to the Petit Coin de France. Although it fell off badly, it is now back in good form, and with a pepping up of service could get back to its former position. I still rate Taverne Française as the best cuisine, whatever the expensive claims of Jimmy's may be. For a quick snack the Regent is not bad but it has no variety of food. I have not yet been to the Carlton Hotel so cannot judge on that. For a good dinner-dance, Shepheard's of course still holds its position, but I am not altogether sold on the quality of Continental dinners.

A somewhat condescending report was made of the first visit to another of the more expensive restaurants: 'We went first to

Maxim's for dinner. It was the first time we had been there and we agreed that it was quite satisfactory and worthy of being put on our list.'

Other visits logged during that period are sufficient to show the wide choice presented to the palate. French cooking was available at Gamache, and the Kursaal remained popular at lunch-time, while the Piccadilly on the Mena Road was a good place for dinner. The Turf Club was a venue where the emphasis seemed to be more on talking and drinking as no gastronomic virtues were recorded at that time despite three visits. Tommy's Bar was good for a snack as were the Bystander and Big Ben.

We leave Cromer's harping on food with an account, written by him on the 1950s as part of an unpublished series of six 'Capital Meals', taken in six capital cities. Long before the American magazine *Gourmet* had settled into its saccharine style, it was pre-empted in this account of a visit during the war to the Casino des Pigeons:

The setting for this meal was ideal – a garden restaurant on a bank of the Nile, the waterway of that surrealist centre of Cosmopolitania, Cairo. A languorous, lazy evening, with palm trees and minarets black against the blue night sky and the heady scent of jasmine completed the background. I ordered an aperitif, which was soon to hand, ouzo, that pale cousin of the absinthe family. Its aniseed freshness strips the palate of all cloying residues and tones it up for the meal to come.

The meal opened with a routine appetiser, the humble prawn mayonnaise. Even in wartime, the standard of this dish seldom fell below satisfactory and frequently reached a very high rating. This night was no exception. The prawns, brought in from the Mediterranean waters around Alexandria, were medium to large, succulent and meaty, immersed in a sticky sea of creamy mayonnaise, in which a judicious mixture of vinegar and oil had been subtly seasoned with the correct quantity of cayenne pepper. Served with a leaf or two of crisp, fresh lettuce from the prolific fields along the river's edge, this first course set the gastronomic barometer at fine.

Two local wines had been ordered, to test the adequacy of the revived viticulture of the country. These wines were revivals of the ancient days of the Pharaohs, when Egypt's vineyards were famed in the Mediterranean basin. The two wines were Clos Mariut, a light white wine, and Clos Matamir, a red. The Clos Mariut was served with the prawns and tasted well in that company. Young, of course, green even, but fresh, bearing a tang rather than a bouquet, this wine had character enough to speak for itself.

It was time then for the main part of the meal, for which the restaurant was famed. This was roast pigeon, a delectable brown, plump bird, sitting comfortably in a pond of rich, non-glutinous gravy. Whatever the failings of Sudanese cooks may have been, when they did set out to produce a meal within their compass, instead of straining after something of which they had only an imperfect idea, the result was usually very much worth while. So it was with the pigeon. Stuffed with liver paste and garnished with slivers of lime, the very sight of the dish made the mouth water. Each guest was always served with an entire bird, skilfully carved and cut so that the flesh fell apart and the tiny bones could be picked clean. Finely sliced game chips added to the attraction, the main vegetables being roast potatoes and runner beans which seemed to have acquired a lushness of taste compared with the often arid dullness of so many of the vegetables which were inclined to grow sterile under the pitiless sun. I attributed this rare quality to the subtle application of butter and lemon.

The bottle of Clos Matamir had been standing upon the table – no etiquette of room temperature here in the open air. It proved a worthy, if timid, companion for the Mariut which had preceded it. It suffered, of course, from having been forced on too quickly, drunk too soon, but the demands of wartime catering were such that one had no right to expect anything more than a harsh apology of a wine. In fact, this was not the case. The Matamir had the weight of a very young claret, paradoxically combined with the sharpness of an over-aged vintage. The latter was due to the over-rapid ripening and drying of the grapes – there was no rain to swell the gourds, so that they were always premature in reaching a maturity which did not carry fulness with it. Nevertheless, wine was enough of a luxury at that time to make an excellent background to the rich, tasty pigeon which went all too quickly.

As the feluccas glided silently along the Nile, only the whine of the mosquito struck a discordant note in that most pleasant garden. The sweet course fell into two parts: a sticky, nutty round of rahat lakoum, covered with sugar; and a ripe, juicy mango, always a problem for the uninitiated to manoeuvre round its large oval stone. The usual coffee followed, sweet, black and thick, served with a glass of fragrant rosewater. The moon rose higher, the crickets cheeped and another capital meal was ended.

We have said nothing so far of the Egyptian reaction to this style of life, so to round off this chapter and end our review of wartime Cairo, let Mursi Saad el Din have the last word:

Anglophiles as we Eygptians were, we always wanted to emulate everything our English friends did. We were always frequenting the places they frequented – especially those of us who could afford the 50 piastres meal, and we were not many. It was some kind of status and, somehow, we felt proud doing it. In fact, to this day, we still visit the restaurants, and surreptitiously, the bars, which we used in the past.

7

The Aftermath

One sentence sums up the situation which faced Egypt at the end of the war. It was written by Tom Little in his book *Modern Egypt*:[116] 'The Egypt which emerged from the war was devoid of people who could lead the country, for there was neither the Zaghloul of the '20s nor King Fuad's cautious manipulation of political life in the '30s.' Nevertheless, the war had brought prosperity to the country and it had also stimulated and intensified every aspect of Egyptian thinking and politics. While we have endeavoured to eschew the details of political evolution, it is inevitable that events in that field would colour and influence the cultural life of the country. The writers, who were concerned with the development and welfare of Egypt, more particularly the Egyptians, for the articulate minority who were shaping its ends were growing in confidence, analysed and mulled over every aspect of events that were affecting the burgeoning nation. We are now in the period when Mursi Saad el Din's career and experience provide a unique source for the literary cornucopia which has continued its flow until today.

The writers whom he met and whose works he knows so well were (and some still are) poets, novelists, short story writers, political writers and journalists. One such was Freya Stark who was a mixture of writer, traveller, politician and diplomat. She is remembered for her war effort and the formation of a movement, if it may be so called, known as 'The Brothers and Sisters of Freedom'. The main aim of that movement was to create political sympathy for the Allies. It had branches in almost all Arab countries. Freya Stark loved the Arabs. She travelled extensively in the Arab World. She was another Lady Hester Stanhope, but with a cause. She wrote a number of books, mostly about the Arab World, but the one that stands out is *East is West*,[117] in opposition to Rudyard Kipling's famous saying 'East is East, and West is West, and never the twain shall meet'. With Freya Stark the twain have met.

In that book, she describes, in a highly literary style, her experiences in a number of Arab countries and devotes five chapters to Egypt: 'Young Egyptians', 'Brothers in the Azhar', 'Three Prime Ministers', 'Lulie', and 'Country Visits'.

We must remember, though, that she is writing about a society that no longer exists in Egypt.

> For a long time it was largely true that the Arabian World was divided between the Pashas and the Poor. And although Egypt is in many ways not typical of the rest of the Arab World, yet it shares its religion and its language, and is the chief centre of its culture; and the difference between the Pashas and the Poor has always, I imagine, been more pronounced here than elsewhere and has remained so to this day.

Freya Stark believed that the young middle-class professionals are the main agents of change. The Pashas might have done some good, she says, but the good they have done 'can be interred with their bones', indeed most of it, she goes on to say, 'was not done by [the Pasha] at all, but was accomplished much against his will in an uphill battle less than eighty years ago, by Lucie Duff Gordon, fragile and dying in Luxor among the Egyptian Arabs who so loved her that they offered her a burial among the holy ones of their Muslim dead'.

Freya Stark's analysis of the new, emerging Egyptian society deserves mention. She believed that there were young men stepping out who, though they may look westwards for inspiration, have their feet firmly planted in the peasant soil from which they spring. It is the task for the future to reach some kind of amalgamation, the weaving of patterns and not separation. It is the task of the middle-class young Egyptian:

> It would be well if the relationship, built upon an identity and not on conflict were better understood by both the Pashas and the British. The professional young man is a new arrival and it has taken both the Englishman and the Pashas some time to understand that he is here at all. I like the young effendi of Egypt and I met him at a time when the British cause and that of democracy in general appeared to be at the very nadir of their fortune.

She thought the wishes of the young Egyptians were simple and that they believed in the principles of democracy and were anxious to help defeat the Axis. The meetings between her and these young men helped them to realise their own beliefs at a time of their life when supports of school and college were slipping out of sight.

> At such a time [she wrote] it is the forces of tradition, the gradual evolution from one generation to the next that alone help the young traveller pushing in his untried boat from shore; they give him, as it were, a coastline with anchorages ever in sight. But the youth of the Middle East, brought up in a Western way, has no such coastline; he steers into open sea; and the passion of devotion with which he looks back to the days of guidance, to teachers in school and college, can best be realised when the loneliness of his further journey is borne in mind; for British traditions are deep, flexible and strong and they help carry most Englishmen from youth to age.

Events turned out differently, with the increasing tensions and turmoil which culminated in the drama that ended the monarchy in Egypt and severed the British connection, thus changing the course of the country's history. The year was 1952. Nahas Pasha, who had signed the Anglo-Egyptian Treaty of 1936, had abrogated it in 1951; there had been riots and a general boycott of labour in the British garrison in the Canal Zone. Alfred Sansom, out of the army but taken into civilian service as security officer at the British Embassy, had flown home on 18 January 1952 for consultation with the Security Department of the Foreign Office. There was another outbreak of shooting in Ismailia, during which the lives of a number of the Buluq Nizam, the Egyptian auxiliary police, were lost – 80 according to the Egyptians, 36 by the British count. Sansom rushed back to Cairo, by which time rioting had started in the city. On 26 January 1952, known thereafter as Black Saturday, the Badia Cabaret was set on fire. Sansom records the scene:

> We entered Opera Square just in time to see the fire brigade arrive. Immediately some youths slashed the hoses. A group of City Police stood watching, but took no action. And that was how Black Saturday began . . . The Rivoli cinema had been set on fire. The Metro cinema was next. Then I had a report that the mob had started on Tommy's Bar. This was just opposite the Turf Club. It was around 1 p.m., an hour when the Club was usually full . . . Some twenty-five British members had ignored advice to leave and were in the club . . . The latest report from Tommy's Bar was that spirits were being poured on the counters and furniture to add to the flames . . . then they attacked the club, and set fire to it, and those who tried to escape were pushed back to burn to death. Later I had the

melancholy duty of taking relatives to identify the bodies. Ten died in this horrible way, including two women and the Canadian Chargé d'Affaires ... There was no apparent motivation in the choice of targets of fire and destruction, except that they were all in the centre of Cairo. Whole streets were burned down at a time. Shops and cinemas, banks and hotels, office blocks and bars, all suffered impartially. Of the 400 buildings destroyed during the day nearly all were Egyptian owned. Famous landmarks disappeared in flames – Shepheard's Hotel, Groppi's, Cicurel, Chrysler's, Barclay's Bank.[78]

The subsequent history of the Turf Club is interesting. The Egyptian Government later replaced the burnt-down club with a flat in a modern block opposite the main offices of the Shell company. The club continued as an exclusive British club, with a board elected from among its members. Even after the Revolution of 1952 and the Suez Crisis of 1956, the club functioned in the same way. Later on the government gave it, free of charge, a beautiful villa built in a marked Arabesque style. Although the membership had dwindled, the club bar was always full and was renowned for having the best cellar of Scotch whisky, Cognac and wine.

The Turf Club still flourishes but nobody knows how. Elections take place every so many years and a new chairman is elected. Its membership has been extended to Americans but not Egyptians. The present chairman is an American. The odd thing is that clubs and associations come under the jurisdiction of the Ministry of Social Affairs, but not the Turf Club. How? Nobody knows, but its continued existence, through the ups and downs of Anglo-Egyptian relations is, in itself, a living example of Egyptian tolerance, kindness and camaraderie.

Returning to 1952, the climax was reached with the revolt of the Free Officers, the ousting of the King and the beginning of a new regime. For a reflective view of this dramatic change, let us turn to Peter Mansfield, who began his career in the British Foreign Service. Learning Arabic at the Middle East Centre of Arabic Studies in Lebanon, he resigned from the Service over the Suez affair in 1956. From 1959 to 1961 he edited the *Middle East Forum* and from 1961 to 1967 he was Middle East Correspondent and was shuttling between Beirut and Cairo with occasional visits to other Arab countries. In addition to a number of books published on Egypt and the

Arabs, one of which is entitled *The Arabs*,[118] he supervised the publication *Who's Who in the Middle East*.

Peter Mansfield was one of the first, if not the first, to observe and record the changes which the 1952 Revolution brought to Egypt. Furthermore, he was enthusiastic about those changes. This enthusiasm comes out clearly in his book *Nasser's Egypt*,[119] published in 1965, since when many revised editions have appeared with changes in the light of events. For a hundred years under Khedives and Kings, Egypt was little more than a corrupt satellite revolving in turn round Turkey, France and Britain. But under Nasser, claims Mansfield, Egypt became a magnet for the Arab World, a force in African affairs and an audible voice in the conduct of international business.

Mansfield's opinions and thoughts on Egypt are reflected more than anywhere else in this book, which was the result of many years of study and can be regarded as a fair and accurate analysis of the situation in Egypt before and after the Egyptian Revolution. That revolution, says Mansfield, 'which deposed a hundred and fifty year old dynasty and destroyed the well entrenched power of an immensely wealthy and self-confident ruling class, can claim to be the least violent in recorded history'. And then he asks: 'Why should a small country, with few natural resources, except one great river, hold such a key position in the world?' 'One factor,' he answers, 'is undoubtedly Egypt's geographical position as the West's gateway to East Africa and Asia, a position which led Bonaparte to call it "the most important country".'

In all his writings, Peter Mansfield reflects a real understanding of the psychology of Egyptians, docile and humorous, who identify exploitation with foreigners, accusing them of benefiting from their country's prosperity rather than the people themselves. He then goes deeper in his analysis. Egyptian revolutionaries do not have to be classified as Marxists, Titoists or anything else. The history of Egypt provides their driving force and their goal. For what those young officers wanted most of all was to make up for the 2,500 years in which Egypt's history was shaped by foreigners. Then he goes on to list the foreign powers who invaded Egypt over the years, as well as the nationalist movements that had erupted, until he reaches the 1952 Revolution. Mansfield then goes into the minutest details about the Revolution, its beginnings, the officers who were instrumental in shaping it and carrying it out, then the differences which later emerged and how they were resolved.

The value of his book lies in its analysis and exposure of the new policies of the Revolution, the political system the young officers were searching for, the economic policies, education, culture, as well as a discussion of Nasser's Philosophy of the Revolution, the Arab circle, the African circle and the Islamic circle. These sympathetic feelings for Egypt are reflected in the chapter entitled 'The Land and the Fellah'. He begins this with a quotation from Father Ariot's book, *The Fellahin of Egypt*: 'Here man belongs to the land, it is not the land that belongs to him.' He then goes on to describe the land, the valley and the Delta of the Lower Nile, the serene palm trees, the brilliant green colour standing against the chocolate earth and a soft blue sky, the somnolent buffaloes cooling themselves in the canals and the overwhelming impression of ancient fertile land carefully and lovingly tended. But the civilised beauty of the Egyptian countryside, as the author calls it, should not conceal the fact that most of the people who inhabit it are as poor as anywhere on earth.

The creators of Egypt's wealth, the fellahin, have been oppressed, neglected and despised for so long that it was not surprising that one of the first acts of the Revolution was agrarian reform. Mansfield then goes on to explain what the reform entailed, the appropriation of large estates and their redistribution among the fellahin, the creation of co-operative societies to assist the new smallholders by supplying tested seeds as well as modern machinery which they could not acquire for themselves, the combined units with doctors and agricultural experts attached. He then describes the High Dam and its effects on the country. He discusses the pros and cons of these policies and comes to the conclusion: 'And if the central problem of the 20th century is to prevent the widening of the gap between the developed and undeveloped nations, the efforts of Nasser's Egypt against formidable obstacles are deserving of sympathy'.

P. H. Newby has a special place in Mursi's heart as he was his professor at Cairo University from 1941 to 1943. Their friendship continued long after that, during Mursi's 12 years in England and beyond. Unlike other writers who lived in Egypt and wrote about it, Newby was closest to fathoming the real country and its people. He had a genuine love for Egypt and when Mursi, as Chairman of the State Information Service, asked him to write the text for a collection of photographs taken by the American photographer Fred Maroon, he accepted without hesitation. The book, *The Egypt Story*,[120] is, to Mursi's mind, the best and most sympathetic survey of the country.

Newby lived in Egypt from 1942 until 1947 and the result was a trilogy, *Picnic at Sakkara*,[121] which is now a text book for the English Section of the Faculty of Arts. The first volume deals with King Farouk's waning power. The second, *Revolution and Roses*,[122] concerns the period of President Nasser's revolution. The third, *A Guest and His Going*,[123] takes place in England but focuses on the Egyptian Question, this time the threatened nationalisation of the Suez Canal Company. In all three volumes Newby is trying to fathom Egyptian life and politics. The central theme is not only the apparent one, the relation between England and Egypt but, as G. S. Fraser says, 'something much deeper, the difference between sadness and sanity, and at a puzzling angle to that, the difference between false logic and true impulse'.

The trilogy is not the only Anglo-Egyptian group of novels. In 1968 Newby published *Something to Answer For*,[124] a novel with a fully Egyptian setting. It deals with the Suez Crisis, although written ten years after it. The main characters are British. The hero is an ex-sergeant who served with the British Army in Suez. He is a crook and the novel is about his efforts to acquire wealth by crooked means. But the whole background of the novel is Egypt.

Some of the points made by Newby in *The Egypt Story*, referred to above, are original. For example, writing about the Pyramids, he refutes the thesis that these great monuments were erected under a *corvée* system. He is of the opinion that the Egyptian workers who were engaged for their building were doing it as an act of faith. It was their religious enthusiasm which drove them to work. Like those who built the Christian cathedrals in Europe, it was belief and not compulsion that was in the background. Another point he makes is about the Egyptian peasant. He thinks of the Egyptian fellah as the backbone of the country. The fellah is the reason behind this Egyptian continuity of character. Traders stick to the big cities but the Egyptian peasant kept his purity and his traditions. Newby also questions what Herodotus said: that Egypt is the token of the Nile. He believes that Egypt is the token of the peasant.

Newby continued to visit Egypt as a tourist or as a lecturer

for the British Council. His interest in the country never stopped. His novel *Kith*, published in 1977,[125] had Egypt as a setting.
His characters are both British and Egyptian, whose lives are
interwoven. Yet he believed that there was a distinction between
the English and Egyptian character. In an article he wrote for
the *Listener*, entitled 'Having Drunk of the Nile', he expresses
his opinion that both characters are based on illusion. English
fantasy is rooted in mystery, he says:

> The East will cease to be mysterious, but to walk down an English
> street or ride in an English train will give us food for infinite wonder
> and speculation. This is because in England we never get to know
> one another. We have the greatest difficulty in establishing ordinary
> human relations. In a nation which admires eccentricity, each and
> every Englishman, thus impressed by a sense of his own unique
> personality, is determined to keep his secret to himself. We do not
> know, therefore we have to invent.

Newby's Englishmen are forever protecting their essential
unknowability by the invention of little illusions of order. The
Oriental, the Egyptian, on the other hand, thinks he knows.
Nothing about human behaviour surprises him. His sense of
fantasy, which Newby terms 'the supreme Oriental luxury', is
founded on instinctive acceptance of the improbable and the
contradictory. Newby believes that there is no reconciliation
between the two. Egypt remains Egypt and England adamantly
England.

As has become apparent in this book, Egypt has long fascinated women writers, and that prolific writer Ethel Mannin was
another such. She wrote a number of books on Egypt and the
Middle East, the best known, perhaps, being *A Lance for the
Arabs*.[126] In all of these she reflected a real sympathy for the
Arabs and for the Palestinian cause. She had been attracted to
Egypt since, at the age of 12, she underlined Cairo as a place
to visit in her school atlas. Later on she began to read stories
about what she calls 'sophisticated people who sat on the terrace
of the Shepheard's Hotel' and she pictures herself sitting on that
terrace, sipping her drink and looking at Cairo. Unfortunately,
by the time she came to Cairo, the old Shepheard's was no
longer there. Instead there was a new ten-storey hotel overlooking the Nile instead of the Ezbekieh gardens. Her book describes
whatever she saw in the city, its sights, its people, its customs.
Taken to see the Son et Lumière at the Pyramids, she is not

impressed at all. In her delightful style, with a pinch of humour, she deplores what she calls 'the Middle Class English voices delivering a banal dialogue of which I understood every word'. She said she would have preferred to listen to it in Arabic, of which she knew not a single word, or French, which she understood imperfectly. 'The Pyramids and the Sphinx do, of course, look very wonderful floodlit but the least said about the rest, the better.'

She records her visit to the Arab League Headquarters and her meeting with Abdel Khalek Hassouna, the then Secretary General of the League. She simply wanted to know more about the League. She heard the usual talk about Arab unity, how the Arab world is like a large family and in large families there are always quarrels, but they are still all brothers and sisters. After her two visits to the League, she said:

> On both occasions I left the Arab League building feeling the whole Arab world suffused in a golden glow of amity, a splendid unity imminent and all problems solved ... The glow lasts for just about as long as it takes to cross the courtyard garden, with its lush green grass and its white roses, its weeping white roses.

Ethel Mannin was very kind to Egypt. At times she was critical but without that air of condescending or patronising which characterises many writings of lovers of Egypt. When she criticises, she does so almost as an Egyptian, with a glow of love and compassion and with no malice or disrespect. At other times she is supportive of projects started by the Revolution. She discusses land reform. According to her, this is revolution in itself. She was, however, concerned that progress might mar some of the glory. She was impressed by Aswan. She liked:

> the lagoon-like effect of the Nile since the Cataract has been dammed; in the still, glimmering lagoon rise red granite rocks of strange, dream-like shapes, and there are wooded islands, and the tall white sails of feluccas which glide like fantastic birds over the translucent water. There is the quality of the light, too, in which everything, red rocks, white sails, tawny hills, tall palms, stands out with luminous sharpness.

But she shows the other side of the story:

> Aswan is very beautiful. How long it will remain so is another matter, for there is iron ore in the surrounding hills, and the Aswan Dam (not to be confused with the mighty project of the High Dam) has been electrified and there is already a fertiliser factory, and one

way and another Aswan is well on the way to being an industrial centre of the South as Helwan is of the North.

Our chronology in this chapter has been somewhat erratic and we would like to bring it to a close with a reference to *Egyptian Service, 1902–1906* by Sir Thomas Russell Pasha, KBE, CMG[54] because that title sums up so well a dedication and a period of time which, as the author wrote in his foreword, 'contributed much to the country's development and of which little record has been made: I mean the late [Lord] Cromer and immediately subsequent period of the English Advisers and their provincial inspectors'. As those days came to an end, that spirit of service ended with them and it would be a pity if the work done by this great public servant were to be forgotten. As he went on to say:

> Time passes, memories are short, records are destroyed, and many of the present generation are unaware of the constructive work done in those days by the Inspectors. We were happy in our lives as being unconcerned with politics; our duty was to get the greatest efficiency possible out of the material at our disposal, and to keep ourselves in the background, while helping to build up the great administrative machine necessary to the governing of a country of seventeen million people.

Russell Pasha started his career in Egypt with the Coastguard Service in Alexandria, and as an Interior Inspector he came to know village life and the underside of smuggling and drug-running. After two years as Assistant Commandant of the Alexandria Police under Hopkinson Pasha he was transferred to Cairo in 1913 in the same capacity under Harvey Pasha, who was a martinet of the old school. His account of bribery, corruption, prostitution and white slave trafficking reveals the difficulties of preserving integrity and upholding the rule of law in the seething cauldron of the Cairo underworld, with mob rule and mass hysteria being used on the surface as political weapons. Russell took over command of the Cairo Police from Harvey Pasha in 1917 and from 1919 to 1924 his main concern was with political riots and assassinations.

Russell is best known throughout the world for his pioneer work in combating drug traffic. His early days had been spent tracing sources of contraband hashish but in 1916 cocaine began to make its first appearance in Cairo, to be followed by what he calls 'the pleasanter and more potent heroin'. We are almost enured today to the world-wide presence of these lethal drugs, which have led on to the even more potent peril of AIDS, but in 1928 Russell:

> began to realise that something was happening which was producing a new slum population in Cairo, the like of which we had not seen before. For the first time we heard of the method of intravenous injection of heroin and soon came across its victims. Within a short time we found a new element in our Bulaq slums ... We began to find human wreckage lying about in the Bulaq lanes, pale-faced semi-corpses evidently not of the Bulaq type who when spoken to replied in educated Arabic or even English and admitted that it was the heroin habit that had got them there ... The Bulaq settling-pit quickly filled with the human debris of every class of Egyptian society. One night I netted the whole area and collected a couple of hundred of those pitiful creatures and cross-examined many of them myself. They were from every class, working men, sons of small shop-keepers, cabmen, artisans, clerks for Government offices and even sons of well-to-do citizens. All ruined by heroin.

The widespread and devastating effect of heroin addiction alarmed the Egyptian Government and in 1929 Russell was empowered to set up a Central Narcotics Intelligence Bureau of which he was made Director, a post he held until his retirement. The last part of his book is devoted to the excellent work done by the Bureau and its input to the United Nations and International Committee on Narcotic Drugs.

Looking back on his career, he recalled that in 44 years' service he had been the servant of 32 Egyptian Governments. As Commandant of the Cairo Police he had taken orders from 29 different Ministers of Interior in as many years.

> In the ebb and flow of politics there were many Ministers whom I had, at one time or another, to arrest or intern, under orders from on high, and yet I think I can say that, in spite of this severe strain on personal relationships, no one of them has borne me lasting unfriendliness for having carried out my orders.

His final words reflect the feelings of so many of those public servants who have come under the spell of Egypt: 'Egypt's friendliness and hospitality have never failed me and I have spent many happy years in this country of immense charm and beauty.'

8

The Continuing Interest

On through the second half of the twentieth century, the fascination of Egypt has continued with unabated strength. In the 1960s, writers who had been in the country in whatever capacity looked back in reminiscence and description. Alan Moorehead, whose *African Trilogy* (comprising *Mediterranean Front, A Year of Battle* and *The End in Africa*, published during the Second World War) was a journalist's account of the events of the time, took the Nile as his theme for a deeper look at the country and its neighbours, in his two-volume study *The White Nile*[127] and *The Blue Nile*[128]. The definitive book on the great river is, of course, *The Nile*, written by Emil Ludwig,[129] strangely enough not mentioned in either the chapter notes or the select bibliography given in Moorehead's books. Moorehead describes Harry Johnson's *The Nile Quest* as 'one of the earliest attempts to give a connected history of the river, and it remains probably the best general introduction to the subject'. He pays tribute to the books of the explorers, splendid to behold but now well out of print and collectors' items, quoting Livingstone's *Last Journals*, Burton's *Lake Regions of Central Africa*, Speke's *Journal*, Baker's *Albert N'yanza*, Stanley's *Through the Dark Continent* and Thomson's *Through Masailand*, and remarking that there are many others. He also mentions 'a second class of books about African exploration and the Nile which are of much later date and which might be described as standard works, since they are the result of devoted scholarship in the present century'. These we leave to readers of Moorehead's work to discover.

In his two books, he traces both the history and the course of the Nile from its sources to its mouth. The eternal Nile, as it is often called, is the longest river in Africa and possibly in the world. Its length from Lake Tanganyika to the entry of the Rosetta branch of the Delta is over 4,000 miles. Against a background of many facts, Moorehead draws his colourful pictures of history and adventure. Like most Europeans, he is interested in both the White and Blue Niles, the search for the sources of which seems to have intrigued people since Pharaonic times.

The White Nile, which includes some interesting illustrations and nine maps (including the endpapers) is concerned with the years between 1856 and 1900 and mentions only very briefly the early history of the river. The book, which, incidentally, is dedicated to Freya Stark, is in four parts, the titles of which give a clue to the way the subject is treated: 'The Exploration'; 'The Exploitation'; 'The Moslem Revolt'; and 'The Christian Victory'. Moorehead ends the book by recapitulating on the outstanding characters whose work and influence he has traced in the text and concludes:

> The river binds them all together. Each of them was drawn towards it by an irresistible attraction, and it makes very little odds whether we think of the stream as it is in this present century or as it was in the age of Ptolemy. The Nile seems to be impervious to change. It flows on now, as it has always flowed, perpetually renewing itself from year to year and from century to century, a never-ending flood of warm, life-giving water that spans half Africa from the Equator to the Mediterranean, and it is still the mightiest river on the earth.

The Blue Nile deals with events from 1798 to 1869 on that part of the river and the mainstream that descends from Ethiopia through the Sudan and Egypt to the sea, complementing the previous volume. Part One is entitled 'The Reconnaissance' and is a curtain-raiser for the historical events that follow. Part Two, 'The French in Egypt', deals with Napoleon's expedition. The French leader thought that, once conquered, Egypt would not be difficult to govern, but he wrote later: 'There is no country in the world where the government controls more closely, by means of the Nile, the life of the people. Under a good administration the Nile gains on the desert, under a bad one the desert gains on the river.' Moorehead wrote much more about the Napoleonic battles on land and sea but also uses the river to write about Egypt and describe Cairo, its craftsmen and its bustling life. The book does not stop at Egypt, Part Three being 'The Turks in the Sudan' and Part Four 'The British in Ethiopia'. But the author cannot get away from the dream of Napoleon. He returns to the theme in his epilogue:

It is remarkable that the French, who set in motion the whole nineteenth-century upheaval on the Nile, and who did so much for the exploration of the river, should have had so disproportionate a share in its government and development. Britain, Italy, Belgium and Germany were all destined to found colonies in this part of Africa: never the French. Yet of all the people mentioned in these pages Bonaparte is the one who appears to have had the clearest notion of what was involved in the conquest of the Nile. All the schemes for the regeneration of the river that were eventually carried out – the dams and canals – the land reforms and the local government, even the study of the ancient past – were originally his, and he understood the strategical importance of the Nile better than anyone else. At the Pyramids he not only felt he was being watched by the past; he had a vision of the future centuries as well.

A writer whom Mursi knew well in the 1960s was Desmond Stewart, at that time giving his services free as adviser to *The Arab Observer*, a weekly magazine published by the Ministry of Culture in English and French, of which Mursi was Editor-in-Chief. Going through a list of Stewart's published books, one is impressed by his preoccupation with the Arabs and things Arabic and Egyptian: *Early Islam, The Pyramids and Sphinx, The Temple of Janus, T. E. Lawrence, The Sequence of Roles*, a trilogy involving three generations of a Scottish family with the Egypt of Lord Cromer, Saad Zaghloul and Gamal Abdel Nasser. He also wrote a novel about the Egyptian Revolution entitled *Men of Friday* and translated the Fathi Ghanem novel, *The Man Who Lost His Shadow*.

Stewart's love for Egypt was such that he eventually rented a flat in the middle of Cairo on a permanent basis. He died suddenly in early June 1981. One of his last books was about Cairo, called *Great Cairo, Mother of the World*.[130] About this book he wrote:

It is a product of a love affair with a city, spanning in my case the late 1950s and early 1960s. Although the passion has mellowed into affection, Cairo still seems to me – for its history and what survives of its buildings – one of the most fascinating cities in the world.

This love of Egypt is reflected in every word in the book and the author's deep and genuine understanding of its problems can be felt all through it. Cairo was, for him, the capital not just of Egypt and the Arabs, but the entire Third World.

Moving on from a general survey of the city, Stewart writes

about Memphis and Heliopolis in detail, then goes on about Babylon-in-Egypt, its occupation by the Persians and its liberation from them by Alexander. He devotes a great part of the book to Islamic Cairo, throughout its whole history to today. Like all other books Desmond Stewart has written about Egypt or with the country as a setting for his novels, this book reflects his love and admiration for what he sometimes called 'my second country'.

As with Desmond Stewart, Cairo was a lure to which the American, James Aldridge, with a dozen novels under his belt, fell victim. Having lived in the city for many years, he, too, has provided an in-depth account of its history and its inhabitants. *Cairo*,[55] subtitled 'The Biography of a City', was first published in the USA in 1969 and in London a year later. The author states in his preface:

> This is not an academic study of Cairo, nor is it an amateur history. It is really a passionate involvement in the place by someone who has long admired the city and its people . . . My task was to treat the subject as a living, breathing entity, and tell the full story from primitive gestation to modern metropolis. I have to admit that I am primarily a novelist, and though there is an extensive and sometimes unique historical documentation in this account, I have tried to extract the drama rather than accumulate the dust. There are far too many bloody moments in the story of Cairo, but on the whole I have underplayed rather than emphasised that aspect of it.

The June war was very much in the author's mind when he wrote in his last chapter:

> Nobody can breathe in this city and not feel its nervous whispers and its carefree ecstasies for simple things. You don't need to give yourself to this city because it gives itself to you, and there is hardly a man, woman or child in it who, in the space of an hour or two, wouldn't lay his entire life bare for you to judge and admire or condemn . . . The modern city beats like a hot bat against the outside walls of its dusty sky and its clean, dry deserts. It grows like a cactus, becomes noisier, harsher, less credulous, more efficient, and it fills itself hungrily with the four winds of fate. Day by day it lives a little more and dies a little less, and like the Egyptian himself it offers to a visitor more heart than sense. But it still guards for itself the prospects of the future it has only just defined.

As a *jeu d'esprit*, we feel we should mention a little book in the Nick Carter series which appeared in 1972. Also entitled *Cairo*,[131] it bears little relation to the city and tells even less of the country. Like the 40-odd other titles in the Carter stable, it is another yarn of brutality, murder and bloody vengeance. There are shoot-outs in the tombs and temples of Luxor and in the Egyptian desert. As for descriptions, the best one can hope for is the following: 'The next morning was as cool, bright and clear as the Star of Africa. The eternal Nile ran placidly, an oiled metallic blue sheet. Beyond that twisting ribbon of life glowed the burnished copper of the desert and hills.' If the seal of approval for violence is sought for, it may be found in the dedication, 'To the Men of the Secret Services of the United States of America'.

Let us now return for a moment to two *Personal Landscape* personalities, whom we have already mentioned. The first, Robin Fedden, having written a civilised, sympathetic and nicely illustrated book under the title *The Land of Egypt*, recast it, brought it up to date, added a bibliography, two maps and travellers' notes, for it to be published as *Egypt, Land of the Valley*[132] in 1977. He writes of the people, their work and crafts, the landscape, the monuments, and life in town and country. He, too, has a description of Cairo in the 1970s:

> A first impression is the graceless impact of the 20th century. In a single generation the population of Cairo has trebled; the spacious green gardens and villas have disappeared; unkempt crowded streets are racked by the ceaseless blare of motor-horns; concrete blocks, rising in unplanned disarray, overshadow tenements. Yet from hotel windows, ten storeys up, the stranger glimpses to the east of the modern town a startling forest of minarets; on the street laden camels wait, with an air of disdain, for traffic lights to change; feluccas slip quietly downstream while cars and lorries roar across the Nile bridges; on the pavement by the river's edge, facing the high-rise blocks, men prostrate themselves at sunset towards Mecca; and, bound for Mecca, the Holy Carpet sets out each year, not indeed with the Great Caravan as it did for seven centuries, but by aeroplane. Such inconsistencies betray the survival, amid the Westernising present, of another city, the historic capital of Islam.

Like all true friends of Egypt, Robin Fedden looks to the future:

> There is reason to hope. A great fund of character and vitality resides somewhere in this ancient people. In a country where there was never a caste system even in pharaonic times, a new corporate identity comes naturally. Given a rule they respect the fellahin and

their river are capable of untold achievement. A long historical hibernation, which proved impervious to the passage of dynasties and the pressures of imperial policy, seems to have reached its term. The Egyptian is perhaps aware that an inheritance awaits him. After all this time, he deserves it.

Olivia Manning's Balkan Trilogy began publication in the late 1970s, the last two volumes, from which we have already quoted, being concerned with Egypt. *The Battle Lost and Won* and *The Sum of Things* followed the fortunes of Guy and Harriet Pringle, thinly disguising Reggie Smith and Olivia, whose writing, while fluent, does little more than skim the surface, rarely showing insight into character, or elucidating some of the apparent inconsistencies of behaviour and action. The spirit of the British Council hangs heavily on the air and those outside its circle, including Harriet Pringle herself, have to fend for themselves as best they can. The absurd Lord Pinkrose is one who is barely believable, although his murder by two Stern gangsters is probably based on the assassination of Lord Moyne, a very different sort of peer, needlessly lost. The inaccuracies of facts about Cairo are likely to be noticed only by those who were there when the events depicted in the novels were taking place, but when realism is sought, things real should be right. When the books were later made into a television series called 'Fortunes of War', certain of these errors were carried over on to the screen, despite Mursi's efforts to correct them when acting as a consultant to the series.

Moving into the 1980s, we come to a revival of the Salamander group, which began in 1976 when Erik de Mauny, G. S. Fraser and Victor Selwyn set out to reprint *Oasis* in a more permanent form. It was sheer chance that John Cromer, flying back from London to his post in Brussels in the EEC Commission, ran out of reading material and happened upon a copy of the *Daily Mail*. To his surprise, he came across a letter headed 'Poets Call', signed by de Mauny and Fraser, seeking contact with former contributors. Meetings followed; Cromer, still titular President of the Salamander Society, threw in his lot with the others and, with former contributors to the original *Oasis*, banded together to form the Salamander Oasis Trust, with Cromer as first President. Funds were raised, sponsors and publishers found after a prodigious amount of work by Victor Selwyn, with the result that *Return to Oasis* was published in September 1980, this time in substantial hardback form. The sub-title shows the expanded form of the book: 'War Poems and Recollections from the Middle East 1940–1946'. The editors were Victor Selwyn, Erik de Mauny, Ian Fletcher, G. S. Fraser and John Waller, with Tambimuttu and John Cromer as consultants. Two contemporary cartoons of the 'Two Types' by Jon formed the frontispiece and there were two sketches by Keith Douglas, whose colourful 'Cairo Street Scene' decorated the back of the dust cover, the front of which was a reproduction of the original *Oasis* cover. Introductory prose contributions consisted of a preface, setting the scene by Selwyn and John Checkley, an introduction by Lawrence Durrell and pieces by Cromer, Fletcher and Fraser. The whole of the original *Oasis* was included and further sections contained previously published Middle East verse, and previously unpublished soldiers' poems and ballads which had been written at the time and place. Appeals in two newspapers had attracted nearly a thousand replies. As Selwyn wrote, they included 'army ballads that had been written or typed to be passed hand-to-hand. When they reached us, some fell apart. Widows and children often sent us poems a man had treasured, along with his medals and war records, as part of his life.' Other prose pieces were Tambimuttu's descriptive 'Last Lunch with Keith Douglas', a tribute to Keith Bullen and ten vignettes. Louis Challoner's contribution on 'Tracing Oasis Poets' revealed how thorough the search had been to track down 31 poets, leaving some 15 still undiscovered. The original *Oasis* took four months to produce. *Return to Oasis* took four years.

The book was, of course, devoted solely to the poets who had been in uniform and a reception at the Imperial War Museum underlined this exclusivity. It had been a difficult task to select the poems and a good number would not have made a more literary anthology. But that was not the task of that particular exercise, which was to show how much poetry, good, bad and indifferent, had been written by men and women in the forces in the Middle East during the war years. As a further record, a representative cross-section of the poems has been put on tape, with the verse being spoken by Martin Jarvis, Irene Richard, Edward Wilson, Mick Ford and Erik de Mauny, arranged by the late Michael Croft, who was Director of the National Youth Theatre of Great Britain. An extract from Field Marshal Lord Montgomery's recorded speech of 13 August 1942, on assuming command of the Eighth Army, can also be heard, as well as an introduction by Field Marshal Lord Carver.

The Salamander Oasis Trust followed up with a sequel, *From Oasis into Italy*,[133] published in 1983. Sub-titled 'War Poems and Diaries from Africa and Italy 1940–1946', the format was similar to that of its predecessor, with exclusively servicemen's verse and prose (no contributions from women as in *Return to Oasis*), with a quarter of the book being devoted to the Middle East. The editorial panel was a little changed, Dan Davin coming in for John Waller and George Fraser (who had died), aided by two wholly military advisers, Field Marshal Lord Carver and General Sir John Hackett. The introduction explains the editorial policy:

> In contrast to many collections, the selecting and editing of this series has been carried out by people who themselves served in these campaigns and have written about them and during them, and so they are familiar with the subject material . . . There is one feature common to all the pieces: a direct relation to experience. They are sincerely written, true to themselves and to their background.

Two paragraphs are devoted to justifying the inclusion of ballads and doggerel. Another passage in the introduction explains one of the differences between the two anthologies:

> The second volume is an attempt to continue the process of recovery, redemption, revelation and adjustment to long-established prejudice. The accident of material available, and changes of military scene, have produced some differences: the proportion of prose to verse is greater and it is noticeable that, for whatever reason, the poems tend to be written by those who had written before serving in North Africa and Italy. The spontaneous act of creation in the Western Desert and in Cairo would not be repeated. It had become a different war.

It had. Egypt had been left behind. It was the aim of the Trust to retrieve and publish as much as possible of the writing of the time, albeit not all of the highest quality, and in keeping faith with the writers, that aim was achieved.

Broadening the horizon still further, to embrace all theatres of war, the Salamander Oasis Trust, then under the chairmanship of R. D. Smith, went on with its work, to publish in 1985 *Poems of the Second World War – The Oasis Selection*.[134] In a preliminary note, General Sir John Hackett explains something of how the choice of poems came to be made.

The poetry we look for need not be concerned only with experience in battle. It should, however, be such as would be unlikely to be written except in wartime. It is the product of the pressures and tensions, the pangs and passions, the fears and frenzy, the loneliness, excitement, boredom and despair, the disgust, the compassion and the weariness, and all the other stimuli to self-expression which, though they are not uniquely found in wartime, react then upon the human condition with special force. Poetry that could as easily have been written in peace tells us little about the explosive creative urge which develops so strongly in men and women under wartime stress. It is the cry from the heart which is wrung from quite ordinary people by what happens to them in war that we look for, a cry that probably would never have been heard at all in peace.

We are in danger of drifting away into the nostalgia of the ex-soldier for scenes of past glories, whereas our task is to show how writers have been influenced by their stay in Egypt. We shall therefore leave this anthology, remarking only that the part of it relating to the Middle East contains poems already published in earlier *Oases*, unites the contributors to both *Personal Landscape* and *Salamander* and contains such unexpected names as Quintin Hogg and Enoch Powell.

Another book upon which we have already drawn is G. S. Fraser's *A Stranger and Afraid, Autobiography of an Intellectual* published in 1983, three years after his death. The book was written at the end of 1949 when the memory of his Cairo period was still strong. It is with those times that we have been concerned and his contribution to these pages through quotation we acknowledge with the thanks of those who were privileged to know him and to benefit from that knowledge. In his review of the book, Robert Nye posed a question: 'Was he really an intellectual?' and answered it himself – 'Not on the evidence presented here. A deeply reflective man, yes; and one deeply responsive to literature, people, and events. But the drift of his mind was intuitive rather than deductive, more concerned with feelings than ideas.' Intellectual or not, George was a good writer and good company.

Another of the writers about whom Mursi is qualified to comment from personal knowledge is Norman Mailer, whom he met in New York when representing Egypt at the PEN Congress. During that Congress, Mursi had many opportunities to meet him, when the American insisted on calling him Said and not Saad. They spoke about Egypt and Mailer's ambitious novel *Ancient Evenings*,[135] published in 1983, which is about ancient Egypt. It was natural that Mursi's first question to him was why had he chosen ancient Egypt as a setting for his novel? Mailer referred to an interview he gave to the *Harvard Magazine* in which he gave vent to his ideas and views.

It took Mailer ten years to finish writing what he calls his Egyptian novel. He announced his intention of writing it in 1972 and it was not published until 1983. It started as an excursion into Egypt. He said:

> I was going to dip into Egypt for a chapter or two, then get out, move on to Greece and Rome, then the Middle Ages. I was thinking of a sort of picaresque novel. That was in the first half year of working on it. But I began to realise that I was in Egypt for a long haul. So I started studying and I've learnt about ancient Egypt these ten years.

Mailer admitted that he took a great risk in writing about Egypt, a greater risk than with any book he had ever written. But, he says, 'I think I have used every bit of inspiration I've had on this book. If the book is not good enough, then I am not good enough. I feel that kind of peace about it.' Reading about ancient Egypt gave Mailer an understanding of certain things. He came to know more about the wealthy, by dealing with Egypt, its gold and Pharaohs. When he was asked, 'Why Egypt?' he answered, 'I don't know enough about history to be able to answer that. Egypt was one of the places, I think definitely one of the places, where magic was being converted into social equivalence, in effect, used as an exchange.'

But there was more than that to interest him. He made one assumption, which was that ancient Egyptians had minds which are easily as complex and interesting as our minds. 'They had an intellectual discipline that was highly unscientific from our point of view. But I suspect no farther off the mark than ours.' Mailer expresses some brave views about the gods of ancient Egypt. It was before the Judeo-Christian era, it was a pagan era more or less. But while writing the book he found that the ancient Egyptians had a tremendous influence over the Hebrews. 'Much of the Old Testament you find in Egyptian prayers. Some of it is startling. The early pages of Genesis could be taken from certain prayers to Amon and the ways in which he created the universe.'

When asked whether his novel bears any resemblance to the

Egypt of today, or what was in it for the modern writer, Mailer answered:

> Well, I've failed if we start reading the book that way. And I think that is going to be one of the difficulties for people, because most historical novels perform a service or pretend to teach something about today. And I will have failed if that's the way people react to my book. I want people to realise, my God, that there are wholly different points of view that can be interesting as our own. And as thorough-going as our own. In other words, probably a social evening in Egypt – and this is one of the reasons why I ended by calling the book *Ancient Evenings* – in that period 3,000 years ago was as interesting as an evening in New York today.

While Mailer was writing his book, another American, Laurie Devine, was also engaged on a 500-page novel, *Nile*, also published in 1983.[136] In this book, the interaction between Egyptians and Hebrews is brought up to date in the conflict between the nations of Egypt and Israel and the effect it has on the lives of an Egyptian girl, Mona, born in the village of Karnak, and Youssef, the son of a wealthy Egyptian Jew of Alexandria, who becomes an officer in the Israeli Army. The outward and inward tensions, political, religious and personal, permeate the pages.

Even after the revolution the restaurants and the night clubs continued to prosper, just as they had during the 1940s. Devine describes the Casino des Hamam (the pigeon restaurant on the Nile, praised earlier by John Cromer) and his picture of another wartime haunt shows how little things had changed:

> After midnight they finally reached Auberge des Pyramides, the gaudiest nightclub in Cairo – and by the looks of the limousines and the taxis parked outside, the capital's most popular cabaret. Everywhere on the walls and the dance floor were silver tinsel, and purple cutouts of cupids, and flashing neon. A forty-piece band was playing, it seemed, at least three different tunes, and at the same time a red-faced comedian was bawling bawdy jokes into a squealing microphone.

Devine has captured the two extremes of modern Egypt – village life and the metropolis. He writes of Karnak village:

> There was even a comfort in the sameness and slowness of every inevitable night and day. Each shuffled past, much the same as the one before . . . Lateness was calculated not in minutes or hours but in days. A man was to come on Thursday morning, but when he arrived the next Monday night, no apologies were offered or

expected. Malesh. Thursday or Monday, it was all the same. All
that was required was breathing out and breathing in, until a man
or woman breathed no more.

In the vocabulary of not only Karnak but every other village in
Egypt, there was even a word for this comfortable trance. Kaif, it
was called, when a man or woman, worn down by the impossibility
of relief from every vexing problem, succeeded in entirely turning
off the mind. A fellah in the fields, a fellaha by the river, could sit
for hours without movement or action or thought, drowsy in the
dry white heat under a cobalt sky.

Coming from that suspension of life in a country village, it
was a shock to arrive by train at Bab el Hadid station:

> The mother and son paused on the threshold of Cairo. A mammoth
> granite statue of an ancient pharaoh rose smack in the middle of
> the square before them, staring as if in perpetual disdain at what
> swirled at his feet. Cars, taxis, trucks, donkey carts, camels, horse
> carriages, and bicycles careered in every direction, even high in the
> air on swaying concrete-and-steel overpasses. Old men, young men,
> women, and children moved with dogged determination on the
> streets, over the fences, alongside the cars. Garishly painted kiosks
> and food carts fought for position along the street under the angry
> red and orange and green gashes of neon signs. Over it all was the
> constant hellish howl of horns: tooting, beeping, crying, wailing,
> nearly talking in their own hooting jargon that is Cairo.

When the late Noel Barber started writing his successful series
of novels at the age of 70, after a lifetime of top-flight journalism
as a foreign correspondent and editor, with a string of non-
fiction books to his credit, it was inevitable that one of his
experiences, Egypt, would figure high on his list of locations.
So it was that after his first bite at the cherry of fiction, *Tana-
mera*, written round the fall of Singapore, and *A Farewell to
France*, a self-explanatory title, *A Woman of Cairo*[137] appeared
in 1984, another long book of 600 pages. As he says in his
acknowledgements:

> Though this is a novel, a few real characters flit through its pages,
> and their activities, as told by me, are based on truth, given the
> poetic licence of dialogue . . . I lived in and out of Cairo for several
> years as a foreign correspondent based in the Middle East . . . I was
> a member of the Gezira, which features so often in this book, and
> in those balmy days of long ago when the Egyptians hated Britain
> but still loved the British, an Egyptian friend did me the honour of
> toasting me 'as an honorary Cairene'.

Both Mursi Saad el Din and John Cromer were able to give a few pointers to the author when he was writing the book and both have an affection for it. It is a steamy love story with all the stresses, frustrations, tragedy and ultimate happiness which are the hallmarks of the Noel Barber stories. Cairo is the setting and the sense of place is anchored as securely as are the historical facts which act as a frame round the fictional characters and events. The period covered by the book is from 1919 to 1953, taking the reader through the political events from the arrest of Saad Zaghloul to the presidency of Gamal Abdel Nasser. The wartime period and the overthrow of the King are dealt with in factual newspaper style, particularly the riots which led to the burning of the Turf Club and Shepheard's Hotel.

A flavour of the descriptive parts of the book may be tasted in Barber's account of the reaction the news that Britain had agreed to negotiate a treaty of full independence for Egypt:

> Cairo went mad with joy on the day the news was announced. Three million people jammed the streets – two million of them crowding into the capital by every train, ancient bus, bicycle, felucca, even camel and donkey that could be used as transport. For infants there were makeshift creaking roundabouts made of wood and turned by hand. For the older children picnics on the green of Cairo's squares. Hookahs were passed round as they watched the rope-players, fire-eaters, glass-eaters, even live snake-eaters and other sideshows; the Ghawazi girls [girl dancers] and girls from the cheap brothels near Clot Bey and the fish market did a brisk business; while so, for that matter, did male prostitutes dressed as Ghawazi.

Barber crammed his works with authentic facts and incidents, weaving into them the running torrent of his text with consummate ease. He also had a trick of signalling his punches, dropping a clue in one part of the book to lead to a dénouement later. Thus, having written that Farouk and Narriman were married in Abdin Palace on 6 May 1951 and that within a few weeks of the wedding the King 'had melted down every ounce of wedding-gift gold into more easily disposable ingots', he later describes the preparations for the King's departure from Egypt after his abdication:

> Farouk and Narriman, all pretence of royal dignity forgotten, were engaged in a frenzied attempt to finish their last-minute packing. Every time they came across more personal belongings they found they didn't have enough suitcases. Officials made a dozen trips to

the souk to buy tin trunks. Farouk had the feeling that he might be made to abdicate, and so had taken everything he could lay his hands on to Alexandria – including, of course, the wedding gifts, now in the convenient form of gold ingots which Nasser agreed he could take as they were his personal property.

The Nobel Prize winner, William Golding, admits to a life-long attachment since his schooldays to 'things not so much just Egyptian as Ancient Egyptian'. He did not visit the country until he was past his middle years but when, ten years later, he was asked to write a book on the country, he happily agreed. To his two essays, then, and his novella *The Scorpion God*, he added a fourth work on Egypt, *An Egyptian Journal*,[138] which was published in 1985. It is a return to the traveller's tale approach, a generalised personal diary of everyday events, with its reflections, observations and descriptions of the usual hazards and eccentricities of life aboard a motor boat and its crew of five in a journey from Cairo to Luxor and back. Many of the accompanying photographs are his own, others from more professional hands. Let the writer give his own judgement on his books:

> What I have tried to describe and what these sixty pictures show is a touristic commonplace, the *fact* that Egypt is a land of wonderful beauty. Perhaps I have been able to contribute a rider to that fact – if a fact can have a rider – call it a proposition – that proposition: namely that Egypt suffers from the indifference of its inhabitants to that beauty; and that those with power and influence in the land have missed a golden opportunity of counteracting the drab and dangerous ugliness of its domestic buildings ... In our defended wanderings we have been forced into a deliberate mistake, that of trying to look at everything and having an opinion on everything. Of course the result is that you end with opinions on nothing. It must remain an expanded journal in which I have been able, by consulting my notes, to put back to some extent what I felt and more often what I was thinking ... It was, after all, a kind of challenge to see what would arise in an unusual juxtaposition of two cultures and two wildly differing sets of experience.

From one prizewinner to another. Penelope Lively, born in Cairo in 1933 and living there until the last year of the war, was awarded the Booker Prize for her novel *Moon Tiger*,[139] published in 1987. It was, in fact, the third prize she had won, the Carnegie Medal and the Whitbread Award having been gained from children's books. Once again we are back in wartime Cairo, the book being a flashback in the life of a popular woman historian who is dying in a London hospital and through dreams and conversations with visitors, builds up her story, dwelling particularly on an episodical brief encounter when she was a war correspondent during the Alamein campaign. As the author was a child then, the whole period is imagined, reconstructed and brought to life from what she must have heard and read. Yet it rings true. She catches the spirit of the time:

> You lived from day to day. That, of course, is a banality but it had a prosaic truth to it then. Death was unmentionable and kept at bay with code-words and the careless understated style of the playing fields. Women whose husbands had bought it during the last push were seen a few weeks later being terribly plucky beside the swimming pool at Gezira Sporting Club.

As with most of the writers whose works we have looked at, it is always Cairo, Cairo:

> Cairo, polyglot and multi-racial, both absorbed and ignored what had happened in the desert. At one level the place exploited and manipulated the situation, at another it simply went on doing what it had always done. The rich got richer; the poor continued to wade in the mud of the canals, make fuel out of buffalo dung and beg in the streets.

Then comes the post-war erasure of those days:

> You can no longer climb the Great Pyramid. There is an admonitory sign in English and Arabic: 'Don't climb the Pyramids' . . . Nor are there any house-boats moored on the Nile banks. The egrets no longer roost by the English Bridge and the polo grounds are gone.

The diary at the end of the book has the descriptive matter of the fighting in the desert and the reactions, perhaps of a tired tank commander. But it is somehow improbable. Would it have been written? Could it have been written? It is this kaleidoscope of reality and fantasy which is the essence of the writer who is infected with the waters of the Nile. It runs through the weft and warp of the culture of the Western mind as it becomes bemused by the Middle Eastern dream.

At the beginning of 1988 a first novel appeared in the Collins Crime Club series, written by Michael Pearce, who grew up in the Sudan and returned there later to teach. *The Mamur Zapt and the Return of the Carpet*[140] is an unusual book with an unusual title. The time of the novel is 1908 and the place is, inevitably, Cairo. As the author writes in his forenote:

> Egypt was a country of many potential masters. It had four competing legal systems, three principal languages, and several religions, apart from Islam. It had many, many nationalities. It was a country ripe with ambiguities. A country bright with sunlight and dark with shadows. And in the shadows, among the ambiguities, worked the Mamur Zapt.
>
> In this story I have tried to stay close to fact. The streets were those of Cairo in 1908. The terrorist 'clubs' were a feature of the period too. There really was a national newspaper called *al Liwa* and in 1908 Kitchener's famous screw-gun battery really did accompany the Return of the Carpet. There was even a Mamur Zapt, although perhaps he was not quite like this one.

On the first page we are introduced to the Mamur Zapt of the book, a Welshman and an Army Captain, who is called from his office by the Assistant Commandant of Police, Bimbashi McPhee, to handle a case of attempted assassination. That is the fictional account. In these pages we have met Bimbashi McPherson, who *was* the Mamur Zapt from 1918 to 1920, and Sir Thomas Russell Pasha, who was Assistant Commandant, first of Alexandria and then of the Cairo City Police. These facts give some indication of the source of the novel. The events which weave round the return of the Holy Carpet could be as factual as they are fictional, so tangled were the political webs of the day. The central event, for the benefit of the uninitiated, is described by the author thus:

> The Return of the Holy Carpet was one of the two great processions of the Cairo year. The other was the Departure of the Carpet. The Carpet departed with the annual caravan of pilgrims and returned from Mecca some months later, usually well after the pilgrims had returned, the actual date depending less on position in the religious calendar than on how far behind administrative arrangements had fallen. It also depended on the Desert Tribes between Mecca and the coast, who were still inclined to harass the pilgrimage and had been particularly difficult this year: so much so that the Sirdar had sent an escort of the Fourth Battalion, a troop of cavalry, and two machine-guns, not to mention the famous screw-gun battery which Lord Kitchener had wanted to buy for the Boer War.

The author's description of the Carpet seems to have derived from the texts of Douglas Sladen and Edward Lane.

The Carpet, of course, was not a carpet. It was a piece of tapestry made to go round the Kaaba stone at Mecca. It was of the stiffest possible black silk – black because that was the colour of the Abbasid dynasty – and embroidered heavily with gold. Making it was a hereditary privilege of a certain family, necessarily well-to-do; and a new one had to be made every year, since the Khedive cut up the old one, or the part of it that was returned to him, to present pieces of it to great Mohammedan personages.

It was Lane who said of the procession: 'The Mahmal is borne by a fine tall camel, which is generally indulged with exemption from every kind of labour during the remainder of its life.'

9

Alexandria

Although the subject of this book is Egypt as a whole, it is dominated throughout by the centrality and force of Cairo, which is inevitable once the archaeological importance of Upper Egypt has been removed from the arena. It would not be possible, however, to discuss the influence of the country on writers without devoting one chapter to Alexandria as a city and centre of interest in its own right. As Jasper More wrote in his *Land of Egypt*,[141]

> The astonishing characteristic of Alexandria, occupying the best site in Egypt, is that until modern times it had led a life apart. The Ptolemies were Greeks and the Alexandrians in the main were Hellenes; they had little in common with the mass of Egyptians and led a largely self-contained life, supported obviously by the taxes levied on the Egyptian natives but spiritually and economically living in an almost private world of their own.

This private world becomes more accentuated when we look at the writers. Leaving the classical world aside, it was because E. M. Forster could find no monograph on Alexandria – and his research was deep and wide – that he wrote his own book, *Alexandria: a History and a Guide*[56] which was first published in the city itself, in 1922. Today, when one thinks of Alexandria in terms of writers, two names stand out – E. M. Forster and Lawrence Durrell.

Forster was a great admirer of Alexandria in a way different from Durrell's attitude towards the city. Whereas Durrell looked upon Alexandria as an extension of Greece, and a bad one at that, Forster admired it as a centre of learning and of a civilisation for which he nurtured great feelings. He had a kind and sympathetic attitude towards Alexandria and warm memories, which are reflected not only in this book but in his letters from that city to his friends in England. Mursi Saad el Din remembers talking to him at Leiden University, where the English writer was given an honorary Doctorate, during a PEN Congress presided over by Charles Morgan. Forster said:

> You Egyptians do not appreciate the value of Alexandria. You look upon it simply as a summer resort, beautiful beaches, lovely sea breeze with all the delights of a holiday. This is your Alexandria. But mine is different. It is Alexander the Great; it is the Pharos lighthouse. It is the great Library, which stored the best books in the world and which was the centre of research in all branches of knowledge: language, literature, science, astronomy, art, philosophy, mathematics, geography and medicine. Alexandria exported knowledge to Europe and to the whole world.

Forster's book is in two parts, a history and a guide. In the history section, Forster traces the development of the city from the time of its establishment by Alexander until the present time. In dealing with Alexander, Forster expresses his great admiration for that fine leader. In his own words,

> Few cities have made so magnificent an entry into history as Alexandria. She was founded by Alexander the Great. When he arrived here he was only twenty-five years old. He went to Memphis (near modern Cairo), then he descended the Nile to the coast and ordered his architect Dinocrates to build round the nucleus of Rhakotis, a magnificent Greek city. This was not mere idealism on his part, or rather idealism has happily combined with utility. He needed a capital for his new Egyptian kingdom, and to link it with Macedonia that capital had to be on the coast. Here was the very place – a safe harbour, a perfect climate, fresh water, limestone quarries and easy access to the Nile.

Mark the way Forster talks about Alexandria as a she, and note the style, which only a writer of Forster's calibre can wield, a combination of the descriptive and the literary. This happy combination becomes more noticeable with the development of the book, and it is not only in the history section but in the guide as well, which, written from a practical point of view, is intended for use on the spot, with maps and plans.

But we have to look to Durrell, in his introduction to the 1982 edition, to give Alexandria the particular aura and warmth it deserves:

> [Alexandria] plays, even today, a somewhat unwilling role as a second capital for Egypt, the only relief offered a resident of Cairo – that burning-glass of a city, wedged between deserts. It opens

upon a dreaming sea and its Homeric waves are rolled and unrolled by the fresh breezes from Rhodes and the Aegean. Going ashore in Alexandria is like walking the plank for instantly you feel, not only the plangently Greek city rising before you, but its backcloth of deserts stretching away into the heart of Africa. It is a place for dramatic partings, irrevocable decisions, last thoughts; everyone feels pushed to the extreme, to the end of his bent. People become monks or nuns or voluptuaries or solitaries without a word of warning. As many people simply disappear as overtly die here. The city does nothing. You hear nothing but the noise of the sea and the echoes of an extraordinary history.

That history is meticulously, if succinctly, traced by Forster, and Durrell leaves the detail, to comment on the decline of the city:

> The classical Alexandria is never in question save as an historical echo – how could it be? With the arrival of Amr and his Arab cavalry the famous resplendent city nosedived into oblivion; the sand dunes encroached and covered it. Between Amr and Napoleon stretch nearly a thousand years of silence and neglect. It had been something of an artifact, born of a whim of the boy Alexander who had not stayed to see it actually built, but whose body had been brought back to be buried in the centre of it, thus to become its tutelary god. The despatch Amr sent back to the Caliph of Arabia mentions his conquest of the city with a beautiful succinctness. 'I have taken a city of which I can only say that it contains 4000 palaces, 4000 baths, 400 theatres, 1200 greengrocers and 40,000 Jews'. No trace of this elaborate beauty remained to greet Forster when he stepped ashore in 1915.

Yet, as Jasper More explains:

> For a whole century, from the 1840s to the 1940s, it was the first Egyptian landfall, both for the traveller to Egypt and for the traveller to India. The curiously named 'Overland Route' came into fashion. Disembarking at Alexandria, the Indian traveller would proceed, in early days by canal, later by railway, to Cairo and would then drive in a horse-drawn vehicle across the desert to Suez to take ship for Bombay. All this was made possible by the resurgence of Alexandria and indeed of Egypt by the extraordinary tyrant Mehemet Ali. With the opening of the Suez Canal, Alexandria lost its monopoly. Port Said became a rival port and Indian travellers preferred to do the whole journey by sea. But it is the aeroplane that has almost wiped the city off the tourist map. Travellers to India no longer travel by sea at all and visitors to Egypt land at Cairo airport.

The relationship between Cairo and Alexandria has been well described by Russell Pasha, making the comparison in 1911.

> Alexandria, with its docks, its Bourse and its large cotton industry is the Manchester and commercial centre of Egypt, whereas Cairo has always been the seat of Government. Cairo with its Citadel and magnificent ancient monuments is essentially an oriental city, while Alexandria has little Eastern character or remains of her Hellenic origin, and strikes the newcomer merely as a bustling Levantine port and business centre.

Ronald Storrs made the same point:

> Officially, as well as commercially, Alexandria was nearer to Europe than Cairo; and, remarkably for those old Islamic days, the repos hebdomadaire was kept, both in the city and on the quays, not as elsewhere on Friday, but on the Christian Sunday.

He went on to remark,

> Alexandria is not an obvious city; she requires, before revealing herself, time, study and love. I liked her well, from the Sharia Sharif Pasha, which has something of the brilliant narrowness of Bond Street, to the sinister rowdiness of the Anastassi, the Gumruk Quarter and the Attarin Caracol.

To many people, Lawrence Durrell became identified with Alexandria through his four books, *Justine*,[142] published in 1957, *Balthazar*,[143] 1958, *Mountolive*,[144] 1958 and *Clea*,[145] 1960, collectively known as *The Alexandria Quartet*. Durrell arrived from Greece in Alexandria with his first wife Nancy and small daughter in the spring of 1941 and John Cromer, on security duty, was the first to greet them as they stepped ashore. The family went to Cairo, to stay at the Luna Park Hotel, and Durrell found work writing humorous columns and leaders for the *Egyptian Mail*. In August he was taken on by the British Embassy as Foreign Press Officer and it was not until 1944 that he returned to Alexandria as Press Attaché, mainly on account on his knowledge of Greek and the Greek people, in a city where there were some 300,000 Greeks, with several daily newspapers in their own language and a number of weekly journals. At the time of 'The Flap', Nancy went off to Palestine with her daughter and did not return. A year later, Durrell married an Alexandrian Jewess, Eve Cohen, to whom *Justine* is dedicated. Alexandria lies at the heart of the novel. Durrell himself explained:

When I started, I wanted to set my novel in a purely historical plane, using Alexandria as a foundation, one of the real nerve-centres of our civilisation. And as I went along, through all this ordure, through this orgy, I stumbled on what is perhaps the most interesting part: the pure and dedicated quest for a new asceticism.

Much has been written about these four novels, one of the closest analyses having been made by G. S. Fraser in his book *Lawrence Durrell, A Study,*[146] published in 1969. Durrell's own note, which appeared in *Balthazar*, tells us nothing about the city and as little about the characters. He is concerned with form and tells us:

> Modern literature offers us no Unities, so I have turned to science and am trying to complete a four-decker novel whose form is based on the relativity proposition. Three sides of space and one of time constitute the soup-mix recipe of a continuum. The four novels follow this pattern. The first parts, however, are to be deployed spatially and are not linked in a serial form. They interlap, inter-weave, in a purely spatial relation. Time is stayed. The fourth part alone will represent time and be a true sequel ... This is not Proustian or Joycean method – for they illustrate Bergsonian 'Duration' in my opinion, not 'Space–Time'. The central topic of the book is an investigation of modern love.

Fraser takes us a little further:

> Sensuality and mysticism are the two traditions of Alexandria, and the tension between these polarities defines the city's soul. Between these tensions, Durrell's characters, though they may not be 'dis-crete', are living and real. They can be related less to Freud's theory of the Id than to Groddeck's theory of the It, 'a cosmic process which transcends mind and body', a process of which 'what we call mind and body are interactive functions'. The realm between pure reflection and brute sex could be called the realm of the imagination, and it is in the erotic imagination that Durrell's characters are most alive.

As to the form, Fraser says:

> Perhaps a little too much has been written about Durrell's ideas about time in relation to *The Alexandria Quartet*. The idea that the order in which events should be presented in a narration is not the order in which they occurred but the order in which they acquire significance for the narrator is, of course, not Durrell's invention ... The pattern of the first three members of the quartet is an explor-ation of a given area of space–time in growing depth; in the fourth volume time, within the magnetic area of Alexandria, moves

forward, but is still dominated by what has been explored before, and particularly by two characters who reach their fullness of being for the imagination only in death . . . The sense of eternal recurrence, the turning of the great wheel, is therefore as important in *The Alexandria Quartet* as the space–time continuum idea, the revelation, as in a detective story, of 'what really happened' in successive layers . . . The Quartet constantly, as it were, questions its own status in time: it moves from a level of jumbled chronicle, of the deceptions of perspective and memory, to the timeless level of fable. An extremely sophisticated attitude to time merges into an extremely primitive one, tentative factuality is drowned in real magic: 'Once upon a time . . .' It is this problematicism that gives *The Alexandria Quartet* its real originality. To put it pompously, we move from a radical scepticism and relativism on the level of phenomena to a cosmic mysticism on a level of ontology. Less pompously, Durrell the joker is always there, who likes his little mystifications, who enjoys pulling our legs.

Fraser says much more – about the themes of love, death, art and power – and illustrates his exegesis with vignettes about the characters – but our proper interest here is not Durrell's insight or cleverness but the influence upon him of the city. His Alexandria was a special one. The city is there but it was more the people who preoccupied him. And yet Durrell's characters could live only in Alexandria; their very lives were shaped by the city. The genius of the place played havoc with their lives and their relations with each other. Durrell's Alexandria was harsh, all-engulfing and unsympathetic, at times even devouring. Alexandria's characters suffered from deeply rooted frustrations.

What is of interest is the author's attitude to Alexandria and how the city features in the novels. Also important are the political insinuations which Durrell makes. For instance, the heroine of the Quartet is Justine, Jewish, married to a Copt, Nessim. It is some kind of alliance, a political alliance conspiring against the presence of the British in Egypt and the Middle East, and smuggling arms to Palestine. G. S. Fraser believes that although Justine's relations with Darley and Pursewarden are purely physical, yet they are fundamentally political, with Justine acting as a secret agent. Darley and Pursewarden, with their teaching and writing jobs, are British Embassy intelligence agents, Darley a very minor efficient one and Pursewarden a highly placed one.

Durrell has said that it took him years to evolve *Justine* because he was having to work on so many levels at once:

> history, landscape (which had to be fairly strange to symbolise our civilisation), the weft of occultism and finally the novel about the actual process of writing. What I was trying to achieve was a canvas that was both historic and ordinary; to get that I made use of every modern technique. To my eyes, Proust had exhausted the literary potential of our society; I had to find something else, to turn, for example, to Einstein, or to go back to the origins: The Book of the Dead, Plato, to the occult traditions which are still alive in the East . . . In the Quartet, I drew on all my poetic resources, including word-painting. It's very difficult to construct four novels around one subject. That's why you often find three or four metaphors in one sentence.

Durrell's writings about Egypt reflect a love/hate feeling. It is the same love/hate feeling of his characters. The contradictions which characterise his heroes and heroines are, in his opinion, a reflection of the contradictions of the city itself. The spirit of his Alexandria he could grasp only when he was away from it, having returned to his Hellenic dream of a world. In the isolated village where he lived after leaving Egypt, Durrell ruminated on what had happened in the past and came to the conclusion that it was not they, Justine and Darley, who should be convicted but Alexandria and that they, as its children, should pay the price. The personification of the city reflects the fact that it is Alexandria which is the main hero. G. S. Fraser is also of the opinion that the true heroine of the Quartet is Alexandria. According to him, she manifests herself in many selves, in many roles, but it is in the end the single source, more real, more potent than the various manifestations. 'She hurts,' he says, 'she can kill but she also resurrects.'

D. J. Enright was another Englishman who, like Durrell, wrote about Alexandria, which was to him, also, an extension of Greece. But, unlike Durrell, his Alexandria was not a Greek city but an Egyptian one with a Greek flavour. Enright, as a university lecturer, dealt with Egyptians but he could not help thinking in terms of Greek history. Nothing could be more different than these two poets' treatment of Alexandria and its inhabitants. Enright, like Forster, is more sympathetic, more understanding and more interested in the city and its people than Durrell.

Enright worked in Egypt from 1947 until 1950 and the

country became the setting for his novel *Academic Year*.[147] At that time Egyptian schools and universities had English teachers, a tradition which had started with Robert Graves. These were the last years of King Farouk's regime. The country was astir with indignation and rebellion and in writing his novel, Enright could sense this. In his own words, the time was one of 'a mixture of anarchy and repression, nihilism and nerves, riots and rumours of riots and coups d'état, as well as the more customary students' strikes'. His appreciation of his students' attitude towards these strikes also reflects the affability of Egyptians and their inherent respect for their teachers. When the students decided to go on strike, one of them said to him, 'We all honour you, sir, you are our teacher. But we cannot work today – it is Down with Britain day, if you will excuse it, sir.'

The years 1947–50, when Enright was there, saw the end of the British Mandate in Palestine in 1948 and the foundation of the State of Israel, which resulted in the first Arab-Israeli war. As Anthony Thwaite says in his introduction to the novel, 'It was a time of apprehension and of a different kind of scrutiny from that which Enright had experienced at Cambridge. Farouk's secret police and so-called Moral Police were everywhere.'

Like all novels written by English writers who lived in Egypt, *Academic Year* deals with the lives of Englishmen and English institutions in Egypt. Egyptian characters are secondary and they are there only inasmuch as they have something to do with the main English characters. The central performers are three: Bacon, an oldish lecturer at the University, an Egyptianised pagliacco, as he is described by Enright, an affable and boozy cynic; Packet, a younger lecturer and in some sense the mouthpiece of Enright; and Brett, a young prig newly arrived and employed at the Cultural Centre, presumably the British Council. These three characters (in the words of William Walsh in his book, *Enright: Poet of Humanism*[148] are 'embodiments of the experienced, ardent and intolerant in the English character, and present a kind of English solidarity in the face of the aspiring and impalpable Egyptian sensibility'.

The novel is about the lives of these three characters, their work, their loves and their problems, as well as their attitudes to the city and its people, revealing Enright's feelings about Alexandria and Egypt. Packet is coming back from England after spending his annual holiday there. He was the first to run

down the gangway of the ship that brought him from England,
when it berthed at the Alexandria docks. He asks himself:

> Should he go straight to his flat? No, first of all let him say hello,
> with a new and unexpected appreciation, to Alexandria. Packet
> walked happily up and down, dropping in at the bookshops to
> announce his return, beamed at a student who had given him inordi-
> nate trouble the previous year, scattered a few piastres among the
> familiar beggars and stared appreciatively at the girls in their pretty
> summer frocks – they were all, he felt sure, either past or future
> students of his. And then, in this state of mild intoxication, he
> strolled towards the sea. Home? he asked himself. Well, it would
> do nicely for the time being.

This paragraph, and many others like it, reflects the kind, chari-
table and loving attitude of Enright towards Alexandria and its
people. Even Brian Brett, the newcomer, nurtures good and
kind feelings towards his new city. Walking out of his hotel, he
describes the scene that faces him: 'The air was full of fantastic
good will, the sun forbore to oppress, there was a gentle motion
of warm breath. The streets were pleasantly moist, the little
shops neat and tidy.' All through the novel, Enright shows deep
and genuine understanding of Egypt and things Egyptian, of the
manners and customs and the idiosyncrasies that govern the
lives of Egyptians. This is why his Egyptian characters are real.
In fact in many cases one can discover the actual people he
writes about.

Enright is devastating on the education of the time:

> There was a considerable amount of education in Egypt, of one
> kind and another – English, French, Greek, Italian, Jewish, Moslem,
> Armenian, Berlitz, Fax, Scottish, Swiss, German, American, private,
> public, several kindergarten establishments (one had been closed
> down recently when an unannounced tax inspector had discovered
> a number of rather old girls plying a different trade there), monastic,
> conventual, and of course Egyptian. In addition there was a con-
> siderable amount of plain illiteracy.

Durrell and Enright both had a love–hate relationship with
Alexandria, the latter being more benign for the most part but
also forthright in using his characters to damn the attitudes
which exasperated him.

> The city was a colossal lie. Its very name was an empty pretension
> – and the palatial dollar-studded headquarters of the World Health
> Organization, the King's yacht in the harbour, the scores of

chromium-plated travel agencies, the Greco-Roman Museum (a give-away at the best of times since an insecure roof kept it closed to the public for the past two years), the multiple stores, the fine cuisine of Le Petit Coin de France, and Bacon's farcical university . . . What had held the whole thing together so long? A tacit conspiracy of appeasement on the part of people like Bacon, a conspiracy of pretence, of turning a blind eye and nodding and winking. And what possible compromise could there be between Bacon's taste for poetry and this bestiality in the street? Only shiftiness, quibbling, at the best, a long-term dishonesty.

We have said something already about Laurie Devine's *Nile*, which begins and ends with Alexandria. In 1954, the restaurant/teashop Pastroudis had changed little in the last 50 years.

The soft Persian carpets, the dark wood panelling, and the hazy smoked-glass lighting transformed café into haven. Prosperous Muslim matrons, with their heavy black eye makeup and their stiff lacquered hair, sat plumply squeezed beside their spoiled children. Gray clouds of cigarette smoke hung in dark haloes over the heads of frowning middle-aged Arab men leaning over splayed newspapers. Aging foreign women sat alone at tables for one, their raisin eyes searching the crowd for faces which would never again appear.

Sadly, Alexandria has fallen from grace and although from a distance it may still attract, the real city is in decline. It is even worse today than it was in 1978. As Devine described it:

A sun haze hugged the waterfront. From this far away Alexandria was still jewel-like, with its shining minarets and mosques and steeples. It was only up close that the city was bigger and dirtier and rowdier. There was more and yet less of it. It had increased in quantity but lost in quality . . . Alexandria had been glorious. It had been so easy once to believe that it had been Cleopatra's city. Walking the Corniche used to be like strolling the seaside promenades of the Riviera. But Egypt had reclaimed Alexandria . . . A film of dirt and decay glazed the colonnaded arcades and the consular centres and the sweeping stone squares. In Midan Saad Zaghloul, ragged old men slept on broken marble benches while the wind riffled discarded newspapers. The flat rooftops of ornate Italian Renaissance villas were a jumble of laundry, animal pens, and the date-palm shacks in which the poor lived and died. It would have been more merciful to burn Alexandria to the ground than to let it become like this.

Yet Alexandria, which E. M. Forster guided us through and which Lawrence Durrell saw as an extension of Greece, and which was eclipsed after the creation and flourishing of Cairo, is now getting its second wind. With the initiation of a UNESCO-backed and partly financed project for rebuilding the ancient Library of Alexandria, the city, Egypt's capital under the Ptolemies, is beginning a new phase of recognition. Suffice it to say that when the Library Commission met in Aswan in the winter of 1989–90, it was presided over by President Husny Mubarak of Egypt, with President Mitterrand and some European monarchs as members. They adopted and sent out the Alexandria Appeal for international co-operation and solidarity for the revival of the Library, which, during its existence in ancient times, was known as the Cultural Lighthouse of the World. The revival of the Library means the rebirth of the city which was once the throbbing capital of Egypt.

10

Under Their Own Spell –
Egyptian Writers

In the preceding chapters we have dealt with writers and others who have come to Egypt and fallen under its spell. It would be a grave omission if we were to say nothing of the way the country has been the inspiration of its own literature: the inter-action of East and West has been a two-way process.

Poetry has always appealed to the Arab mind and heart and has a long tradition in Egypt. It preceded the development of prose and is closest to the story-telling which later became the short story. Language has been the base upon which literature is built and Egypt, as with other Arab countries, has had great difficulty in bridging the gap between the spoken and the written word, largely because, as James Aldridge has pointed out, there are three Arabic languages to be found in Egypt, 'classical, modern and colloquial. In general, classical Arabic is the lan-guage of literature, modern Arabic is the language of news-papers, and colloquial Arabic is the language of the uneducated. The uneducated or half-educated Egyptian cannot understand classical Arabic, even when it is spoken.'[55]

It is particularly difficult for poets because the qualities, gram-mar and skill required to handle the art have been moulded into a particular style which became conventionalised as far back as the twelfth and thirteenth centuries. For example, a strict set of comparisons was elaborated then and although this did not last long, other conventions took its place, leaving Egyptian poetry with a deep sense of form.

Abbas Mahmoud El Aqqad is regarded as the founder of the new school of poetry. He was greatly influenced by English literature, especially the Romantics. His interest in English literature was wide and varied and he translated into Arabic Shakespeare's *Venus and Adonis* as well as selections from

Romeo and Juliet, *Othello* and poems of Burns and Cowper. His master of criticism was Hazlitt.

The main innovation in the poetry of this school was in the structure of the poem. They made the poem an organic unity, as it were. The unit of Arabic poetry was the line. A classical poem can be shuffled and re-shuffled without seriously affecting the whole. El Aqqad and his school would produce a complete poem in the Aristotelian sense, that is with a beginning, a middle and an end.

Mahmoud Hassan Ismail belonged to this school. He was very prolific and his theme of the countryside and the open air led to him being known as the 'Wordsworth of Egypt'. His fame spread through the Arab World through his songs, which were sung by many prominent singers. He died in 1977. Other followers of El Aqqad were Ibrahim Abdel Kader el Mazni (also a novelist), Zaki Abu Shadi, Ibrahim Nagui, Aly Mahmoud Taha, Saleh Gawdat, Abdel Rahman Sidky and more besides. It is significant that many of their poems were set to music by leading Egyptian composers, which clearly reflects the lyrical nature of their poetry.

A further development came after the Second World War. This school came under the influence of W. B. Yeats and T. S. Eliot. It was through English writers – many of them university professors – who lived in Egypt during the war and of whom we have already written, that young Egyptian poets, and writers generally, were introduced to these two outstanding modern poets. At the head of the group was Salah Abdel Sabour, who died in 1983. He wrote verse drama and was an expounder of Sufism. Abdel Mooti Hegazi is another poet in this group whose innovation was in breaking away from the basic metres of classical Arabic poetry and writing in free verse. The members of the group did not use rhyme, concentrating instead on internal rhythm. They also used symbolism, not so much the complicated, mythological symbolism of Eliot, but rather a simpler kind, closer to that used by the poets and dramatists of the Celtic Twilight movement.

Here we may quote what Salah Abdel Sabour wrote explaining his and their concept of modernism. It was a revolution in the whole style of life and thinking, as a result of their contacts with Western culture. This modernism parted from the ancestral traditions: 'The old heritage did not reflect the individuality of the poet, while in modern poetry we find that each poet wants to express his own self, to speak from inside himself, as it were.'

Drama, too, was a late innovation in Egypt. The play was unknown in ancient Arabic literature. Egyptian thinkers and philosophers explained this in an interesting manner. The absence of drama from the ancient Arabic literature should not be taken as a sign of backwardness. The Arabs were so proud of their literature that they refused to borrow from Greek drama. They translated treatises from Greek philosophy and science but no other literature than their own was considered to be worthwhile.

It was only after the Second World War that the play became a popular form in Egypt, and many Egyptian novelists now write plays which are performed on stage. The Egyptian theatre is flourishing, both in the public and private sectors. There is a Governmental Theatre Organisation which is responsible for the actual theatres, and this has helped greatly in developing drama.

Until the twentieth century, Egyptian literature had been rooted in the Arabic tradition of story-telling, with the accent on form and beauty rather than on realism. The stories would be told in the villages and in the cafés of crowded Cairo and provincial towns. It needed the overwhelming effect of the European, including Russian, literary cornucopia of the nineteenth century to bring alive a virtually new art to embrace the novel, the short story and drama. It did not find favour with the entrenched literary world. The emerging literature was criticised as being a corruption of the classical Arabic language and form and the ruin of taste and morals of readers, particularly girls and young women.

The country having the most influence initially on writing as distinct from the reading of literature was France, in some measure through the establishment of Napoleon's Institute, and the use of French as the diplomatic language but equally as much because the educated Egyptians tended to be sucked into literary Paris when they went to finish their degree courses. The predominance of the French language in this respect carried through the century, so that today some writers of the Arabic novel may also write in French. It would be difficult to find an Egyptian writer of any standing who has written a novel in English. This, despite the great influence that English writers have exerted and the avidity with which English literature has been studied by Egyptians in colleges and universities. We have to rely on translations to appreciate the nature and content of those novels which have given their authors an international reputation. For it is on the world scene that the true stature of a writer must be measured. The really great are translated into the major languages of the world and even minor writers will earn the accolade of translation into three or four European languages. English, of course, opens up the markets of the British Commonwealth, particularly Australia and Canada, as well as the bookshops and universities of the United States.

It is hardly surprising, therefore, to find that the first Egyptian novels were not written in Egypt but in Europe. The first, in chronological order, was the eponymous *Zeinab*, subtitled 'Scenes and Manners of Egyptian Country Life by an Egyptian Fellah', published in 1914. The author, Mohammed Hassanein Heikal, wrote the book in Switzerland, where he spent his holidays when studying law in Paris immediately before the First World War. Very much in the French romantic style of Alexandre Dumas, the novel pictures the Egyptian countryside in all its seasons and divides its characters into three clearly distinguishable classes: the poor peasants of whom Zeinab and her family form a part; the small farmers who have some land of their own; and the landowners, from which class the author himself came. Nevertheless, he was able to portray, with great accuracy, the life in the fields along the narrow green strip beside the Nile. This pioneering novel set the tone of many to follow – the difficulty of establishing an individualism against the overwhelming pressure of the set social pattern. It remained a lonely trail-blazer, for not until the 1930s was there another novel to challenge it in the hierarchy of Egyptian letters.

Admittedly, there was one book in the 1920s which reflected the idiosyncrasy of the Egyptian poet Beiram el Tunisy but his curious work *Sayed and His Wife in Paris* sprang from the travails of the author. He had been banished to Tunis by King Fuad and thence by the authorities to Paris, where he spent the 1930s as a hack journalist. His book is in the form of dialogues between Sayed and his wife, written in colloquial Cairene Arabic. The traditional Egyptian sense of humour is given a cutting edge by Beiram's own bitterness.

The period between the two World Wars was characterised by the emergence of the struggle between the old traditional legacy and the newly introduced European thought. The question began to impose itself on men of letters and intellectuals: what is the means by which these two cultures can be combined in an organic unity which does not turn its back on the distinct traditional local stamp yet at the same time can fit in with the contemporary world?

To this question there were three kinds of answers coming from three groups of thinkers and based on three styles of writing. One propagated and adhered to the inherited old thought and style. The leader was Mustafa Sadek el Rafei. The second group, represented by its leader Salama Mussa, aimed at eliminating completely the old inherited thought and style and turning to European culture, its science, literature, style of writing and life. The third group tried to find a middle ground, combining the previously mentioned styles. When its advocates wrote, they adhered to the rules of the Arabic language, while embracing a combination of old and new subjects. This group included Mahmoud el Aqqad, Taha Hussein, Hussein Heikel, and Abdel Kader el Mazni. They published articles which were later published in book form. Going through any of these books today, one cannot fail to find Western culture moulded into old Arab culture or the other way round.

For example, one could find a chapter on Homer or Shakespeare, followed by one on Umri El Qais, an old classical poet, El Roumy or El Mutanabby. Taha Hussein was a clear example of this mélange. His method was to combine the two by treating an old subject in a new Western style. One of the best-known Egyptian writers outside his own country, Taha Hussein, as well as being a scholar and writer, became Minister of Education in the early 1950s. Born in 1889, he became blind at the age of six, yet this did not hamper his writing career, which began in the opening years of the twentieth century, as an angry young man turning out heated prose and poetry. In 1914, like many of his predecessors, he left for Paris, where he soon responded to European culture which enabled him to grow in stature and become a leading intellectual when he returned to his own country. This experience convinced him that the future of Egyptian culture, and literature in particular, depended upon its ability to take advantage of European developing ideas and to absorb the Graeco-Roman-French elements.

In 1926 Hussein exploded what one may call a rational intellectual bomb, which nearly landed him in prison. The bomb was in the form of a book on pre-Islamic poetry, in which he compared the style of the Quran with the style that had existed before the emergence of Islam. Taha Hussein can be regarded as a personification of the amalgam of cultural unity and literature. He expounded his theory in a book entitled *The Future of Culture*, published in 1939. In it, he expressed his opinion that it is essential for Egyptians to borrow from Greek cultural origins as a continuation of what their forefathers had done at Alexandria in their intellectual renaissance, when they copied from Greek scientific and philosophical treatises without any embarrassment or hesitation. He was firmly of the opinion that culture was not necessarily embedded in education and that education could only succeed if it was modern, secular and free as 'water and air', to use his own phrase. He propagated these ideas in his university lectures and many writings, not least in his monthly magazine *El Katib el Masri* (The Egyptian Scribe), which was published between 1945 and 1948.

Taha Hussein was the author of some 50 books, many of which have been translated. His acknowledged masterpiece is his autobiography, *El Ayyam* (The Days), written as a trilogy, published first as a monthly serial and in book form in 1932. The first volume, *An Egyptian Childhood*, is remarkable for the way in which Taha Hussein expresses the awareness of a blind person and it is extraordinary that he was able to write about films and plays he had been to without the reader being aware that he was blind. It was a great achievement to overcome this handicap which he referred to as 'the source of wretchedness which would never dry up until the source of my life is spent'.

Another discussion which followed was about Egyptian identity. What are the origins to which Egyptians should resort? Are they ancient Egyptian first and Arab second? A group of intellectuals, including Salama Mussa, Hussein Heikal and others, adopted the concept of the Pharaonic origin. They believed that all the changes that had taken place in Egypt since ancient times separated Egypt from its original Pharaonic roots. A second group answered back, ridiculing that idea and claiming that any effort to go back beyond the Arab period would get one lost in a labyrinth. Among them was Ahmad Hassan el Zayat, who wrote accusing the first group of wanting 'to change the minarets of mosques into obelisks and the mosques and churches into temples and altars and its scientists into high priests'. El Zayat summed up his idea as follows: 'The spiritual aspect of our civilisation and culture is based on Christianity

and Islam, the literary aspect on the Arab and Western literature, the scientific side on Europe. The Papyrus culture has
nothing to tie us up with Arabic, Islamic or Coptic Egypt.'

It was Taha Hussein who was able to strike the balance
between the different arguments. In an article in *El Rissala* (The
Message), in June 1933, he wrote:

> Of what does the spirit of Egypt consist, since it has been Arabised?
> It consists of three origins: the first is the pure Egyptian origin
> inherited from Ancient Egypt; the second is the Arab origin, which
> comes to us from the language, religion and civilisation; the third
> is the foreign origin which has always influenced Egyptian life and
> will always influence it. It is obtained through Egypt's constant
> contacts with the civilised nations of East and West. In ancient
> times it was obtained from the Greeks, the Romans, the Jews and
> the Phoenicians; in the Middle Ages it was obtained from the Arabs,
> the Turks and the Franks. In modern times it is obtained from
> Europe and America.

One of the many lawyers who became writers was Tewfik el
Hakim, who was born in Alexandria in 1898 and died in Cairo
in 1987. After studying law in Cairo, he, too, went to Paris to
continue his studies for his doctorate, which he never achieved.
He seems to have spent much of his time in and around the
Odeon Theatre, Montparnasse and the Latin Quarter, while
steeping himself in the works of Ibsen, Shaw and Pirandello.
He wrote his first novel, *Audat el Roh* (Resurrection), in 1927
but it was not published until 1933 and has not yet been translated into English. He dedicated his book to Saad Zaghloul and
it was an immediate success. The character Mohsen barely
disguises Hakim himself and the novel struck a chord in Egypt
because, as in *Zeinab*, but in a very different way, it asserted
an individuality by stressing the national character of the
country which had come through the 1919 Revolution. In this
novel, the myth of Isis and Osiris is evoked and used as a
symbol. Isis collecting the scattered parts of Osiris, until she
restored his body and soul, is Egypt through the ages. Someone
would tear her to pieces, but not for long. It only needs a leader
to come from among the people, rise to power, collect the
dismembered parts and make of them an integrated nation, full
of all that motivates life.

The character Mohsen appears again in *Asfour Men el Shark*,
which was published in 1938 and in 1966 in an English translation as *A Bird from the East*. The Odeon Theatre comes into

the novel, for it is the girl in the box-office with whom the Egyptian falls in love, watching her from his usual café across the street. The East–West cross-fertilisation of cultures comes across very clearly in this important novel.

In between these two books, Tewfik el Hakim had used his professional experience as a provincial public prosecutor, or District Attorney, to write *The Maze of Justice*, published in 1937 and translated into French and Spanish and into English in 1947 by another lawyer, Abba Eban, who was for a time Foreign Minister of Israel. Like all novels dealing with law courts in all countries, this one shows up the seedy side of life, particularly as lived in the villages and small towns.

Hakim left novel-writing for what was really his true love, the theatre. His dialogue, which is a feature of his novels, became sharper and more sparkling as he perfected his technique in scores of plays, ranging from social studies of Shavian proportions to his contribution to the Theatre of the Absurd, *The Tree-Climber*, written in 1962 and translated into English in 1966. His range was even wider, as exemplified by his earlier works, *The People of Cairo*, based on the Quranic version of the Christian Seven Sleepers of Ephesus, and *Sheherazade*, written in 1933 and 1934 respectively. His debt to Pirandello was acknowledged in 1963 with *Food for Every Mouth* and in 1967 his play *The Bank of Anxiety* reflected the political turbulence of Egypt in the 1960s. His enthusiasm for the new republic of the 1950s waned in the 1960s and by the early 1970s his criticism of the regime came to a head in a book published in 1974, *Audet el Waei* (Return of Consciousness), which brought angry responses from the ruling socialist politicians and also from Islamic fundamentalists.

Ibrahim Abdel el Kader el Mazni was another who took off in the 1930s with his first novel *Ibrahim el Katib*, which was published in 1931. His inspiration came from the Russian school but was firmly grounded in the Egyptian scene. The novel was a personal translation of the writer's life, analysing the phenomenon of love between a man and a woman. He died in 1949. *Sarra* by Abbas Mahmoud El Aqqad, published in 1938, also deals with love, and one wonders whether this preoccupation was due to the emancipation of women. These novels can be regarded as a response to the call of Kassem Amin, the great male supporter of Feminism, for women's emancipation.

Another contemporary was Mahmoud Taymour, who established himself about the same time as a strong writer of novels and short stories. His brother, Mohammed Taymour, had preceded Tewfik el Hakim to Paris and, like him, had failed to obtain his doctorate, having been seduced by the theatre. He returned to Cairo to act at the Opera House and to write libretti for the composer Sayyid Darwish, but tragically died while still a young man. To return to Mahmoud, he lived into his eighties and was the first Egyptian writer to have his works translated into English. A collection of his short stories was translated by Denys Johnson-Davies under the title *Tales from Egyptian Life*, with an introduction by Abdel Rahman Azzam Pasha, the then Secretary-General of the Arab League.

Although Egyptian writers, like their European counterparts, have been mostly city dwellers of middle-class background, all have become adept at evoking the spirit and earthiness of the countryside when they have chosen to depict characters who are rooted in the soil. This was certainly so with Abdel Rahman el Sharkawi and Youssef Idris, who, although they were born in the country, were educated at school and university in Cairo. The former, born in 1920, studied law and the latter, born seven years later, studied medicine. Sharkawi's first novel was published in Arabic in 1954 and, as *Egyptian Earth*, in English in 1962. It has been described by Fatma Mussa[149] as 'probably the first specimen we have of the "Socialist novel" in the true sense . . . it tells of a rural crisis unprecedented in Egyptian fiction, of the struggle of little people for their living . . . and ends by being tied up with a nationwide action against an oppressive government'. The significance of the book was the emergence of the fellah as a real person, working under difficult conditions, replacing the more romantic picture painted by earlier novelists. The landless peasant spoke up for himself as the Revolution produced widespread agrarian reform.

The theme was developed in *The Fellah*, published in 1967, in which the struggle develops between the peasants, who now have some land, and the survivors of the old regime who try to cheat them out of their rights by taking control of the new co-operative society. The works of Sharkawi reflect his socialist zeal and repeated warnings to the people against attempts to filch from them their newly-won rights. He died in Cairo in 1987.

Youssef Idris turned his Delta background and ward training

to good account, entering literary life through the medium of short stories, his first collection, *Cheap Pastime*, being published in 1954. His first novel *El Haram* (The Sin), was published in 1958 and has much the same motivation and country background as Sharkawi's first novel, although the story is, of course, different. The diverse characters come very much to life. It was one of his plays, *El Ghafeer* (The Overseer), that created great interest in 1966 when it started a new direction in the Egyptian theatre, a seriousness tinged with irony. In this play, Idris highlighted the character who would always tell someone else what to do, taking the credit if it turned out well but blaming others if things went wrong.

Some remarks made by Idris in his contribution to the book of excerpts from the interviews filmed for the documentary *The Year of Maya*[150] to celebrate the 50th anniversary of the British Council in Egypt, give an accurate insight into the relationship between Egyptians and the British, as depicted by Mursi in our opening chapter:

> I began joining the demonstrations against the British in '46 and '47 . . . in the mornings until 2 or 3 o'clock when everything was finished and then I would go in the afternoons to the British Council to learn English and see British films . . . When I started taking writing seriously, I read nearly all the classical English literature. I read the Irish writers, Indian writers, Australian writers and American writers, but it was English literature all the time. I read it all.

He went on to make a very profound remark:

> The first world is very rich in technology, in industry, in chemicals, in know-how, and all kinds of things that we lack in the third world. But here we have a surplus of imagination. We are going through the same experiences that produced the great artists in Europe in mediaeval times and at the beginning of the Renaissance.

This is as significant an observation, and an exciting foretaste of things to come as his next remarks:

> If I were from a European country, England in particular, I would be very keen on translating this kind of imagination into English, not for us to become international writers, we do not care about that, but for English writers to be exposed to other imaginations. I think the same thing happened with French and British culture when Dostoievsky, Chekhov and Tolstoy were translated. They enriched European culture very much.

The idea of exposure to other imaginations goes to the root

of the international exchange of national literature through translation, and since the learning of many languages to enable readers to read original texts is very far off, we should look forward to increasing numbers of translated versions of Egyptian novels becoming available throughout the world.

In reverse, is there a danger of the deep-rooted and rich culture of the country being eroded and eventually replaced by the bland anonymity of modern techniques and way of life? Idris had his answer:

> I don't think there is any contradiction between modernity and retaining the authenticity of our culture. Importing culture will not stop us from producing original culture because culture is not a disease. It is health; and importing another culture means that we will become healthier. It means that we will get the vitamins of other cultures . . . Let us be invaded by culture. Let us be infected by culture because then we will produce our own culture on a healthier and more stable basis. I am not afraid of culture at all.

It seems almost as if this was a challenge both to Egyptian writers and to the world. Was Idris aware when he made it of the honour about to be bestowed on Egypt's outstanding novelist, Neguib Mahfouz? Probably not, but in 1988 the Nobel Prize for Literature was awarded to him, the first Egyptian and the first writer in Arabic to win the award in its 87 years of existence. Born in Cairo in 1912, he has 35 novels, 20 collections of short stories, over 30 film scripts and plays to his credit and he shows few signs of exhaustion, although there have been times when he has been silent. With a degree in philosophy from Cairo University, he turned to writing, beginning with an historical romance about the ancient Egyptians which sprang from an exercise in English translation of James Baikie's *Ancient Egypt*, done while he was still an undergraduate. This was published in 1939. The same Pharaonic period provided the background for his next two novels, *Radopis*, published in 1943, and *Theban Struggle*, a year later. Already, despite the setting, the disillusionment of the Egyptian people with their lot was being displayed both in their relations with their monarch and their oppressors (the Hyksos being a thinly veiled reference to the British).

Throughout his literary career, he has been a civil servant, working in the cultural section of the Egyptian Government from 1934 until his retirement in 1971. In all that time he has lived a café life, listening as a boy to the poets declaiming their folk epics in the Gamaliyeh district of Cairo, now replaced by radio and television, and consorting with intellectuals in his later years. He has likened the café life to the French literary salons of the nineteenth century. It was this densely populated, teeming alley world of craftsmen and small traders that inspired him to change his style from the quasi-historical novel to the social realism which has become his hallmark, in the Western tradition of Dickens and Balzac. Between 1945 and 1949 five works appeared, depicting the grinding poverty and the daily frustrations of the life of the lower middle classes in Cairo in the immediate pre-war and wartime years of the 1940s.

These books are self-descriptive. *Modern Cairo* needs no elaboration. The second, *Khan el Khalili*, was the first of the 'alley' novels and marks the clash of cultures, tradition and progress which was biting deep into Egyptian life, seething beneath foreign occupation in a period of a war being fought around the country, which had no way then of determining its own fate. It was the next novel, published in 1948 under the title *Zuqaq el Middaq*, which brought Mahfouz the popular acclaim which has grown steadily ever since.

'Zuqaq' is the Arabic for 'blind alley', a term of double meaning, as exemplified at the outset of the novel where an electrician is installing a second-hand radio set in a café, thereby putting out of business the blind old bard who had been used to reciting his epics there. Blindness persists in the alley, which provides a sort of cocoon around the inhabitants, sheltering them from the outside world. The other novels were *The Mirage* and *Bedaya wa Nehaya*, published in English by the American University in Cairo Press in 1985 and by Doubleday as a paperback in 1989.

The further significance of these 'alley' novels is that Mahfouz established a new language, the traditional literary Arabic form having no place in the realistic settings. The use of idiomatic dialogue was an innovation and the author himself has said that the problem of language arose not only in the dialogue but also in the narrative itself. It had to take 'its inspiration and tone from the place, time and the people. I found, without even planning or thinking about it, that language must change to suit the theme.'

Another change of theme came with Mahfouz's 1,500-page *Trilogy*, published in the years 1951 to 1957 and cited by the

Nobel jury as his most outstanding work. It is largely autobiographical and the author has said that it was written before the Revolution of 1952 but left fallow as it could not have been published under the old regime. It carries in it the very essence of Egyptian life as lived in the old Islamic part of Cairo, and covers three generations of a family from 1917 to 1954, reflecting the impact on individual lives of a period in which there were a number of political upheavals. Part One of the trilogy is *Bein el Kasrein*, establishing the family of Sayyed Ahmed Abd el Gawad, a merchant who rules his family with a rod of iron. The action is carried through the 1919 Revolution and through the Zaghloul period. The second part, *Kasr el Shauq*, goes through the second generation, the central character being Kamal who, with his contemporaries, is dissatisfied with postrevolutionary Egypt but does nothing, his socialist politics being diffused in the philosophy which, as he is a teacher, keeps him apart from the rough and tumble of the ferment around him. Part Three, *El Sukkariyya*, brings in the third generation, represented by Kamal's firebrand nephews, one a Socialist, the other a member of the Moslem Brotherhood. The end of the trilogy comes with the death of the patriarch and the end of an era, with the curtain about to rise on a new phase of Egyptian history and the end of the old feudalism.

Mahfouz then felt that he had little more to say. The main targets of his criticism had been removed. Then, with *The Children of Gebelawi* came a new phase and a new direction. As he records it:

> I felt a new urge bringing me back to literature and a new form, not based on reality but as symbols blended with reality. I had first to find a suitable place for it and the place where I feel comfortable is in the alley. This place represents the world, which is larger than any alley so you have to have a kind of unreal or completely imagined alley.

The book is allegorical, a search for spiritual values, showing humanity trying to regain an earthly Paradise, believed by the children of the alley to be their true inheritance. As the 'children' included Mohammed, Jesus and Moses, the book created an uproar in strict Islamic circles. It was promptly banned by the authorities of el Azhar and can be obtained in Egypt only in a pirated Lebanese edition. Mahfouz claims that he has been misunderstood:

The objections made against the book were comical; they were all the result of misinterpretation. Our men of religion do not usually read novels, so when they are faced with an allegory, they do not understand it. It is ridiculous for them to think that Mohammed would be described as smoking hashish. It was all a problem of misinterpretation.

In 1960 a serial by Mahfouz in the newspaper *El Ahram* was published as a short novel, *El Liss wal Kelab* (The Thief and the Dogs), changing his technique yet again. With this and six short novels which were published in the following seven years, he rejected realism and the usual wealth of background detail in favour of symbolism, leading into a changed method of narration, including stream of consciousness and a new range of imagery.

In 1961 Mahfouz shifted his locale from Cairo to Alexandria in his novel *Autumn Quail*, the trapped birds symbolising the life of a man trapped by circumstance and politics, ending, as the birds do, in out-of-season Alexandria. The theme carries into *Pension Miramar*, which has been described as the Egyptian *Alexandria Quartet*, the story being told through four separate characters much as Lawrence Durrell's Quartet did. John Fowles has written that in this work, Mahfouz allows us 'the rare privilege of entering a national psychology in a way thousands of journalistic articles or television documentaries could not achieve'.

The latest novel of Mahfouz, *Talk of the Morning and the Evening*, returns to the theme of the family but, 30 years later than the Trilogy, shows it in a state of breakdown. The close-knit ties of and within the alley have been broken and morality has taken on a new meaning. Individualism and opportunism have replaced the family ethos and loyalty. Mahfouz has become disillusioned at so-called progress. He says: 'We are leading a sick life and we are hoping for a cure.' Where does this cure lie? Political Socialism points in one direction, religious fundamentalism in another.

Let Mahfouz have the last word on where he stands today:

I have a strong desire to write but there is no theme or situation to make me write. There is nothing to inspire me. All the themes that occur to me I find unconvincing. I once read in a doctoral thesis that I flourish for seven years and dwindle for seven years. I don't know how he calculated this but I hope that I am not at the beginning of a lean seven years.

In 1989 three English translations of the works of Mahfouz appeared as paperbacks. Mursi himself has collaborated with John Rodenbeck in editing and revising *Wedding Song*;[151] John Rodenbeck has revised *The Thief and the Dogs*;[152] and Mason Rossiter Smith has edited *The Beginning and the End*[153]. *Palace Walk* is the first volume of the *Cairo Trilogy* to appear in English, as a hardback, in 1990.[154] We look forward to the remainder of the trilogy in English and hope that this burst of activity is merely the forerunner of a continuing stream of Egyptian novels being made available to Western eyes in translation.

Perhaps one of the aspects of the Egyptian spell is the production of literary quartets. Yet another, *The Man Who Lost His Shadow*, was written by Fathi Ghanem, originally a short-story writer and editor of the weekly magazine *Sabah el Kheir*, in which his Quartet was published serially before appearing in book form between 1960 and 1962. As the first parts of Durrell's *Alexandria Quartet* were already on sale in Cairo, Fathi Ghanem had to point out that his own work was not imitative but had been in his mind for some time. Indeed, he had postponed reading Durrell's book until he had finished his own. The technique is, however, similar, with soliloquies by two men and two women weaving the narrative in their own way, taking events from the mid-1930s to the dénouement of the Cairo conflagration of 1952. The Quartet is of particular interest because it contains what is probably the first example of stream of consciousness writing in Arabic fiction.

Once again the alley theme surfaces, this time against the background of Alexandria, in the work of Saleh Mursi, another short-story writer whose *Zuqaq el Sayed el Bolti* (Bolti Alley) was published in 1963. Bolti, an Egyptian fish, is a cul-de-sac near the harbour where the fishermen live. The book bears all the authenticity of seamen's lives, as indeed it should, as Saleh Mursi spent seven years in the Egyptian Merchant Service.

He went on to become one of Egypt's leading novelists and short-story writers. He is the first, and possibly the only, Egyptian writer who has written espionage novels, based on actual files supplied by the Department of General Intelligence. His TV serial (over 60 episodes) *Raafat el Haggan*, deals with an Egyptian spy who was planted as a mole inside Israel, and his long life and relations with Israel (he was never unmasked), and his business life there and in Germany. It is now the most popular serial on Egyptian TV.

Among the later generation of writers, Gamal el Ghitani has also used the alleys for his locale, very much influenced by Mahfouz. Having lived for over 30 years in the crowded quarter which forms so much a part of 'alley' writing, in his *Treatise on the Fates of People*, published in 1969, he deals with the Sadat era and shows that the frustration and corruption which runs through the history of life as depicted in the Egyptian novel continued to grip the imagination of writers.

It may be that the changes wrought during this period have been sufficient to break down the old alley life and open its frontiers to the outside world and technological innovation. It is no longer possible to live a cul-de-sac existence when the pace of the world has accelerated and caught up even the most backward areas. Values have changed, family life has ceased to be patriarchal, morals have declined. East and West have become closer within the concept of One World.

Youssef el Sebai, who died in 1978, like Ihsan Abdel Kuddus, represents the Romantic movement in narrative. An ex-cavalry officer, the son of Mohammed el Sebai, also a writer, he became one of Egypt's leading novelists, most of his novels being made into films. He may be regarded as the Revolution's leading writer, giving it a humane character. His masterpiece, also made into a film, was *Rud Qalbi* (Give Me Back My Heart), a love story between the daughter of an aristocrat (an enemy of the Revolution, as they were called) and one of the free officers who started the Revolution. It is knee-deep in romanticism, and, at times, sentimentality.

El Sebai, being close to the military leadership, was able to render great services to writers. He established 'The High Council of Arts and Literature' in 1954, the Writers' Union and the Story Club, and managed to have writers and artists represented in all delegations to international conferences. When he became Minister of Culture, there was a real flourishing of the arts and literature. He signed many cultural agreements with other countries which resulted in the exchange of writers, theatrical troupes, musical ensembles and orchestras, such as the Royal Ballet London, Bolshoi and so on. During his leadership of the High Council of Arts and the Ministry of Culture there was a big expansion of translations, both from foreign languages into Arabic and vice versa.

Ihsan Abdel Kuddus is one of the most controversial writers. He was always criticised, at times attacked, by literary critics and even religious figures, yet his novels sold more than any other writer, apart from Youssef el Sebai. Both he and Sebai can be regarded as the leaders of the Romantics. Both were very popular, especially among the young, who constituted the majority of, if not all their readers.

Ihsan was born in an artistic family, his father being one of the leading actors in Egypt. But it was his mother, Ros el Yussuf, who gained greater fame. A successful actress herself, she started the most influential political magazine in the history of the Egyptian Press, *Ros el Yussuf*, after her own name. The magazine became the channel for the most vehement attack against corrupt governments. It was also a school which produced some of Egypt's most successful writers and cartoonists. Eventually Ihsan became the editor-in-chief of the magazine and his political articles fired the minds of the young. In fact, in many ways, he was behind the 1952 Revolution. When the young officers were planning their coup, Ihsan was taken into their confidence.

Yet, in spite of his lashing political pen, he wrote the most romantic, almost sentimental novels. Love was the main theme but always with more than a touch of politics. His heroes are famous journalists, well-known politicians, as well as artists, dancers, actresses. Both he and Sebai almost monopolised the film industry. It could be said that over 50 per cent of Egyptian films are either based on their novels or specially written for the cinema. Ihsan had a unique ability for expressing the emotions of women in a way that can be the envy of women writers. His delineation of the innermost thoughts of women is quite remarkable. It is regrettable that none of his works has been translated into English. Ihsan died in 1989 and his funeral became a popular demonstration.

Louis Awad, the Copt writer who died in 1990 as this book was going to press, was a great admirer and translator of European literature. Having studied English at Cairo University, where he won scholarships to Cambridge and Princeton, he was appointed in 1940 to the English Department of Cairo, the first Egyptian with a British degree to hold such a post. He it was who introduced the tutorial system to the University.

Mursi has referred to the influence on modern Arabic poetry of the poems of T. S. Elliot which was largely due to Awad who first brought them into the syllabus. His own collection,

Plutoland and other Poems, published in 1947, startled the Arabic literary world by its introduction which called for a change from traditional metrical form.

Although he was expelled from the University in 1954 for his anti-Nasser views, he returned after a term of imprisonment and in the 1960s published a number of literary studies and critical works, among which were *Studies: Arab and Western, The Revolution and Literature* and his two-volume *History of Modern Egyptian Thought*.

Awad's academic career was followed by one in journalism, first as literary editor of *El-Gumhuriyya*, then as an established writer with *El Ahram*. He not only studied, taught and wrote about English literature but also wrote in the language; one of his later works, *The Literature of Ideas in Egypt: Selection, Translations and Introductions*, was published in Atlanta, USA in 1986. Among his many translations into Arabic perhaps his greatest was that of *Prometheus Unbound*. His free-ranging mind and desire for liberation from strict classical rules resulted in a remarkable review of the Arabic language, *Memoirs of a Student Mission Member* which he wrote in colloquial Egyptian.

There has been a significant gap in this review of Egyptian writing: no mention of women writers. Yet the development of the novel itself has not failed to reflect the changing nature of society. Women have always been avid readers and have, by their own emancipation, however slow it may have been, ensured that their total role has been understood and interpreted by male writers. This evolution has been traced by Fatma Mussa in her book (developed from a series of radio talks) *The Arabic Novel in Egypt*.[149] She points out that female characters have been historically depicted in their usual roles of mothers, daughters, sisters and so on but that the greatest interest lies in the character of sweetheart or love-object, ranging from the victim of social customs and parental tyranny to the early novels to the idealised female as depicted by Tewfik el Hakim.

It is Mahfouz, once again, who has brought into his female characters the same realism as he applies throughout his major works. He reflects the changing place of women in Egyptian society and in the last part of his Trilogy, 'he presents for the first time an idealised image of the new woman, Sawson . . . she is handsome, modest and independent. Her marriage is based on a free understanding between equal partners.' His later novels sketch out other girls living independent lives, although they are not developed in depth.

Youssef Idris, too, has written female characters into his books, depicting them as bread-winners and taking their proper place, doing a man's job in a man's world, even if he does not wholly succeed in *The Taboo*, published in 1962, in fully satisfying the demands put upon him as a novelist.

Fatma Mussa makes the point that most of the activity of women writers has, in the past, been devoted to journalism and feminist propaganda, working towards legislative reform of their social and marital position. The militancy and single-mindedness that such a struggle requires does not fit easily into the role of the creative artist and, as with their European counterparts, Egyptian women were more successful in earlier days with poetry and short stories. The segregated society of the Arab World has not been conducive to women writers, an outstanding exception being the literary Cairo home of the Taymour family. Ahmed Taymour Pasha encouraged his two sons, Mohammed and Mahmoud, in their literary and dramatic careers and his sister Aisha Taymouria, who lived from 1840 to 1902, was the only female poet of any note to appear in the nineteenth century.

The twentieth century has produced women writers who have carried on the tradition of poetry and essays but have come late to the short story and the novel. Outstanding among them have been two writers with the same surname but who were not close relations. Both progressed through the study of European literature, Latifa el Zayat at the Department of English, Cairo University, and Enayat el Zayat in a German Convent School in Cairo. Latifa's *Open Door*, published in 1960, equates the struggle of a middle-class girl to live her own life with the national struggle for freedom during the period 1946–57. Enayat's novel, *Love and Silence*, was published seven years later and is more poetic in form. Fatma Mussa relates, with some sadness, that Latifa el Zayat produced no second novel and that Enayat could not because she committed suicide.

Somehow, poetry seems to come more easily to Egyptian women writers than prose, or narrative to be more correct, since there are many women in journalism. Among the well-known women poets one can mention Rawhiya el Quilliny, Malak Abdel Aziz and Sherrifa Fathi. There are, however, those who have made names for themselves in prose, some as literary critics and historians, such as Dr Soheir el Qalamawy, Professor of Arabic Literature at Cairo University and author of a comprehensive study on the Arabian Nights. She has also contributed what may be described as a novelette, *Tales of My Grandmother*.

Some female writers have distinguished themselves as TV and film authors; among them are Sekkina Fuad, Editor-in-Chief of *Radio & TV Magazine*, Sanaa el Bissy, Editor-in-Chief of *Nuss el Donya* (Half the World), a women's magazine, and Hosn Shah, Editor-in-Chief of *El Kawakeb*, a film and theatre magazine. All these, and a few others, have enriched the cinema and TV with dramatic serials and films which dealt mainly with women's problems of living in a society which is mainly a male prejudiced one.

But while the writings of these few are moderate and low key, as it were, one woman writer stands out as almost violent, outspoken and rebellious. Nawal el Saadawi, a medical doctor who decided to write at the expense of her medical practice, deserves a special and separate mention. Nawal's fame, one may even say notoriety, stems from her rather unorthodox, and to religious leaders, shocking ideas regarding women's rights. This is not the place to discuss her demands, which she crystallised in her movement 'Arab Women's Solidarity Association'. The adjective 'Arab' is cleverly chosen since, having exhausted the demands of Egyptian women, she is now embracing the cause of women in many Arab countries who still live under a system of slavery and concubinage.

Because of her liberal, rather revolutionary ideas, Nawal el Saadawi is the most translated of women authors (possibly the only one) into foreign languages. She is certainly one of the most translated Egyptian authors, male or female. She is probably better known in the West through her translations than she is at home.

It will surely not be long before new Egyptian women writers emerge on to the world stage. Will there be a Nobel Prize winner among them?

Epilogue

We have sought to illustrate the strength of the effect of Egypt on Western culture, particularly on the literature of the English language. We have been concerned not with linguistic matters or questions of style but with the influence of the country itself on the people who have gone there, tasted of its joys and been inspired to write through the very magic of the country itself.

In turn, we have tried to show how Egypt, too, has responded to the many foreign influences to which it has been subjected, but particularly to Western culture. All through its long and rich history, Egypt has been subjected to one foreign invasion after another but it has never succumbed to the invaders' cultures. It may have extracted certain formulae in one field or another, but never at the expense of its national cultural sovereignty.

Culture is a system of communal perception. It is not simply the ability to read and write. Prophets were mostly unlettered but they were leaders in the cultural field. When considering cultural influences, we must distinguish between three strains: intermarriage, continuity and compromise. Some nations simply refuse any outside influences; they follow an isolationist and separatist policy which discards any cultural interplay. Egypt was never so. It has always been ready to learn from others and has ever received outside culture with open arms.

Whether in ancient Pharaonic times or during its Arab phase, Egypt has manifested great tolerance and understanding. Within the country itself, there has never been what can be termed any ghetto culture. Egyptian culture has always belonged to all Egyptians. If we look at Arab history, in which Egypt has played a major role, we find that right from the Umayyad dynasty, Arab savants embarked on a thorough study of Persian and Greek philosophy and expertise, quaffing from their rich sources and adopting some of the components of their culture, and formulating a mesh of 'civilised culture'.

What has characterised Egypt's attitude is its refusal to accept anything at its face value. It is only after examination and analysis that foreign tenets are embraced. In many cases, foreign influences have been subjected to a process of comprehensive reformulation. Egypt experienced the first kind of cultural exchange – intermarriage – which resulted in the evolution of new rich patterns of diverse sources, French and English in particular, its own culture being continually renewed at the same time. It has not been a matter of imitation or placid reception of other cultures, but a new creation.

The second kind of cultural influence – continuity – accepts foreign patterns without trying to build up something new. So, too, in many cases, Egyptian writers and artists adopted certain foreign forms of expression. The novel form, for instance, was taken from Europe, but the content has always been purely Egyptian. The same thing happened in the field of literary criticism, where we find T. S. Eliot's and I. A. Richards' canons of criticism applied by Egyptian critics. The process has always been one of enquiring into the basis of culture in Egypt and there have always been many schools of thought in this respect. Some have called for a return to old Islamic and Arab origins, some have fought for a complete adoption of European culture, while a third school, that of Dr Taha Hussein and Tewfik el Hakim, proclaimed an intermarriage between ancient Arab culture and European influence, as their writings reflect.

The third kind of cultural influence comes from compromise. Relations between countries should be based on give and take; they should not be a one-way flow but a reciprocal one. There should be no fear of the so-called cultural invasion if the local, national culture is strong and deeply rooted. Egypt does not search for a cultural identity; it seeks to assert its already existing one. But national culture cannot exist in a void. Egyptian culture, in spite of the many influences it has been subjected to, was never interrupted or trodden down by others at any juncture of its history.

Cultural consciousness is no longer individualistic. In our modern age, culture has become in its essence an expression of a relation of sharing and participation in human society at large. It is not enough to believe in one's national culture and heritage; others must, likewise, believe in it and trust its human and historical function. The exchange of culture has been accelerated by the incredible development of communication. We no longer travel to culture, culture arrives on our doorstep, indeed in our sitting room. Armchair travelling has replaced the actual journeying and TV and video have become the traveller's guides. Great plays, concerts, ballet, opera and other artistic manifestations are now available through the mere pressing of a button.

It may be that the pace of all this change has brought us to a new era, through the technological revolution, and that all we have set down in this book will soon be as far distant as the life depicted in Egypt's own hieroglyphs. Whether that be so or not, we feel that this chronicle of a period of cultural interchange has some place in a passing world. Books continue to be written about the fascinating country of Egypt. Reminiscence and nostalgia are being supplanted by historico-journalism which paints a second-hand gloss on the characters and events of half a century ago, while the mysteries of the Pharaonic days tempt writers into imaginative re-creation of a world which is lost in the mists of time. As long as Egypt exists, its spell will remain, a source of inspiration and excitement. Whatever the future may bring, it cannot wholly break the hold of Egypt's spell as we have traced it through the centuries.

Appendix
Art and Architecture

For the most part, nineteenth-century travellers showed little interest in Islamic architecture, their attention being riveted on the antiquities. Lady Duff Gordon wrote that, 'No one has said a tenth part of the beauty of Arab architecture.' Florence Nightingale had her own views: 'In all Egyptian buildings you are no less struck by this – they seem to have thought nothing about effect; their buildings are hardly meant to look at from the outside.' And in another letter: 'The mosques of Cairo are the most beautiful, the most gorgeous, the fairest in the world – those of Constantinople are barns in comparison.'

The earliest examples of painting and drawing by visitors were, perhaps, the engraved illustrations in the books of members of the short-lived Egyptian Society, which were not very good quality, the most accurate being the somewhat military representations done by Frederick Norden. Most of the eighteenth-century travellers from Britain preferred to have the country depicted by Italian, French or German artists who were thought to be better at it. Indeed, the first professional British artist to visit Egypt was Richard Dalton, who went there with Lord Charlemont in 1749, 12 of his watercolours being still in the Royal Collection. Dalton's watercolours were mainly of local people, dancing girls and the like, but for the greater part of the eighteenth century artists concentrated more on the tombs and temples, as exemplified in the work of Willey Reveley, who accompanied Sir Richard Worsley on his visits during the 1780s.

James Bruce was more traveller and adventurer than artist but his copies (probably aided by his companion, the Italian artist Luigi Balugani) of the wall paintings of harpists from the tomb of Ramses III, link him into his place in history as the first European to publish a description of the tomb, which he visited in 1768. The most distinguished painter of the eighteenth century to use an Egyptian theme was William Hogarth, whose oil painting of 'Moses and the Daughter of Pharaoh' was done for the Foundling Hospital in Coram's Fields, London.

The defeat of Napoleon in Egypt gave rise to a number of artistic works, the battle of the Nile itself being depicted in four separate stages by Francis Chesham, aquatints of which, by William Ellis, were published in 1899. The caricaturist Gillray made Napoleon the butt of his biting wit and the etchings in the British Museum portray various aspects of the discomfiture of the French. A painter in the grand style was Sir Robert Ker Porter, whose battle paintings shown between 1799 and 1804 included the large canvas 'The Battle of Alexandria', which depicts the victory of the British Expeditionary Force over the attacking French Army.

J. M. W. Turner was also greatly influenced by Egypt in his early formative years and it is tragic that one of his first great historical paintings, 'The Battle of the Nile at 10 o'clock when the L'Orient [*sic*] Blew Up', which was exhibited at the Royal Academy in 1799, has been lost. The following year his painting 'The Fifth Plague of Egypt' was shown, followed by 'The Tenth Plague of Egypt' in 1802.

The discoveries and subsequent exhibitions of the Italian engineer Giovanni Belzoni provided the impetus for the wave of Egyptiana which swept across Britain in the post-Napoleonic period. Much of what he discovered was bought by Henry Salt who, as Consul-General in Egypt, financed many excavations. Having been trained as a portrait painter, he was no mean artist himself and produced many pen, ink and watercolour studies of the Pyramids and the interiors of tombs.

The line between archaeology and art becomes blurred after the exploits of Belzoni had kindled fires of exploration, excavation and drawing by a mixture of talented men. Between 1824 and 1835, Robert Hay assembled a team of such talents around him to assist in the recording of antiquities and the making of casts, which resulted in further gains for the British Museum. Among the artists were Joseph Bonomi, who was born in Italy but lived most of his life in England, where most of his works are to be found. He was primarily a sketcher and a watercolourist and recorded various details from the temples. One of his colleagues was Francis Arundale, another of the many watercolour artists who had trained as an architect. Another colleague was Frederick Catherwood, also an architect, who executed many drawings of Thebes, Upper Egypt and Nubia.

Edward Lane, the author of *Manners and Customs of the Modern Egyptians*, first trained as an engraver, a skill which stood him in good stead during his trips up the Nile and his life in Cairo, when he was able to make tiny sketches on paper hidden in his palm for, as he said, 'I wished to avoid being seen in the public places engaged in so heathenish an act as drawing.' A number of his watercolours and drawings on cards are to be found at the Griffith Institute, Oxford.

In an essay in the catalogue for the 1933 exhibitions in Brighton and Manchester, *The Inspiration of Egypt*,[1] Patrick Conner wrote:

> The 1820s saw the flowering of a new sub-genre of English painting: the Egyptian capriccio. Paintings which attempted to represent ancient Egypt in an authentic or at least plausible way were very largely a phenomenon restricted to this decade; they seem to have had much less appeal in the post-Georgian era, until Poynter and Alma-Tadema revived the fashion with the aid of a wider and more dramatic array of stage properties.

Among the artists who painted these capriccios was the painter-traveller Benjamin Haydon, who could not resist depicting the Pyramids and sphinxes in his set of biblical pictures.

Of all the Orientalist artists, perhaps the most outstanding in terms of range of subject, faithfulness of reproduction and devotion to scene, is David Roberts, who was born in Edinburgh in 1796 and died in 1864, having become a Royal Academician in 1841. His own journal sums up his aspirations and achievement, which were 'to make drawings of the scenes and the antiquities of Egypt, objects of such interest as could satisfy him'. He went to Alexandria and to Cairo, obtaining permission to visit every mosque he wanted to, a unique privilege for a Christian. He made the journey up the Nile in a three-month trip by boat and before he returned to Cairo he had made drawings of almost every building of note from Nubia to the Mediterranean. The journey resulted in six folio volumes of drawings, *Egypt and Nubia*, published between 1842 and 1849.[2]

A rival claimant to the crown as the greatest of the Orientalist painters is John Frederick Lewis, a representative of the English School, who lived from 1805 to 1876. Writing a letter in June 1875, Edward Lear said of Lewis:

There never have been, and there never will be, any works depicting Oriental life more truly beautiful and excellent – perhaps I may say so beautiful and excellent. For, besides the exquisite and conscientious workmanship, the subjects painted by J. F. Lewis were perfect representations of real scenes and people.

Lear himself made five visits to Egypt and 46 of his watercolours and oils relating to the country have been recorded. In addition, there are many ad hoc sketches with inimitable Lear captions and comments. He described the feluccas on the Nile as 'giant moths' and Karnak made him feel like a 'cheese mite among the giants'. It is a pity that his Nile diaries, which he considered publishing, were never printed.

William James Müller, an artist from Bristol, was in Egypt at the same time as David Roberts but they did not meet as they were travelling in opposite directions. Müller was a fast worker and painted many street scenes and bazaars as well as the almost obligatory tombs and temples. In the early 1840s Richard Dadd spent the winter making watercolours of the tombs of the caliphs in Cairo and it was there that he first showed signs of that subsequent insanity which drove him to murder his father. A year earlier Sir David Wilkie had visited the Holy Land and while in Alexandria waiting for his boat home, painted Mohammed Ali, Pasha of Egypt. This fine portrait, now in the Tate Gallery, was not quite finished as Sir David died on the journey home and the Pasha never received it. William Holman Hunt went to Egypt to gather material for biblical subjects, which were a key feature of Victorian era paintings. He was not very interested in Cairo as such and regarded the Pyramids as 'extremely ugly blocks, as one always knew, and arranged with most unpicturesque taste'.[1] One of his most evocative paintings is 'The Afterglow in Egypt', now in Southampton Art Gallery.

Another painter of biblical scenes was Thomas Seddon, who spent a few months with Hunt in the winter of 1853–4. His pictures did well enough for him to return three years later but he died in Cairo shortly after his arrival. A year or so later, Frederick Goodall made his first visit, living in the Coptic quarter of Cairo with his friend Carl Haag, a Bavarian who had studied watercolouring in England. Both artists were very successful and sold many of their works.

Other artists substituted imagination for experience and never visited the country at all but could not resist the subject matter which had gained such a hold over the public mind. Among these was Edward Poynter, who later achieved a knighthood, Presidency of the Royal Academy and the Directorship of the National Gallery. His extraordinary oil, 'Israel in Egypt', executed in 1867, can be seen at the Guildhall Art Gallery in London and is a favourite for loan exhibitions. Edwin Long was another non-visiting painter and although Sir Lawrence Alma-Tadema did, indeed, visit Egypt in 1902–3 for the inauguration of the first Aswan Dam, nearly all his pictures of the country were painted before that visit, being based on books about ancient Egypt and visits to the British Museum.

Although Lord Leighton, the eminent Victorian painter and President of the Royal Academy, visited Egypt twice, he was never captivated by the country as most other painters have been. The Khedive lent him a steam yacht for the journey up the Nile. Some of the resultant oil sketches are to be found in various galleries but he did nothing on the large scale to which his admirers are accustomed.

Two artists whose travels in Egypt followed closely on each other in the late 1860s were John Dibblee Crace and Frank Dillon, both of whom have depicted the exteriors and interiors of houses in Cairo, usually in watercolour, which was the favourite medium of most of the painters to whom we have referred. The marine artist Edward William Cooke was a visitor in the 1870s and exhibited the oil-finished results of his pencil sketches in the Royal Academy. A watercolourist whose works have found increasing favour was Hercules Brabazon Brabazon, who made three journeys up the Nile, drawing extensively, but did not hold an exhibition until 1882, when his show at the Goupil Gallery brought him into the limelight.

Henry Andrew Harper was another traveller in Egypt and the Holy Land and his delightful watercolour 'The Nile at Cairo', painted in 1874, may be seen in the Wallace Collection. Joseph Austin Benwell worked mainly in watercolour and gouache, his Egyptian scenes often depicting camels on the move. He exhibited in London and leading municipal galleries in Britain and his work is gaining increasing respect.

Our text has mentioned the return of the Holy Carpet, which has been depicted by Frederick George, whose drawing of the event in 1865 is to be found in the extensive Searight Collection of Egyptian paintings and drawings, now in the Victoria and Albert Museum. Also in the collection are works by Howard

Carter, best known, of course, for his amazing discovery of the tomb of Tutankhamun.

The son of the Irish painter Robert George Kelly had some difficulty in establishing his personality to distinguish himself from his father. Born in Birkenhead in 1861, he worked in his father's studio and first exhibited as Robert George Kelly Jnr. He travelled in the Middle East, settling down in Cairo, painting under the name of Talbot Kelly, but as his 1915 watercolour 'Tombs of the Khalifs, Cairo' shows, he also used the signature Robert G. Talbot Kelly.

He was a member of the Royal Institute of Painters in Water-colours, as was Walter F. R. Tyndale, who was born in Bruges of English parents. His watercolours were of landscape and architectural subjects but he was also a portrait and genre painter in oils. He was a constant traveller and used his water-colours to illustrate his books, two of which were *Below the Cataracts* and *An Artist in Egypt*.

There is a wealth of lesser professional and highly talented amateur artists whose works demonstrate the attraction that Egypt has held for pencil and brush. Apart from the galleries which specialise in Orientalist art, such as the Mathaf Gallery in London, which has been very helpful to us, many a library contains books with fine illustrations of all aspects of Egypt, done by artists for writers or by artist/writers themselves.

The long and continuing influence that Egypt has exerted over architecture and architectural furnishings has been extensively documented and can still be seen in those buildings which survive and in the museums which hold so wide a range of artifacts and fine arts. The early nineteenth century saw that surge in interest in Egyptian culture known as 'The Egyptian Revival', more particularly applied to architecture and the decorative arts and chronicled by Sir Nikolaus Pevsner and S. Lang in their article in the *Architectural Review* (May 1956) and more substantially in the books by Professor G. Carrott[3] and Dr James Stevens Curl.[4] Indeed, with these two books in hand, the search for information and enlightenment on the subject need go no further.

Dr Curl's book, *The Egyptian Revival*, sums up:

Throughout the ages, and especially in the eighteenth, nineteenth and twentieth centuries, Egyptian art and architecture have inspired designers. The Nile style was particularly important in furniture design, and has been a highly significant element in the style known as Art Deco . . . An awareness of the persistence of Egyptian ideas in religion, art and iconography creates fresh and enlightening perspectives . . . The pyramid, the obelisk, the pylon, and the symmetrical temple are pure shapes that are best seen within a luminously clear landscape, set among Horatian verdure, where the colours are strong, and the light is not dissipated in mist or in haze.[4]

The influence of Palladio on all types of buildings in Great Britain and Ireland is discussed and explained by Dan Cruickshank in his indispensable *Guide to the Georgian Buildings of Britain and Ireland*.[5] We are concerned only with that aspect of Palladianism which has been influenced by Egypt and is exemplified by the buildings referred to in that book. The seminal work is the Egyptian Hall, described by Vitruvius and illustrated by Palladio, manifested in Lord Burlington's Assembly Rooms, York (1731) and elaborated further in the City of London's Mansion House as designed by George Dance the Elder in 1737. Holkham Hall, Norfolk, had the benefit of designs by William Kent and Lord Burlington for the Great Marble Hall, also based partly on Palladio's illustration of a Roman basilica and partly on his Egyptian hall.

The Egyptian Hall was also the inspiration for St Lawrence Church, Mereworth, Kent. St Laurence's Church, West Wycombe, Bucks, created from a mediaeval church in 1763 for the founder of the Hell-Fire Club, Sir Francis Dashwood, has also been likened to a very superb Egyptian Hall.

Visitors to historic houses in Britain will be familiar with the sphinxes on pedestals and obelisks designed by William Kent for Lord Burlington's villa at Chiswick; the Sphinx Gate of this villa was copied in 1768 for Temple Newsam House, Leeds; other sphinxes at Blickling Hall, Norfolk, which also has a Pyramid Mausoleum designed by Joseph Bonomi; and Castle Howard, Yorkshire, which boasts an obelisk, a pyramid and Vanbrugh's Pyramid Gate.

Ireland's obelisks mark a grandeur that has gone: one based on rock, built by Sir Edward Lovett Pearce around 1732, still stands at Stillorgan House, Co. Dublin, although the house was demolished in 1880; and at Powerscourt, Eniskerry, Co. Wicklow, it is sad to see the pedimented obelisks flanking the nine-bay centre block, which was gutted by fire in 1974, thus destroying the Egyptian Hall.

The Egyptian Revival showed through amid some of the

more florid touches of Vanbrugh and Hawksmoor, the use of pyramids being one example. For Sir John Soane, the grandeur of Egyptian architecture had 'colossal', 'awful' and 'majestic' properties. Dr Curl claims that 'the inventor of the fashion for Egyptianising forms used in a Rococo manner was Giovanni Battista Piranesi. His Vedustista often include Egyptian or Egyptianising objects, but the most promiscuous array of exotic elements can be found in the *Antichita Romane*'.

Egyptian influence was reflected in interiors, such as the red and gold Greek/Egyptian Empire-style saloon designed by Henry Holland at Southill Park, Bedfordshire, in 1795 and James Playfair's Egyptian billiard room, which was being put into Cairness House, Grampian, at about the same time. Thomas Hope went the whole hog in designing a whole range of Egyptianised furniture, putting his own models into his house in Duchess Street, London. Interior decorating continued in the same vein with George Dance introducing the theme into Lansdowne House and Stratton Park. Further details appeared in the Gallery at Attingham Park and at Bayfordbury. Goodwood's dining room is said to be based on illustrations by Dominique Vivant Denon, as is the Egyptian Hall under the north portico at Stowe.

A wave of interest in things Egyptian followed the failure of Napoleon's campaign and Nelson's victory. In 1812 the Egyptian Hall in Piccadilly, London, designed by Peter Frederick Robinson, apparently based on the temple at Dendera, opened but has been demolished long since. The neo-Egyptian Library, now Oddfellow's Hall, in Ker Street, Devonport, was designed by John Foulston in 1821 as part of a mixed group of buildings in different styles. Existing buildings were Egyptianised, such as 144 Fore Street, Exeter and 42 Fore Street, Hertford. Perhaps the most outstanding of existing Egyptian-style houses is the Egyptian House, Chapel Street, Penzance, now owned by the Landmark Trust and available for renting. The front elevation is almost identical with the Piccadilly building and was built for Mr George Lavin as a museum and geological repository.

One of the finest examples of the open-air Egyptian decorative effect are the gardens at Biddulph Grange in Staffordshire, now being restored by the National Trust after a period of neglect. These were the creation of James Bateman and his wife, who laid out the gardens in the 1840s with the help of the painter and designer Edward Cooke.

The erection of the Crystal Palace at Sydenham in 1854 gave a further opportunity to Joseph Bonomi to exercise his skill, for, with Owen Jones, he created the Egyptian Court, which was a most imposing structure, consisting of 'a series of rows featuring models of bas-reliefs, columns, deities, Graeco-Roman columns, hieroglyphs, Karnak lions, Egyptian monarchs, Roman-Egyptian columns, the Rosetta Stone and a mock-up of the tomb at Abu Simbel'. Within ten years, a further example of inspiration from a Denon temple illustration was provided by the Freemasons' Hall at Boston, Lincolnshire. A doorcase in High Street, Warwick, reminds us that there, too, was an Egyptianised Masonic Lodge.

Theatregoers to the London Palladium will be aware of the Egyptian features on the nearby Palladium House, built in 1929. In north London, the Carreras building in Hampstead Road, Greater London House, was once a colourful addition to the urban scene with its strong Egyptian colours and style, but drab modernism has taken its toll: the columns have been straightened and the bright decoration has been removed. Pevsner never did like it, his adjectival comment being 'abominable'.

The exuberance of the cinema world has provided so many Egyptianised buildings that there are few major urban centres that have not felt a touch of it. Kensington High Street, Regent Street (the New Gallery), the Astoria Streatham, the appropriately named Luxor, Twickenham, have been singled out among others, including the Pyramid, Sale, in Cheshire, as good examples.

We should not ignore Scotland in this brief survey, especially Glasgow, that fine Victorian city, now enjoying a renaissance and named the European City of Culture for 1990. Alexander Thomson was the leading architect in the use of the Egyptian idiom, his St Vincent Street church of 1859 being probably the most outstanding example of his work. We have not seen his Queens Park church, which was destroyed during the Second World War but from illustrations it is clear that this building, too, emerged from Egyptian inspiration. Thomson did not confine himself to ecclesiastical buildings, his secular work ranging from the columned block of Nos 336–356 Sauchiehall Street and the Egyptian Halls, at Nos 84–100 Union Street, to the villa, No. 200 Nithsdale Road, built in 1871.

John Cromer does not have to walk more than half a mile each way from his home to be reminded of the glory of Egypt.

To the south, the obelisk spire of St Luke's Church, Finsbury, stands above the gutted hulk of what was once one of Hawkmoor's edifices; to the north, the linked villas 46–72 Richmond Avenue, Barnsbury, have doors flanked by sphinxes and obelisks, two marked 'Nile', while further Egyptian influence is evidenced by the lotus-flower motifs on the window surrounds and the low balcony rails at first-floor level. As he approaches his home, he passes the Old Red Lion public house in St John Street, Islington. Built originally in 1415, it was rebuilt in 1899, at which time it sprouted four obelisks at roof height.

The Latin epitaph to Sir Christopher Wren on the wall of the vault in St Paul's Cathedral, where his remains rest beneath a plain black slab, is known the whole world over. In a final tribute to the lasting spell of Egypt, we take the liberty of adding one word to this text to make it read: 'Lector, si monumentum Egyptae requiris, circumspice.'

Bibliography

1. Smith, H.S. – Ancient Centres of Egyptian Civilisation – London – 1985
2. Curzon of Kedelston, Marquess, ed. Peter King – Travels with a Superior Person – London – 1985
3. Sladen, Douglas – Oriental Cairo – London – 1911
4. Lane, Edward (ed.) – Arabian Nights – London – 1877
5. Lane-Poole, Stanley – Cairo – London – 1892
6. Lane-Poole, Stanley – The Story of Cairo – London – 1902
7. Wilkinson, Sir John Gardner – Manners and Customs of Ancient Egyptians – London – 1878
8. Abd el Rahman Ibn Mohammed – Prolégomènes historiques d'Ibn Khaldoun – (tr. Baron Macguckin de Slane) – 1787
9. Abd el Rahman Ibn al Jabarti – Merveilles biographiques et historiques (tr. Chefik Mansour, Abdulaziz Kali, Gabriel Nicholas Khalil and Iskander Ammoun) – Cairo – 1888–96
10. Shaw, Rev. Thomas – Travels or Observations Relating to Several Parts of Barbary and the Levant – 1757
11. Pococke, Rev. Richard – A Description of the East – London – 1743–45
12. Norden, Frederick L. – Travels in Egypt and Nubia
13. Perry, Dr Charles – A View of the Levant
14. Niebuhr, Carsten – Voyage en Egypte – 1841
15. de Volney, Constantin François – Voyage en Syrie et en Egypte – Paris – 1792
16. Browne, W.G. – Travels in Africa, Egypt and Syria from the Year 1792 to 1798 – London – 1799
17. Descriptions de l'Egypte: un receuil des observations et des recherches qui ont été faites en Egypte pendant l'expedition de l'armée française – Paris – 1809–28 (20 vols), 1821–29 (24 vols)
18. de Boisey – Bonaparte au Caire – Paris – 1799
19. Napoleon I and Berthier, Louis Alexandre – An Account of the French Expedition in Egypt – Leeds – 1800
20. Wilson, Sir Robert T. – History of the British Expedition to Egypt – London – 1802

21. A Private on board the *Dictator* – A Faithful Journal of the Late Expedition to Egypt – London – 1805
22. Cameron, D.A. – Egypt in the Nineteenth Century – London – 1898
23. Kinglake, A.W. – Eothen, or Traces of Travel Brought Home from the Near East – London – 1844
24. Thackeray, W.M. – Notes on a Journey from Cornhill to Grand Cairo – London – 1846
25. Clayton, J.W. – Letters from the Nile – London – 1854
26. Stephens, John Lloyd – Incidents of Travel in Egypt, Arabia, Petra and the Holy Land – Edinburgh – 1839
27. Cooley, James Ewing – The American in Egypt – New York – 1842
28. Twain, Mark – Innocents Abroad – London – 1985
29. Lane, Edward – Manners and Customs of Modern Egyptians – London – 1836
30. Steegmuller, Francis (ed. & trans.) – Flaubert in Egypt – London – 1972
31. Trollope, Anthony – Autobiography – London – 1961
32. Pope-Hennessy, James – Anthony Trollope – London – 1971
33. Snow, C.P. – Trollope – London – 1975
34. Dawson Damer, Hon. Mary G.E. – Diary of a Tour in Greece, Turkey, Egypt and the Holy Land – London – 1841
35. Haight, Sarah – Letters from the Old World – New York – 1840
36. Poole, Sophia – The Englishwoman in Egypt – London – 1844–46
37. Martineau, Harriet – Eastern Life – London – 1848
38. Nightingale, Florence – Letters from Egypt: A Journey on the Nile 1849–1850 – London – 1987
39. Duff Gordon, Lucie – Letters from Egypt – London – 1983
40. Edwards, Amelia B. – A Thousand Miles up the Nile – London – 1982
41. Wallis Budge, E.A. – The Nile: Notes for Travellers in Egypt – London – 1985
42. Haining, Peter (ed.) – The Best Short Stories of Rider Haggard – London – 1981
43. Kinross, Lord – Between Two Seas: the Creation of the Suez Canal – London – 1968
44. Blunt, Wilfred Scawen – The Secret History of the British Occupation of Egypt – London – 1907
45. Mansfield, Peter – The British in Egypt – London – 1971
46. Willcocks, William – Sixty Years in the East – London – 1935
47. Boyle, Clara – Boyle of Cairo – Kendal – 1965
48. Lloyd, G.A.L. – Egypt after Cromer – London – 1933–34
49. Chirol, Valentine – The Egyptian Problem – London – 1921
50. Milner – England in Egypt – London – 1892

51. Baring, Evelyn, 1st Earl of Cromer – Modern Egypt – London 1908
52. Cecil, Lord Edward – The Leisure of an Egyptian Official – London – 1984
53. Storrs, Sir Ronald – Orientations – London – 1943
54. Russell, Sir Thomas – Egyptian Service 1902–1946 – London – 1949
55. Aldridge, James – Cairo, Biography of a City – London – 1970
56. Forster, E.M. – Alexandria – a History and Guide – London – 1982
57. McPherson, Bimbashi, a Life in Egypt (ed. Barry Carman and John McPherson) – London – 1983
58. Jarvis, Major C.S. – Oriental Spotlight – London – 1946
59. Jarvis, Major C.S. – The Back Garden of Allah – London – 1941
60. Jarvis, Major C.S. – Heresies and Humours – London – 1942
61. Jarvis, Major C.S. – Happy Yesterdays – London – 1948
62. Elgood, Lt-Col. P.G. – Egypt – a Brief History from Ancient to Modern Times – Cairo – 1949
63. Seymour-Smith, Martin – Robert Graves, His Life and Work – London – 1982
64. Graves, Richard Percival – Robert Graves – the Assault Heroic 1895–1926 – London – 1986
65. Morgan, Janet – Agatha Christie – London – 1984
66. Waugh, Evelyn – When the Going was Good – London – 1951
67. History of the Second World War – Vol II J.R.M. Butler – London – 1959
68. Moorehead, Alan – African Trilogy – London – 1944
69. Stark, Freya – Dust in the Lion's Paw – London – 1961
70. Fraser, G.S. – A Stranger and Afraid – Manchester – 1983
71. Selwyn, Victor *et al.* – Return to Oasis, War Poems and Recollections from the Middle East 1940–1946 – London – 1980
72. Rhys, Keidrych (ed.) – Poems from the Forces – London – 1941
73. Hewison, Robert – Under Siege, Literary Life in London 1939–1945 – London – 1977
74. Bullen, Keith – Bells on the Breeze – Cairo – 1940
75. Bullen, Keith and Cromer, John (eds) – Salamander, a poetry miscellany – London – 1947
76. Rhys, Keidrych (ed.) – More Poems from the Forces – London – 1943
77. Pitt, Barrie – The Crucible of War (Vol. 2, Year of Alamein) – London – 1942
78. Sansom, Major A.W. – I Spied Spies – London – 1965
79. Manning, Olivia – The Danger Tree – London – 1977
80. Churchill, Winston S. – The Second World War (Vol. IV) – London – 1951

81. Speirs, Ruth (tr.) – Selected Poems of Rainer Maria Rilke – Cairo – 1943
82. Craig, Norman – The Broken Plume – London – 1982
83. Bullen, K.B. (tr.) – Albert Samain, Un Pastelliste exquis – Cairo – 1943
84. Waller, John – Spring Legend – Cairo – 1942
85. Gawsworth, John – Legacy to Love – London – 1943
86. Personal Landscape, an anthology of exile – London – 1945
87. Manning, Olivia – The Battle Lost and Won – London – 1978
88. Manning, Olivia – The Sum of Things – London – 1980
89. Schimanski, Stefan and Treece, Henry (eds) – Leaves in the Storm – London – 1947
90. Cromer, John – In Battle – Cairo – 1942
91. Douglas, Keith – Alamein to Zem Zem – London – 1947
92. Graham, Desmond – Keith Douglas – 1920–1944, A Biography – London – 1974
93. Waller, John and Fraser, G.S. (eds) – The Collected Poems of Keith Douglas – London – 1951
94. Bullen, K.B. – Charles Baudelaire, un pòète maudit – Cairo – 1942
95. Bullen, K.B. – We Stand Alone . . . and other War Sonnets – Cairo – 1942
96. Blake-Reed, J.S. – Twentyfive Odes of Horace rendered into English – Alexandria – 1942
97. Parme, Raoul – Poèmes d'Angleterre – Cairo – 1942
98. Bullen, Keith – Alfred de Musset's Souvenir, rendered into English – Cairo – 1942
99. Oasis, the Middle East Anthology of Poetry from the Forces – Cairo 1943
100. Almendro – Heaven's Tramp – Cairo – 1943
101. Almendro – Jan Christian Smuts, Field Marshal – Cairo – 1943
102. Wayment, Hilary – Egypt Now – Cairo – 1943
103. Almendro, Juan – Tomorrow is Soon – Cairo – 1944
104. Blake-Reed, J.B. – More Odes of Horace – Alexandria – 1944
105. Uren, Martyn – Kiwi Saga – Cairo – 1943
106. Cossery, Albert – The Men God Forgot – Cairo – 1944
107. Howarth, Herbert and Ibrahim Shukrallah – Images of the Arab World – London – 1944
108. Fraser, G.S. – Home Town Elegy – London – 1944
109. Waller, John and de Mauny, Erik – Middle East Anthology – London – 1946
110. John, Evan – Time in the East – London – 1946
111. Spencer, Bernard – Aegean Islands – London – 1946
112. Cossery, Albert – The House of Certain Death (tr. Erik de Mauny) – London – 1947

113. Waller, John – The Kiss of Stars – London – 1948
114. Fraser, G.S. – The Traveller Has Regrets – London – 1948
115. Gawsworth, John – Collected Poems – London – 1948
116. Little, Tom – Modern Egypt – London – 1967
117. Stark, Freya – East is West – London – 1945
118. Mansfield, Peter – The Arabs – London – 1976
119. Mansfield, Peter – Nasser's Egypt – London – 1965
120. Newby, P.H. – The Egypt Story – London – 1979
121. Newby, P.H. – The Picnic at Sakkara – London – 1955
122. Newby, P.H. – Revolution and Roses – London – 1957
123. Newby, P.H. – A Guest and His Going – London – 1959
124. Newby, P.H. – Something to Answer For – London – 1969
125. Newby, P.H. – Kith – London – 1977
126. Mannin, Ethel – A Lance for the Arabs – London
127. Moorehead, Alan – The White Nile – London – 1960
128. Moorehead, Alan – The Blue Nile – London – 1962
129. Ludwig, Emil – The Nile, the life story of a river (tr. Mary H. Lindsey) – London – 1950
130. Stewart, Desmond – Great Cairo, Mother of the World – London – 1969
131. Carter, Nick – Cairo – London – 1972
132. Fedden, Robin – Egypt, Land of the Valley – London – 1977
133. Selwyn, Victor *et al.* (eds) – From Oasis into Italy – London – 1983
134. Selwyn, Victor, Ed.-in-Chief – Poems from the Second World War, the Oasis Selection – London – 1985
135. Mailer, Norman – Ancient Evenings – London – 1983
136. Devine, Laurie – Nile – London – 1983
137. Barber, Noel – A Woman of Cairo – London – 1984
138. Golding, William – An Egyptian Journal – London – 1985
139. Lively, Penelope – Moon Tiger – London – 1987
140. Pearce, Michael – The Mamur Zapt and the Return of the Carpet – London – 1988
141. More, Jasper – Land of Egypt – London – 1980
142. Durrell, Lawrence – Justine – London – 1957
143. Durrell, Lawrence – Balthazar – London – 1958
144. Durrell, Lawrence – Mountolive – London – 1958
145. Durrell, Lawrence – Clea – London – 1960
146. Fraser, G.S., Lawrence Durrell, A Study – London – 1969
147. Enright, D.J. – Academic Year – London – 1985
148. Walsh, William – Enright: Poet of Humanism – London – 1974
149. Moussa-Mahmoud, Fatma – The Arabic Novel in Egypt, 1914–1970 – Cairo – 1973
150. The British Council in Egypt – The Year of Maya – Cairo – 1988

151. Mahfouz, Naguib – Wedding Song – London – 1989
152. Mahfouz, Naguib – The Thief and the Dogs – London – 1989
153. Mahfouz, Naguib – The Beginning and the End – London – 1989
154. Mahfouz, Naguib – Palace Walk – London – 1990

Appendix

1. Conner, Patrick (ed.) – The Inspiration of Egypt – Brighton – 1983
2. Roberts, David – Egypt and Nubia – London – 1842–1849
3. Carrott, Richard G. – The Egyptian Revival, Its Sources, Monuments and Meaning 1808–1858 – London – 1978
4. Curl, James Stevens – The Egyptian Revival – London – 1982
5. Cruickshank, Don – A Guide to the Georgian Buildings of Britain and Ireland – London – 1985

Index

Arabic names are indexed under surnames, those with 'el' prefixes being listed under 'el'.

Abbas Theatre, 38
Abbott & Costello, 150
Abdallah, Amir, 40
Abdel Aziz, Malak, 221
Abdel Kuddus, Ihsan, 218, 219
Abdel Sabbour, Salah, 61, 204
Abu Shadi, Zaki, 204
Abdin Palace, 187
Addison, Herbert, 93
Afton, Richard, 142
Ain Shams University, 6
Al-Hilal, 67
Aldridge, James, 17, 64, 178, 203
Alexander the Great, 178, 193, 194
Alexander, Lieut.-Gen. Sir Harold, 84, 85
Alexandria Library, 193, 202
Alexandria Police, 173
Ali, Mohammed (also Mehemet Ali), 13, 23, 194, 230
All Saints Cathedral, Cairo, 132, 135
All Souls College, Oxford, 51
Allen, Adrienne, 143
Allenby, Lord, 39, 42, 49, 50
Allin, Norman, 137
Alma-Tadema, Sir Lawrence, 229, 231
Almendro (see Saunders, Denis)
American Embassy, 97
American University of Cairo, 71, 97, 113, 132, 214

Amin, Kassem, 210
Amis du Livre Français en Orient, les, 110
Amr, 194
Anglo-Egyptian Bookshop, 118, 120
Anglo-Egyptian Union, 32, 72, 73, 74, 76, 77, 80, 86, 91, 93, 94, 105, 130
Anglo-Russian Music Festival, 133, 134
Arab Bureau, 43
Arab League, 172
Arab Observer, 177
Arab Womens' Solidarity Association, 222
Aragon, Louis, 79
Ariot, Father, 169
Aristophanes, 42
Arizona, the, 155
Armstrong, Neville, 100
Arnaz, Desi, 150, 151
Arnold, Alan, 91, 125
Arnstein, Laura, 137
Arundale, Francis, 228
Arvers, Felix, 79
Ashour, Nooman, 61
Ashton, Sir Frederick, 148
Asquith, Earl of, 52
Assia, 150
Astley, Sir Francis ('Bones'), 156
Auberge des Pyramides, 155, 156, 185

Auberge du Turf, 87
Auchinleck, General Sir Claude, 84
Auden, W.H., 74, 101
Awad, Louis, 61, 219
Azzam, Abdel Rahman (Pasha), 211

Bach, Johann Sebastian, 135, 136, 139
Bachauer, Gina, 137
Badia's (Mme Badia Massabni), 156, 166
Baikie, James, 213
Bailey, Leonard, 143
Baker, Samuel, 175
Ball, Lucille, 150, 151
Balugani, Luigi, 227
Baly, Colin, 61, 88, 93, 96
Balzac, Honoré, 214
Barber, Noel, 186, 187
Barbitch, Ivo, 89, 119, 126, 130
Baring, Sir Evelyn (see Cromer, Lord)
Barnard, Leslie Stephen, 108, 110, 138, 139, 140, 153, 156, 160
Bateman, James, 234
Baudelaire, Charles, 61, 79, 110
Beattie, Cecil, 136
Beethoven, Ludwig van, 135, 136, 138, 140
Belzoni, Giovanni, 228
Benet, William Rose, 110
Bennett, Arnold, 52
Bennett, Joan, 150
Benois, Nadia, 148
Benwell, Joseph Austin, 231
Bergen, Edgar, 150
Berger, Munroe, 16, 17
Bergson, Henri, 196
Berlioz, Hector, 134
Bettelheim-Foscolo, Ida, 135
Big Ben Bar, 161
Billam, George, 143
Bielatowicz, Jan, 115
Bishop, George, 114
Blake-Reed, J.S., 61, 84, 88, 90, 111, 119, 123
Blanc, Charles, 30
Blunden, Edmund, 51
Blunt, Wilfred Scawen, 31
Bolshoi Ballet, 218

Bonaparte, Napoleon, 9, 11, 13, 15, 18, 30, 50, 94, 168, 176, 194, 205, 228, 234
Bonomi, Joseph, 228, 233, 235
Booker Prize, 188
Bouchier, Chili, 142
Bouilhet, Louis, 20, 21
Bourse Egyptienne, La, 115
Bowden, Max, 80
Boyle, Clara, 33
Boyle, Harry, 32, 33, 37
Brabazon, Hercules Brabazon, 231
Bracale, Signor, 39
Bracebridge, Charles, 23
Bracebridge, Selina, 23
Brahms, Johannes, 39, 44, 135, 138
Bridges, Robert, 52
Bristol et du Nil Hotel, 57
British Broadcasting Corporation (B.B.C.), 57, 95, 107
British Council, 5, 6, 66, 73, 74, 96, 159, 171, 180, 199, 212
British Embassy, 37, 97, 166, 195, 197
British Information Office, Palestine, 121
British Institute, 5, 60, 72, 98
British War Fund, 143
Britten, Benjamin, 6, 148
Brooke, Rupert, 69, 109
Browne, W.G., 10
Browning, Elizabeth Barrett, 112
Browning, Robert, 110
Bruce, James, 227
Budge, Sir Ernest A.T. Wallis, 28
Bullen, A.H., 77, 79, 123
Bullen, Keith B., 61, 77, 78, 79, 80, 84, 85, 86, 88, 91, 109, 110, 111, 112, 116, 118, 119, 123, 124, 125, 130, 181
Buluq Nizam, 166
Burckhardt, John Lewis, 93
Burk, David, 72, 86
Burlington, Lord, 233
Burns, Robert, 204
Burt, Oliver, 142, 148
Burton, Sir Richard, 93, 175
Busoni, Ferruccio, 139
Byrd, William, 137
Bystander Bar, 161

Cage, Sergeant, 133
Cairo Area Military Band, 133, 139
Cairo Calling, 106, 108, 109, 110
Cairo City Police, 173, 174
Cairo Symphony Orchestra, 133, 136
Cairo University, 6, 60, 132, 169, 213, 219, 221
Calligrammes, 119
Cambridge University, 60, 199, 219
Cameron, D.A., 13, 27
Cameron, Edme, 143
Campasse, Gina, 137
Campbell, Roy, 109
Campion, William Mangan, 99
Carlin, Joan, 143
Carlton Restaurant, 160
Carlyle, Thomas, 122
Carnegie Medal, 188
Carrott, Professor G., 232
Carter, Howard, 232
Carter, Nick, 178
Carver, Field Marshal Lord, 182
Casino des Pigeons, 161, 185
Casino Opera, 155
Catherwood, Frederick, 228
Catullus, 130
Caulfeild, James (1st Earl of Charlemont), 10, 227
Cecil, Lord Edward, 35, 36
Central Narcotics Intelligence Bureau, 174
Challoner, Louis, 181
Charles, Dudley, 88
Checkley, John, 181
Chekov, Anton, 212
Chesham, Francis, 228
Chesterton, G.K., 112
Chirol, Sir Valentine, 33, 49
Chopin, Frédéric, 38, 134, 139
Christie, Agatha, 54, 55, 56
Churchill, Sir Winston S., 18, 84
Citadel, 97, 98, 99
Clarke, Jeremiah, 133
Clarke, Roma, 146
Cohen, Eve, 195
Cordell, Frank, 146
Clayton, J.W., 15
Cloquet, Dr Jules, 20

Coates, Percy, 136
Colman, Robert, 136
Conner, Patrick, 229
Connolly, Cyril, 75
Continental Hotel, 87, 160
Cook, Edmund, 56
Cook, Thomas (and Son), 14, 23, 28, 30
Cooke, Edward, 234
Cooke, Edward William, 231
Cooley, James Ewing, 16
Cooper, Gary, 150
Cormack, George, 143
Corneille, Pierre, 79
Cornell University, 51, 52
Cory, William Johnson, 112
Co-Services Players, 143
Cosmo Cinema, 149, 150
Cossery, Albert, 120, 121, 125, 127, 129
Couperin, François, 137
Cowan, Harold, 143
Coward, Nöel, 145
Cowper, William, 204
Crace, John Diblee, 231
Craig, Norman, 87, 153
Craven, Mae, 144
Crewe, Quentin, 27
Croce, Benedetto, 119
Croft, Michael, 181
Cromer, Lord, 32, 33, 35, 39, 173, 177
Cronin, A.J., 110
Cruickshank, Dan, 233
Cumberbatch, Pat, 143
cummings, e.e., 110
Curl, Dr James Stevens, 232, 234
Curzon, Lord, 7, 32

Daily Mail, 29, 180
Dadd, Richard, 230
Dalton, Richard, 227
Dance, George, 233, 234
D'Annunzio, Gabriele, 130
Dante, 42
Dashwood, Sir Francis, 233
Darwish, Sayyid, 211
d'Auvergne, Lois, 146
Davies, Bryn, 72
Davies, Reginald, 64

Davin, Dan, 182
Davis, Bette, 56
Dawson Damer, Hon Mary G.E., 22
de Boisey, R. Luis, 11
de Havilland, Olivia, 152
de Knevett, Edgar, 62, 78, 79, 85, 86
de la Torre, Raf, 93, 110, 148
de Lesseps, Ferdinand, 15, 30, 31
de Mauny, Erik, 79, 81, 91, 100,
    125, 126, 129, 130, 180, 181
de Musset, Alfred, 30, 79, 112
de Nemes, Eric, 117, 119
de Volney, Constantin François, 10
Debussy, Claude, 139
Delany, Arthur, 93
Denon, Dominique Vivant, 234, 235
des Baux, Cyril, 125, 127, 130
Devine, Laurie, 185, 201
Devonshire, H., 118
Diana Palace Cinema, 149, 150
Dickens, Charles, 109, 214
Dickson, Dorothy, 144
Dillon, Frank, 231
Dinocrates, 193
Disney, Walt, 152
Disraeli, Benjamin, 30
Dixon, Kay, 146
Doll's Cabaret, 87, 156, 157
Dominion, The, 79
Donat, Robert, 153
Dossor, Lance, 135, 137
Dostoievsky, Feodor, 212
Douglas, Keith, 99, 104, 105, 106,
    181
Douglas, Melvyn, 152
du Camp, Maxime, 20, 21, 23
Duchess Theatre, London, 143
Dugdale, T.C., 131
Dumas, Alexandre, 30, 206
Dundas, C.A.F., 60
Dunlop, Douglas, 33
Durrell, Lawrence, 43, 73, 74, 89,
    93, 95, 97, 99, 103, 110, 181,
    196, 197, 198, 200, 201, 216, 217
Durrell, Nancy, 195
Dvořák, Anton, 134
Dwyer, Leslie, 143

Eastern Times, 115
Eban Abba, 210

Edward VII, King, 38
Edwards, Amelia B., 23, 27, 28
Edwards, H.R., 60
Egyptian Expeditionary Force, 43
Egyptian Exploration Fund, 26, 28
Egyptian Gazette, 38, 57, 72, 111,
    114, 115
Egyptian Institute, London, 5
Egyptian Officers Club, 93
Egyptian Society, 227
Egyptian State Broadcasting Service,
    106, 107, 108, 136, 148
Egyptian University, 37
Einstein, Albert, 198
El Aqqad, Abbas Mahmoud, 203,
    204, 207, 210
El Bissy, Sanaa, 222
El Elfi, Mohammed (Bey), 11
El Ghitani, Gamal, 218
El Hakim, Tewfik, 118, 209, 211,
    220, 224
El Jabarti, Abd el Rahman, 9
El Katib el Masri, 208
El Makrizi, Ahmed Ibn Ali, 9
El Manzalawi, Mahmoud, 61
El Mazni, Ibrahim Abdel Kader, 204,
    207, 210
El Mutanabby, 90, 207
El Qais, 207
El Qalamawy, Soheir, 222
El Quilliny, Rawhiya, 221
El Rafei, Mustafa Sadek, 207
El Rai, Aly, 61
El Roumy, 207
El Rissala, 209
El Saadawi, Nawal, 222
El Sebai, Mohamed, 218
El Sebai, Youssef, 218, 219
El Sharkawi, Abdel Rahmnan, 211,
    212
El Tunisy, Beiram, 206
El Yussuf, Ros, 219
El Zayat, Ahmad Hassan, 208
El Zayat, Enayat, 221
El Zayat, Latifa, 221
Elgar, Sir Edward, 134
Elgood, Lt. Col. P.G., 50, 51
Eliot, T.S., 60, 61, 69, 101, 109, 122,
    204, 224
Elliot, Frank, 88

Ellis, William, 228
Elson, Robert, 143
Empire Cinema, 149
Empire Club, 133
Enright, D.J., 198, 199, 200
ENSA, 133, 135, 140, 142, 145, 148, 154
Eppler, Johannes, 155
Ermitage Restaurant, 160
ESFAM, 99
Eugénie, Empress, 15, 31
Ewart Memorial Hall, 132, 133, 134, 135, 137, 138, 139, 144, 152
Exeter University, 6
Ezbekieh Cinema, 149
Ezbekieh Theatre, 132, 142, 143, 144

Fairfax, Lance, 140
Fantazio Cinema, 149
Farouk, King, 59, 156, 170, 199
Farrow, Mia, 56
Fathi, Sherrifa, 221
Fedden, Robin, 60, 74, 91, 92, 93, 99, 103, 104, 106, 110, 179
Femina Cinema, 149
Ferguson, Ronald, 107
Flaubert, Gustave, 20, 21, 23
Fletcher, Ian, 125, 181
Follett, Ken, 155
Fonda, Henry, 150, 152
Ford, Mick, 181
Forster, E.M., 43, 52, 192, 193, 194, 198, 201
Forsyth, Matthew, 143
Foulston, John, 234
Fowles, John, 216
France, Anatole, 86
Franck, César, 134
Fraser, G.S., 67, 68, 69, 70, 72, 73, 74, 75, 76, 77, 86, 89, 91, 93, 97, 99, 101, 102, 103, 105, 117, 123, 124, 125, 129, 130, 170, 180, 181, 182, 183, 196, 197, 198
Freud, Sigmund, 196
Fritsche, Stuart, 156
Fuad, King, 50, 164
Fuad, Sekkina, 222
Fuad University, 74, 107, 121

Gabin, Jean, 152
Galsworthy, John, 40

Gamache Restaurant, 105, 161
Garbo, Greta, 152
Garland, Judy, 150
Garnett, David, 148
Garrison Theatre (ENSA), 133, 135, 136, 139, 142, 144
Garson, Greer, 150
Gaster, Bertha, 118
Gautier, Théophile, 30, 79
Gawdat, Saleh, 204
Gawsworth, John, 89, 91, 103, 125, 130, 131
Gayer-Anderson House, 67
Gen, 158
George, Frederick, 231
George V, King, 50
Gezira Palace Hotel, 54
Gezira Preparatory School, 61, 77, 80, 93
Gezira Sporting Club, 41, 57, 58, 63, 189
Ghanem, Fathi, 217
Gibson, Beatrice, 136, 137
Gilbert, W.S. and Sullivan, Arthur, 140
Gillray, 228
Gilmour, Barbara, 137
Gilmour, Sally, 148
Gin, 158
Gladstone, William Ewart, 18
Glazunov, Alexander, 139
Glinka, Mikhail, 134
Golding, William, 188
Goldstein, Ella, 137
Gollancz, Sir Isaac, 52
Goodall, Frederick, 230
Gordon, Lady Lucie Duff, 25, 26, 27, 57, 165, 227
Gore, Walter, 148
Gorst, Eldon, 37, 39
Gottschalk, Laura Riding (see Riding, Laura)
Goupil Gallery, London, 231
Gourmet, 161
Gover, Gerald, 135, 136, 137
Graham, Desmond, 105
Grant, Cary, 153
Graves, Alfred Percival, 52
Graves, Richard Percival, 51, 53
Graves, Robert, 51, 52, 53, 54, 199

Greene, Graham, 60
Greenwood Prize, 130
Grew, Joyce, 141
Grieg, Edvard, 135
Griffith Institute, Oxford, 229
Groddeck, Georg, 196
Groppi's, 71, 159, 167
Gudenian, H.K., 69, 99, 100
Guichard, Léon, 110
Guildhall Art Gallery, London, 231
Guizeh University Concert Hall, 133, 134
Gutteridge, Bernard, 125

'H.E.', 121
Haag, Carl, 230
Hackett, General Sir John, 182
Haggard, Rider, 28, 29
Haight, Sarah, 23
Hamilton, John, 64
Hamilton, Lady, 12
Handel, George Frederick, 138
Hardy, Thomas, 51
Harker, Clifford, 136
Harper, Henry Andrew, 231
Harrow School, 9
Harrison, Kathleen, 143
Harvey Pasha, 173
Haskal, Jack, 143
Hassouna, Abdel Khalek, 172
Hawksmoor, Nicholas, 234
Hay, Robert, 228
Haydon, Benjamin, 229
Hazlitt, William, 204
Hegazi, Abdel Mooti 204
Heikal, Mohammed Hassanein, 206
Heikel, Hussein, 207, 208
Hell-Fire Club, 233
Hemans, Dorothy, 12
Henson, Leslie, 144
Hepburn, George, 91, 125
Herodotus, 7
Hewison, Robert, 76
Hickman, H., 137
Hicks, David, 98
High Council of Arts & Literature, 218
Highsmith, Johnny (Ali Ali Ahmed Hussein), 156
Hill, E. St Leger, 119

Hill, J.R. & Co., 15
Hinton, Pamela, 148
Hogarth, William, 227
Hogg, Quinton (Lord Hailsham), 183
Holland, Anthony, 143
Holland, Henry, 234
Holloway, Frank, 143
Holman Hunt, William, 230
Holy Carpet, the, 179, 190, 231
Homer, 42, 194, 207
Hope, Bob, 150
Hope, Thomas, 234
Hopkinson Pasha, 173
Horace, 61, 111, 119, 123
Horizon, 66, 75, 76
Horus Editions, 110, 117
Hotel des Roses, 155, 156
Housman, A.E., 79, 112
Howard, Andrée, 148
Howard, Arthur, 142
Howard, Leslie, 150
Howard, Professor Worth, 71, 113
Howarth, Herbert, 121, 122, 127
Hughes, Pennethorne, 127
Hunt, Leigh, 12
Hussein, Taha, 118, 207, 208, 209, 224

Ibn Khaldun (Abdel Rahman Ibn Mohammed), 9
Ibsen, Henrik, 209
Idris, Youssef, 211, 212, 213, 221
Images, 126
Imperial War Museum, London, 181
Institut d'Egypte, 11, 30, 205
International Committee on Narcotic Drugs, 174
Ismail, Mahmoud Hassan, 204

Jammes, Francis, 116
Jarmain, John, 127
Jarvis, Albert, 135
Jarvis, Major C.S., 32, 44, 45, 46, 57, 58, 63
Jarvis, Martin, 181
Jefferies, Richard, 109
Jeffries, Francis, 143
Jesuit College, 132
John, Evan, 88, 127, 128
Johnson, Lionel, 79

Johnson, Harry, 175
Johnson-Davies, Denis, 211
'Jon', 181
Jones, Emrys, 143
Jones, Owen, 235
Jouve, Pierre Jean, 130
Joyce, James, 109, 196

Kamel, Prince Hussein, 41
Kar, Ida, 88, 125
Keating, Rex, 148
Keats, John, 12
Kelly, Robert George, 232
Kent, William, 233
Kenyon, Max, 99, 101
Keyes, Sidney, 104, 127
Kilner, Harry, 125
Kinglake, A.W., 13
Kinross, Lord, 30, 31
Kipling, Rudyard, 164
Kitchener, Lord, 35, 36, 37, 39, 40, 190
Kit Kat Cabaret, 155
Kléber, General, 95
Kostelanetz, André, 139
Krige, Uys, 127
Kursaal Cinema, 149
Kursaal Restaurant, 161

Lamour, Dorothy, 150
Landor, Walter Savage, 112
Lane, Edward William, 8, 19, 191, 229
Lane-Poole, Stanley, 8, 23
Lang, S., 232
Langford, Kay, 137
Lansbury, Angela, 56
Laurel, Stan & Hardy, Oliver, 150
Lavin, George, 234
Lavry, Marc, 134
Lawrence, D.H., 60, 66
Lawrence, T.E., 41, 42, 51, 52, 90, 177
Lear, Edward, 117, 229, 230
Ledwige, Francis, 112
Leda & Doris, 141
Lee, Sir Sidney, 52
Leiden University, 193
Leigh, Vivien, 144, 149
Leighton, Lord, 231
Lemass, E.S. 112, 119

Lever, Reg, 146
Lewis, John Frederick, 229, 230
Lewis, Sinclair, 110
Lewis, Wyndham, 76
Liadov, Anatol, 139
Lillie, Beatrice, 144
Little, Tom, 164
Lively, Penelope, 188
Liverpool University, 52, 53
Livingstone, Dr Henry, 175
Lloyd, Lord, 33, 42, 50, 52
Lloyd George, David, 50
Lodge, Sir Oliver, 107
Long, Edwin, 231
Longworth, David Garrick, 34
Loques, 160
Loutfy, Mohammed Said (Bey), 108
Ludwig, Emil, 175
Luna Park Hotel, 195
Lux Cinema, 149
Lycée Française Theatre, 146

MacDiarmid, Hugh, 125
MacGrath, Leueen, 143
MacInnes, Bishop Rennie, 42
MacLeish, Archibald, 110
MacMahon, Henry, 41
MacNeice, Louis, 60, 74
McLelland, Joan, 148
McNair, Crawford, 133, 134
McPherson, Joseph (Bimbashi), 43, 46, 47, 48, 50, 190
Madge, Charles, 122
Mahfouz, Neguib, 213–218, 220
Mailer, Norman, 183–185
Makin, W.J., 97
Mallarmé, Stéphane, 130
Mallowan, Sir Max, 54, 56
Mannin, Ethel, 171, 172
Manning, Olivia, 74, 76, 82, 94, 97, 99, 157, 180
Mansfield, Peter, 32, 33, 167, 168, 169
Mansour Effendi (see Lane, Edward William)
Marconi Guglielmo, 107
Marks, Alfred, 146
Maroon, Fred, 170
Marx Brothers, the, 150
Martineau, Harriet, 23, 26
Masefield, John, 112

Maskelyne, Jasper, 141
Mason, Eliot, 143
'Masses' Publishing House, 120
Massingham, H.W., 40
Mathaf Gallery, London, 232
Matthews, Betty, 137, 140
Maxim's Winter Roof Garden, 154, 161
Mayerl, Billy, 139
Melville, Herman, 17
Mena House Hotel, 154
Menaszes, Adolph, 136
Menjou, Adolphe, 150
Meredith, George, 25
Messenger, Albert, 137
Metro Cinema, 63, 149, 150, 152, 166
Metropole Cinema, 149, 150, 152, 153
Metropolitan Hotel, 109, 154, 158
Miami Cinema, 150, 152
Middle East Centre of Arabic Studies, 167
Middle East Forum, 167
Middle East Symphony Orchestra, 135, 136, 139
Milner, Lord, 33, 49
Mitterand, President François, 202
Moiseiwitsch, Benno, 139
Montagu, Edward Wortley, 10
Montagu, John (4th earl of Sandwich), 10
Montgomery of Alamein, Field Marshal Bernard, 84, 121
Moore, Geoffrey, 125
Moorehead, Alan, 63, 175, 176
More, Jasper, 192, 194
Morgan, Charles, 109, 193
Morley, Christopher, 110
Morley, Robert, 153
Moscatelli, Jean, 89, 91, 126, 130
Moslem Brotherhood, the, 215
Moyne, Lord, 180
Mozart, Wolfgang Amadeus, 135, 136, 139, 140
Mubarak, President Husny, 202
Müller, William James, 230
Mursi, Saleh, 217
Musgrave, Victor, 88, 125, 133

Music for All, 71, 72, 113, 114, 133, 135, 139, 148
Musica Viva, 137
Mussa, Fatma, 211, 220, 221
Mussa, Salama, 207, 208
Mussolini, Benito, 64, 65

NAAFI, 66, 95, 113, 132, 133, 135, 139, 142
Nagui, Ibrahim, 204
Nahas Pasha, 117, 166
Narriman, Queen, 187
Nasser, President Gamal Abdel, 5, 168, 169, 170, 177, 187, 188, 220
National Gallery, London, 231
National Hotel, 71, 158
National Trust, the, 234
National Youth Theatre of Great Britain, 181
Nelson, Admiral Horatio, 12, 16, 234
New Verse, 74
New Vic, the, 142
New Victoria Orchestra, 136
New Writing, 76
New Zealand Listener, 79
Newby, P.H., 60, 169, 170, 171
Newman Greatorex, 140
Newman, Fl. Lt. Norman, 146
Nicholson, Nancy, 51, 54
Niebuhr, Carsten, 10
Nightingale, Florence, 23, 24, 227
Nightingale, Parthenope, 23
Nile Restaurant, 154
Nobel Prize for Literature, 188, 213, 215, 222
Norden, Charles (see Durrell, Lawrence)
Norden, Frederick L., 10, 227
Noury, F.E. (et Fils), 113
Nubar Bey, 21, 22
Nye, Robert, 183

Odeon Theatre, Montparnasse, 209
Okasha, Sarwat, 27
Olivier, Lawrence, 6, 150
Opera Cinema, 149
Oriental Hall, 132, 136
Oriental Music Club, 108

Orientations, 69, 70, 99, 100, 101, 102, 103, 117
Orzel Biaky, 115
Ouspensky, P.D., 78

PEN Congress, 183, 193
P & O Steamship Co., 22
Palestine Orchestra, the, 133, 134, 135, 136
Palestine Post, 115
Palladio, Andrea, 233
Parade, 67, 74
Paradis Cinema, 149
Parc Cinema, 149
Parkinson, Harold, 137
Parme, Raoul, 61, 77, 79, 84, 85, 86, 89, 91, 112, 113, 119, 123, 125, 127
Pascal, Blaise, 24
Pastroudis, 201
Pearce, Sir Edward Lovett, 233
Pearce, Michael, 189
Perceval, John (1st Earl of Egmont), 10
Perry, Charles, 10
Personal Landscape, 86, 92, 93, 95, 103, 104, 105, 106, 123, 127, 179, 183
Petit Coin de France, le (Alexandria), 201
Petit Coin de France, le (Cairo), 87, 160
Petrarch, 126
Pevsner, Sir Nikolaus, 232
Phipps, Nicholas, 144
Piccadilly, the, 161
Pidgeon, Walter, 150
Pirandello, Luigi, 209, 210
Piranesi, Giovanni Battista, 234
Pitt, Barrie, 81, 83
Plato, 198
Playfair, James, 234
Plunkett, Joseph, 112
Pococke, Richard, 10
Poole, Sophia, 23
Pons Lily, 139
Pope-Hennessy, James, 22
Pothecary, Phyllis, 141
Potinière Cinema, La, 149
Pouishnoffleff, 139

Porter, Sir Robert Ker, 228
Pound, Ezra, 122
Powell, Enoch, 183
Powys, John Cowper, 110
Powys, Llewellyn, 110
Powys, T.F., 110
Poynter, Sir Edward, 229, 231
Preston, Tatiana, 137
Priestley, J.B., 110
Princeton University, 219
Prokop, Joseph, 137
Proust, Marcel, 196, 198
Pudney, John, 127
Purcell, Henry, 133

RAF Command Dance Orchestra, 146
RAMC Orchestra, 139
Rachmaninoff, Sergei, 134, 139
Radio Times, 106, 109
Rambert, Ballet, 148
Rashley, Rex, 146
Rashwan, Abdel Rehim, 5
Rassim, Ahmed, 61, 89, 118, 126
Rattigan, Terence, 142
Read, Sir Herbert, 60
Reader, Ralph, 146
Reagan, Ronald, 151
Regent Cinema, 149
Regent Restaurant, 160
Reuters, 57
Revely, Willey, 227
Rex Garden Cinema, 149, 153
Rex Restaurant, 95
Rhys, Keidrych, 75
Richard, Irene, 181
Richards, I.A., 224
Rida, Mostafa (Bey), 108
Riding, Laura, 52, 53, 54
Rignold, Hugo, 133
Rilke, Rainer Maria, 85, 86
Rimmer, Arthur, 137
Rivoli Cinema, 166
Roberts, David, 229, 230
Robertson, S. Farley, 143
Robinson, Peter Frederick, 234
Rodenbeck, John, 217
Rogers, Ginger, 153
Rommel, Field Marshal Erwin, 81, 82, 85

Rooney, Mickey, 150
Ropes, John, 141
Ross, Janet, 25
Rowntree, J.H., 111
Royal Academy, London, 56, 228, 231
Royal Ballet, London, 218
Royal Cinema, 149, 150
Royal Geographical Society, 7
Royal Institute of Arab Music, 108
Royal Institute of Painters in Watercolours, 232
Royal Opera House, Cairo, 30, 31, 38, 132, 134, 140, 141, 142, 149, 211
Royce, Jack, 146
Roxy Cinema, 149
Russell, Herbert John, 107
Russell, Lady, 71
Russell, Rosalind, 152
Russell, Sir Thomas (Pasha), 40, 47, 64, 173, 174, 190, 195
Ruston, Capt. H.L., 67

Said, Mamoud (Bey), 118
St. James's Cinema, 149
St. James's Restaurant & Bar (Jimmy's), 158, 160
Salamander, 78, 79, 80, 86, 88, 91, 92, 93, 103, 104, 111, 119, 128, 183
Salamander Oasis Trust, 180, 182
Salamander Society, the, 78, 79, 84, 85, 86, 88, 89, 90, 91, 93, 95, 102, 103, 111, 112, 113, 116, 123, 124, 125, 126, 127, 180
Salt, Henry, 228
Salzman, Pnina, 133, 134, 137
Samain, Albert, 79, 88, 116, 123
Sandburg, Carl, 110
Sanders, George, 150
Sansom, Major A.W., 82, 152, 155, 166
Sansom, Colin, 152
Sargent, John, 39
Saroyan, William, 71, 110
Sassoon, Siegfried, 51, 52
Sattin, Anthony, 23
Sault's, 155, 160

Saunders, Denis, 72, 86, 87, 117, 118
Schack, Hedy, 137
Schimanski, Stefan, 128
Schindler, R., 117, 118
Schubert, Franz, 135, 148
Schumann, Robert, 135
Scott, Margaret, 146
Scriabin, Alexander, 139
Searight Collection, London, 231
Searight, Sarah, 25, 26
Seddon, Thomas, 230
Seferis, George, 106
Selwyn, Victor, 72, 86, 113, 180, 181
Seymour-Smith, Martin, 51, 53
Shaffer, Anthony, 55
Shadwick, Joseph, 135
Shafto, Thomas, 153, 154
Shah, Hosn, 222
Shakespeare, William, 6, 42, 60, 142, 203, 207
Shaw, George Bernard, 108, 209
Shaw, T.E. (see Lawrence T.E.)
Shaw, Thomas, 10
Shelley, Percy Bysshe, 12
Shepheard's Hotel, 11, 17, 30, 34, 42, 67, 87, 94, 121, 154, 158, 160, 167, 171, 187
Shostakovich, Dmitri, 133
Shukrullah, Ibrahim, 121, 122
Sidky, Abdel Rahman, 204
Sissoieff, Ioan, 137
Sladen, Douglas, 8, 34, 35, 190
Smart, Sir Walter, 64
Smetana, Bedřich, 134
Smith, H.S., 1
Smith, Maggie, 56
Smith, Mason Rossiter, 217
Smith, R.D., 74, 75, 76, 94, 95, 98, 100, 180, 182
Smith, Sidney, 110
Smuts, Field Marshal Jan Christian, 117
Smyth, Dame Ethyl, 39
Soane, Sir John, 234
Solomon (Cutner), 137, 138
Southampton Art Gallery, 230
Sourian's, 160
Sparks, Fred, 141

Speirs, John, 60, 85, 99
Speirs, Ruth, 85, 99
Speke, John Hanning, 175
Sphinx, The, 34, 91, 106, 111, 123, 138, 142, 145, 154, 158
Spencer, Bernard, 60, 73, 74, 85, 93, 95, 99, 100, 103, 106, 128
Stack, Sir Lee, 50
Stanhope, Lady Hester, 93, 164
Stanley, H.M., 175
Stanwyck, Barbara, 150
Stark, Freya, 64, 66, 79, 164, 165, 176
Steegmuller, Francis, 20
Steinbeck, John, 110
Stephens, John Lloyd, 16, 22
Stewart, Desmond, 177, 178
Stewart, Frederick George, 107
Stewart, Margaret, 148
Storrs, Sir Ronald, 37, 38, 39, 40, 41, 42, 43, 69, 195
Strauss, Richard, 39
Studio Misr Cinema, 149, 152
Sturgess, Peter, 143
Suez Canal Company, 5, 170
Swanson, Gloria, 150
Sweet Melody Cabaret, 155
Swinburne, Algernon, 78
Sykes, John, 99
Sykes, Mark, 42

Taha, Aly Mahmoud, 204
Tambimuttu, 104, 106, 123, 125, 128, 181
Tate Gallery, London, 230
Taverne Française Restaurant, 105, 160
Taylor, Paula, 106
Taylor, Philip, 106
Taylor, Robert, 149
Taymour, Ahmed (Pasha), 221
Taymour, Mahmoud, 99, 211, 221
Taymour, Mohammed, 211, 221
Taymouria, Aisha, 221
Tchaikowsky, Piotr Ilich, 133, 134, 135
Tennyson, Alfred Lord, 12
Terry, Walter, 148
Tessimond, A.S.J., 125
Thackeray, W.M., 14, 15

Themeli, George, 137
Theocritus, 42
Thomas, Dylan, 101, 125
Thomas, Edward, 109
Thomas, Iowerth, 137
Thomas, Tommy, 141
Thomson, A.A., 109
Thomson, Alexander, 235
Thomson, D.J.S., 100
Thornton-Bassett, J., 148
Thwaite, Anthony, 199
Tiller, Terence, 60, 73, 74, 85, 93, 95, 99, 104, 106
Times, The, 57
Tolstoy, Count Leo, 212
Tommy's Bar, 86, 159, 161, 166
Towers, John, 88
Treece, Henry, 128
Trinity College, Dublin, 6
Trollope, Anthony, 21, 22
Tuckley, Onslow, 141
Tudor, Anthony, 148
Turf Club, 57, 61, 88, 161, 166, 167, 187
Turner, J.M.W., 228
Tute, Warren, 82
Twain, Mark, 17, 18, 24
Tyndale, Walter F.R., 232

United Nations, 114, 134, 174
University College, London, 28
Uren, Martyn, 120, 154
Ustinov, Peter, 56

Vanbrugh, Sir John, 233, 234
Vaughan Williams, Frank, 134
Verdi, Giuseppe, 30, 135, 139
Verlaine, Paul, 119
Victoria & Albert Museum, London, 231
Victoria College, 61, 119
Victory, 70
Victory Club, 69, 70, 72, 80, 100, 133, 135
Vitruvius, 233

Wadham, Dorothy, 141
Waghorn, Thomas, 14, 15
Wagner, Richard, 38
Wales, 75

Walker, James, 125
Wallace Collection, London, 231
Waller, Sir John, 74, 75, 76, 77, 78, 86, 88, 91, 95, 99, 105, 112, 124, 125, 126, 129, 130, 181, 182
Walton, Sir William, 148
Weill, Kurt, 148
Warren, F.S., 140
Waterfield, Gordon, 25, 26, 57
Watteville, Nicholas de, 91
Waugh, Evelyn, 56
Wavell, General Sir Archibald, 50, 79
Wayment, Hilary, 117
Wells, William, 100
West, Geoffrey, 151, 160
Westlake, Kay, 143
Whitbread Award, 188
Wilkie, Sir David, 230
Wilkinson, Darrell, 88
Wilkinson, Sir John Gardner, 9
Willcocks, William, 32
Williams, Emlyn, 142
Williams, Gwyn, 106
Williamson, Henry, 109
Willner, Dora, 135
Willner, Gerhard, 135, 136

Wilson, Edward, 181
Wilson, General Sir Henry Maitland, 114, 115
Wilson, George, 137
Wilson, Robert T., 11
Winsor, Elsie, 146
Wolfe, Humbert, 116, 127
Wolfe, Thomas, 71, 109
Wolfit, Sir Donald, 142
Woolf, Virginia, 60
World Health Organization, 200
World's Press News, 69
Wordsworth, William, 204
Worsley, Sir Richard, 227
Wren, Sir Christopher, 236
Writers' Union, the, 218

YMCA, 71, 133
YWCA, 133
Yeats, William Butler, 6, 79, 204
Yergath, Arsène, 61, 89, 126, 130
Young, R.A., 44

Zaghlul, Saad (Pasha), 49, 50, 164, 177, 187, 209, 215
Zizinia Theatre, 38
Zola, Emile, 30